THE AKENHAM BURIAL CASE

By the same author

INSTINCT IN MAN

ISSUES IN EDUCATION

THE FAMILY AND MARRIAGE IN BRITAIN

HUMAN NEEDS AND SOCIAL ORDER

THE PARKERS AT SALTRAM
Everyday Life in an Eighteenth-Century House

THE MAKING OF SOCIOLOGY
Vol. 1. Beginnings and Foundations
Vol. 2. Developments

JOHN STUART MILL
A Logical Critique of Sociology

THE SCIENCE OF SOCIETY & THE UNITY OF MANKIND (Ed.)

THE CRISIS OF INDUSTRIAL CIVILIZATION
(The Early Essays of Auguste Comte) (Ed.)

THE
AKENHAM
BURIAL
CASE

RONALD
FLETCHER

WILDWOOD HOUSE LONDON

FIRST PUBLISHED 1974
© 1974 BY RONALD FLETCHER

WILDWOOD HOUSE LTD
1 WARDOUR STREET, LONDON W1V 3HE

ISBN hardback 0 7045 0090 6

Condition of Sale

600364196X

PRINTED IN GREAT BRITAIN
BY EBENEZER BAYLIS & SON LTD
THE TRINITY PRESS, WORCESTER, AND LONDON
BOUND BY G. & J. KITCAT LTD, LONDON

ACKNOWLEDGMENTS

From the back shed in Southwold, the search for this story took me far and wide. Many helped me – and all with shared interest and excitement.

Mr and Mrs Finch long ago gave me the freedom of their shop, shed, and warehouse – and so, many long hours of pleasure. Judy Smith of the reference section of Ipswich County Library, Miss Maynard, Mrs Murton and Mrs Barrett of the Ipswich Borough Library, and the staff of the Ipswich Records Office, gave all the help that libraries and archives can give – which, in East Anglia, is unstinted and very considerable indeed. Mr S. Gothard of the House of Commons Library also helped greatly with *Hansard* advice. Mr John Castle (of Commercial Studios, Northgate Street, Ipswich) managed to photograph difficult pages of nineteenth-century newspapers which would otherwise have taken an eternity to copy. Sir Laurence Grafftey-Smith gave me those details of Rev. Drury he had obtained in correspondence, and has allowed me to include them here. Don Simpson (the present editor) and Colin Chinery of the *East Anglian Daily Times* have helped with much enthusiasm (the discovery of this story coincides with the centenary of the paper's foundation). Rev. Eldridge and Mr Runnacles of the Zoar Baptist Chapel in Ipswich (of which the Ramseys were members) were ready to help as far as their records allowed. The Rev. Brian Toll – the present Rector of Claydon Church – made available all Drury's bits and pieces, gave us access to the church for photographic purposes, and even took us up to the top of the tower (negotiating two thickly pigeon-feathered ladders) to look at Drury's carvings of 'The Saints and the Beasts'. And Mr Hines (who now owns the 'nunnery'), Mr and Mrs Nielsen (who now live in Drury's 'Old Rectory' – and bless his nine-foot wall and the secluded garden it provides), Mr Rowlinson (who now owns 42 Butter Market, where Joseph Thurston used to pore over his newspaper cuttings), and Mrs Molly Hall (who now lives in Rise Hall Farm, and, with a few friends, has been instrumental in keeping Akenham Church in existence) have all generously allowed us to ramble all over their properties in the freest possible way. When I say 'us', it was Ken Griffiths, of course, who rambled with me – for his illustrations. Also, at the last moment, just before going to press, it was my good fortune to 'discover' the Rev. Wickham Tozer's grandson –

5

Mr Wickham Partridge, now a county councillor for Suffolk; he had much carefully preserved material, including some letters and telegrams which had passed between Frederick Wilson (the editor of the *East Anglian Daily Times*) and Wickham Tozer just before the court action, and he allowed me to use the cartoon partly reproduced in the illustrations and the charcoal portrait of his grandfather which has every appearance of a photograph.

To all these – as they well know – my warmest thanks.

And the same, too – it goes without saying – to the 'team' at Wildwood House, who have been with this book from the beginning, and who have made its production an almost (there had to be *some* cuts!) unadulterated pleasure.

CONTENTS

LIST OF ILLUSTRATIONS

between pages 112 *and* 113

Another generation will hear with wonder and with indignation of the law which now, in rural England especially, insults dissenters and all the unbaptized dead.

With still greater surprise and shame will the clergy of that generation remember that it was the wearers of their cloth who clung to an inhuman and unchristian law when all other classes were anxious to remove it . . .

A.Z.

March 22nd, 1879

Sir, – I am not a Dissenter, but I am greatly mistaken if the people of England will allow the decision of the Court of Common Pleas to be final in the case of Drury *v.* Wilson.

If this decision is to be final, then the freedom of the British Press may be considered as a matter of past history in England.

I, personally, care not a straw for the *East Anglian Daily Times*, or any other paper, but if civil and religious liberty are to be crushed out of England and the English people, it shall not be done without the protest of one . . .

WORM

March 15th, 1879

INTRODUCTION

(i)

If you turn right off the Ipswich road – just after the Claydon turn, driving from Henley – the narrow, winding road will take you through a hamlet marked on both road and map as 'Akenham'. Whether you will ever feel that you have *found* it in this quiet corner of Suffolk is questionable. It is certainly not a village. Barely half a dozen houses can be seen from any one point. As you follow the road – past the modern water-works, with electric cables spanning the sky overhead – you will come to the rough stone track, turning sharp right past a small cottage, and climbing gently upwards to the church standing on the top of the hill. Even this will seem alone and remote. The 'Church in the Fields' it is called, and it does, indeed, seem to be the centre of nothing. No community is visible over all the surrounding meadows, beyond the yards and buildings, the placid duck-pond and the leaning elms of Rise Hall Farm – set just a little lower on the hillside. At a guess, you would make the population about seventy. You would be right.

As you will see later, this is exactly – water-works and electric cables aside – the way in which you would have had to describe the place a hundred years ago. In Domesday Book only four manors were recorded. The population has rarely grown beyond a hundred. And during the nineteenth century, only 'five scattered houses' were mentioned – of which Rise Hall was one – together with a few labourers' cottages.

You may ask, however: 'What is there in all this? What interest does this limited hamlet hold for me, *now*?'

The answer to that, of course, is my story.

(ii)

Some months ago, rummaging through a pile of scrap-books, files of old papers, albums, in the back shed of a second-hand bookshop in Southwold, I came across a slim black book. It lies on my desk now. It is about $17'' \times 12''$ and bound in a poor black cloth over cardboard. The pages were originally plain, and it was used as a record of orders, deliveries, and 'copy-letters' – all written swiftly and efficiently with a sharp steel pen, in an ink which has now turned brown. Entries are like these (made on July 15th, 1879):

18

To Mr Moberley, London.
I have this day forwarded to you by Pickfords & Co., the 8 pillows which I hope will prove to your satisfaction.

No. 148

19

Messrs. Jeffery & Co., London.
Will you please send me 3of Paper No. 42281. Please let me have by return.

No. 149

There are occasional pictures of articles of furniture: fashionable bedsteads, for example, with red-painted frames or plentiful bits and knobs of glowing brass fixed into the black iron.

It belonged to an Ipswich 'Cabinet Maker, Etc.,' (to use his own title). Its owner – Mr Joseph Thurston – was obviously a man much interested in the clashes and conflicts of the time between the Established Church and the Dissenters. Its fascination lies in the fact that he pasted into it scores of newspaper cuttings.

The Black Book – a name we can now fittingly give it – had been given a title: The Akenham Burial Case, and it was this that took me at once to the hamlet and the 'Church in the Fields' that I described. An incident occurred in these quiet fields, in this remote churchyard – focused on a simple event, the death in August 1878 of the two-year-old son of a farm labourer – that was to gather about it all those factions locked in a conflict of religious and political power. Within two weeks, the entire country knew of this burial; was stirred into angry disputation. Within two years, the law of the land was changed.

The story would be spoiled if I plunged too much and too early into large considerations. But its nature could not even be seen without its setting, and, as a starting-point, it is necessary to bear in mind only a few things.

First, in the late 1870s (almost exactly a hundred years ago) a Burial Laws Amendment Bill was before Parliament; introduced by Mr Osborne Morgan, Member for Denbighshire – a name that will appear several times in the coming pages. But why a burials reform Bill? This leads us on to the second fact, that from the middle of the nineteenth century the problems of the enormous population increase were beginning to be grimly experienced. The simplest consequence of the large growth in the number of the living was the large growth, also, in the number of the dead. Where were these dead to lie? There was no room in the existing churchyards. The problem was realized in a sickening way.

It was most evident, obviously, in the new, ever-growing towns of industrial England – which had a scale and complexity not known before. And it was a straightforward problem of sanitation. From 1843, press and parliamentary committees were drawing attention to it. The graveyards of churches were crammed with coffins, as were all the vaults under their pavements. Placed one on top of each other, coffins were sometimes no more than a few inches below the surface. Air pollution was so bad that it directly caused disease. A secretive removal of bodies (into nearby pits) went on, and – as we shall see – even a macabre commerce. It is enough to say that a solution was attempted. In 1847, the Cemeteries Clauses Act made it possible for cemeteries to be provided – and this for the burial of members and non-members of the Established Church alike. In 1852, a wide-ranging Burial Act made it possible for new burial grounds to be acquired and managed; whilst burial in the metropolis itself was restricted and finally discontinued by an Act of 1855, which closed the churchyards. Here was a sheer problem of population and sanitation.

But a third fact to be borne in mind is that these provisions were only effective (for many years) in the towns and cities. In the greater part of rural England, cemeteries were unknown. Only the old parish churchyards remained. And fourthly, this was not a simple problem of population and available land alone. Arithmetic and reason could not quickly solve it. Why? Because the rights, the privileges, the property of the Church of England were at stake. All Englishmen had the right to be buried in their own parish churchyards, but only Church of England clergy could officiate in them. If certain conditions were not fulfilled (for example, if the deceased person was unbaptized, or excommunicated, or a suicide), their own law directed them not to read, and not to allow to be read, the 'Christian' Burial Service. A continuous readiness to warfare therefore reigned between Church of England clerics and the often outraged and militant Dissenters. The issue of disestablishment was given a sharp cutting-edge. Throughout rural England, and especially among clergymen, death and burial were fraught with conflict. They were perhaps the most sensitive antennae of the collective unrest. Touch them – and it was likely to explode.

And the fifth and final point that sets our scene is that Edward and Sarah Ramsey – father and mother of Joseph, the two-year-old boy – were Baptists. Baptists, as is well known, do not, on principle, practise the baptism of infants, believing that baptism is a 'rite' of conscious discipleship only to be undertaken by those who have reached years of discretion. When Joseph died, he was therefore unbaptized. In the Church of England's eyes, he was not a Christian. And, furthermore, the Zoar Baptist Chapel which the family attended (in Ipswich) was some four miles away from their cottage – a long way for labouring people a century ago.

All the events at Akenham took place within this context, though, as we shall see, they were exacerbated by some of the individual characters involved.

I said that when the Akenham Burial Case occurred, the Burials Bill was before Parliament. But perhaps it is also interesting to note that when this Bill was finally debated – in 1879–80 – it was then one of no less than *six* such Bills before Parliament, and it was *this* case, taking place in this small Suffolk churchyard, that had unleashed five of them and the whole intensity and variety of this parliamentary concern. The Act finally passed in 1880 is to be seen on p. 268.

(iii)

I have wondered how this story could best be told. Would it be best to write it as a novel? To dramatize it as a play? To attempt a television reconstruction? The characters and circumstances were certainly sufficiently colourful. The story itself is compelling. Each way of presenting it has much to be said in its favour. But – after all – it was *not* a novel, a play or a documentary. And it is no invention of mine. It was an actual incident; written, commented on, worked through, by the people involved in it. And sometimes the ordinary issues and events of life – no matter on how small a scale – have a power, a profundity, a dignity of their own; needing no art to enhance them, and being only in danger of falsification if over-dramatized.

Ultimately, therefore, it seemed to me that you would prefer to piece the story together as it unfolded in the newspaper controversy of the time; as if you were reading the story in the papers now. I thought you would most like to trace the story as it emerged from the cuttings of the Black Book and then in all the newspapers to which these led. For the Black Book was only a beginning. All I had intended doing was to put these cuttings into chronological order (they were pasted into the Black Book in haphazard fashion – without order, some even duplicated) and to edit them slightly: purely in the service of readability. I thought the story would tell itself. Once seized by its interest, however, I found it impossible not to look as deeply as possible into all aspects of it. Every next inquiry turned up something more exciting. Many things emerged.

The first thing to emerge was that Joseph Thurston's cuttings – thorough at first glance – turned out to be casual and partial in some respects. They were the kind of collection a man would put together, day after day, week after week, purely as a matter of personal interest and pleasure. But most of all, they proved to be only the visible glow of a large subterranean volcano. Much more heat and fire lay beneath the surface. For example, Mr Thurston had included cuttings of the report of the case which followed in the Court of Common Pleas in Westminster. These were fascinating, and, at first glance, very full. But when I looked into *all* the Ipswich and East Anglian papers of 1878 and 1879, new aspects of the story came to light. Mr Thurston had taken the case for the plaintiff from one paper (the *East Anglian Daily Times*) that for the defendant from another (the *Suffolk Chronicle*), and had missed out altogether the summary statements of the advocates, and the judgment and verdict of the court. These two papers were, in fact, on the same side of the fence in the argument, but had reported the case in differing degrees of detail. It was necessary, then, and proved possible, to get together the fullest record of all; that of the *East Anglian Daily Times*. But all this led to a further interesting dimension.

The local newspapers were themselves in a state of feud over the issue. The *East Anglian Daily Times* and the *Suffolk Chronicle* were allies, but a third combatant raised its head out of the century-old dust; the *Ipswich Journal*. The first two were clearly the radicals of the time. The Dissenters, and all groups and causes that battered at the stone walls of an ancient Establishment, found ready – though fair – support in their pages. The *Ipswich Journal*, on the contrary, smelt of peers' robes and Anglican vestries. It raised itself up like a Vicar of Bray among newspapers. Rebellious movements got short shrift in its comfortably laid out columns, set out in its ornate typeface, but in them 'anonymous' reactionaries found plenty of room for their voices. The war over a two-year-old child in Akenham churchyard was at once a war between the local papers. And the warfare spread.

Joseph Thurston had snipped out a few 'Opinions of the Press' and

a few 'Letters to the Editor' from the Ipswich papers. But a full examination of the papers of the time revealed literally *scores* of these. The
case stimulated the most fiery indignation, the most hot and angry
replies, throughout the length and breadth of the country. Letters
were written by the score: from 'Worm', 'Full and Free Liberty', A
Disgusted Layman', 'One of the Haters of Humbug', and many other
forceful, protesting, reasoning characters. I have included a selection
of these – in more or less exact chronological order – so that, placed
among the 'leaders' and other incidental press articles (e.g. 'A Visit to
Father Drury's Domain'), and the full details of the cross-examination
in court, they show in colourful fashion the mounting tide of feeling
and argument. They bear powerful testimony, too, to the vitality and
strength of a free press in Britain: rooted in, serving, and continually
safeguarding and enriching a vigorous democracy. I do not know how
you will find the reading of these many styles of journalism and letter-
writing, but they seem to me substantial evidence of a literature going
well beyond that of novelist, essayist, poet. They exemplify the ordinary, manifold literature of a free people involved in thinking, feeling,
acting, arguing, struggling towards a clarification of the ongoing problems and qualities of their ways of living; seeking always to clarify
principle, and to bring it to bear on day-to-day issues. This 'common'
literature of a hundred years ago seems richer to me than many novels;
richer, indeed, in its ordinariness and actuality than much literary 'art'.
It is the *living* literature of a people engaged with their problems in
home, street, market-place, church, court and government. However –
you will see, and you will judge. All I have done is to collect and *order*
these writings of an earlier generation, inserting comments here and
there, but always minimally, and only to help the story to tell itself.

A second point of interest emerged. As the story unfolds, it is the
rector of the Claydon and Akenham churches – Reverend George
Drury – who emerges as the central character; the villain of the piece.
Idiosyncratic, colourful, extreme, obdurate . . . loving a case in the
courts, attacking people with red-hot pokers, throwing bowls of hot
water over them, 'keeping a nunnery', at odds with his bishop . . .
what sort of a man was he? Well, quite apart from press accounts, it
was possible to discover some little information about him, as recol-
lected by his descendants. Sir Laurence Grafftey-Smith – now of
Coddenham in Suffolk, who bought Drury's 'Old Rectory' in 1960 –
had himself written to Drury's grandson, inquiring about the history
of the house. The information he obtained is given later.* One small

* *See* Appendix 3, p. 276.

point worth mentioning here, however, is that this 'ogre' of High Church persuasion (who had to build a nine-foot wall round his house to protect himself and his family from the stones of villagers) gave one of his empty glebe houses to the village schoolmaster – when he was evicted, and all his furniture turned out into the road – a man who had been one of his strongest and most continuous critics. A strange generosity, one might think, for one so inhuman? But again, the information about him goes far beyond this; to his amateur stone-carving (e.g. of the pulpit and gargoyles of Claydon church); to his enjoyment in making magic-lantern slides; and even to the ghost of a Lady in Grey who walked in his rectory.

And the most intriguing fact of all is that the entire scene of this incident, with all its details, is still there to be seen. Akenham and nearby Claydon carry, still, the evidence of their story. The Reverend Drury's family vault is there – quiet, a little overgrown, against a wall at the edge of Claydon churchyard – where he was laid to rest with such splendid High Church ceremony. So is the register of marriages with his much repeated signature and the labourers' 'marks'; the beautifully designed Bible which some of his congregation presented to him after the Akenham case (Signed, however, by only *one* churchwarden!); and the censer he used to swing in the aisles. And so, also, in the Akenham churchyard not far away, is the tiny headstone of Joseph Ramsey, the two-year-old boy, who – unbaptized and 'buried like a dog' – was the innocent centre of this religious and political storm. The whole of the north end of the churchyard, where unbaptized bodies were laid, is now flat. Coarse grass covers it. Only one stone stands – and when I first saw it, and first approached it, following the indications of Mr Thurston's Black Book, I could not believe that, a hundred years after the event, it could possibly be the one stone I was looking for. But, indeed, it was. It is the headstone of Joseph Ramsey, erected by the editor of the *East Anglian Daily Times* when the court case was over.

But also – and we must come to this later – Drury's 'nunnery' is still there to be seen; the Convent House close to the new (present-day) rectory. There *now* is the old chapel roof, the tiny 'silence' room, the back-kitchen, with its old grate, where Drury emptied hot water over the head of Mr Lovely – a village labourer who (as one of a mob) was breaking the windows to get in and 'rescue' one of his friends' daughters . . . But I must stop. The details of the story spill out of my head all too quickly.

Two points are in the forefront of my mind in feeling the relevance of this case. First, religious bigotry is always ready to trample out its causes – unheedingly – over the bodies of innocent dead. It was so a hundred years ago. It is so now. It is not only the hamlet of Akenham that is still the same. Men too, it seems, despite different fabrics of civilization, do not change. But that is not the end of the story. A second point is that men who are prepared to be active – on particular concrete issues, in local and national affairs, through press and Parliament – *can* change the nature of their societies for the better. When men will take a stand, humanity *can* be upheld against the resistant formalities of power and authority. Democracy *can* work. Justice *can* be done. The good *can* triumph.

But now . . . to the Black Book, and its forgotten story.

FIRST REPORTS

1 'A Passage of Arms'

In Mr Thurston's pages – among masses of cuttings on questions of 'Tithes', 'The Church in Wales', 'Priests and Priest-
craft', the 'Irish Church', reviews of John Stuart Mill's *Auto-
biography* ('... that extraordinary but melancholy book ...'), and
other topics all jumbled together – one title stood out with a
stark clarity. Written on August 26th, 1878, in the *East Anglian
Daily Times*, it was this:

BURIAL SCANDAL AT AKENHAM

*A Passage of Arms Between Rev. George Drury and
Rev. Wickham Tozer*

About midway between the Whitton and the Henley Roads, and about
half a mile from both these highways, is the very small hamlet called
Akenham. On rising ground, and at sufficient elevation to make it
observable from a considerable distance, is the parish church of Akenham. There are not half a dozen houses visible at any one point in the
village, and the number of inhabitants can scarcely be more than from
fifty to a hundred, and we doubt very much whether there are anything
like so many as that. The church is a very comely looking building – at a
distance. If you leave the bridle way and ascend the hill on which it
stands, you must immediately be painfully impressed with the fact that
the sacred edifice and its surroundings are grievously neglected. The
fences are badly kept; the graveyard is a perfect wilderness; the windows
of the church are broken, the porch is in a condition which our sanitary
authorities would pronounce dangerous to cattle; and the whole aspect
of the place gives one the impression that it can never be used for the
purpose of religious services. On looking through the broken panes of
glass into the building, cobwebs in profusion, dead birds, and dust and
dirt in abundance, convince us that it has never been swept for months,
if for years. And yet it is a structure that might be made attractive, if
not beautiful. It is not many years since it was restored by a generous
friend at a cost of some £800. The internal fittings are modern and
comfortable, and a very small outlay would make the exterior respectable.

The incumbent of this notable village church is the Rev. George

Drury, B.A., rector of the adjoining parish of Claydon. Some time during Sunday, alternately in the morning and afternoon, the incumbent might be seen taking a pleasant airing in the vicinity of the church, and if it should so happen that any pious parishioner should manifest a desire to worship by loitering about the building, the doors are opened, and service is duly performed. Such a novelty as this occurs perhaps about half a dozen times in the course of the year, and for this laborious duty the incumbent receives the modest stipend of £266 per annum, in addition to the living at Claydon, which is worth at least £240 per annum.

A few days since, a working man, in the employ of Mr E. E. Gooding, of Akenham Hall, lost a child who was about two years old. Both parents being Baptists, the child was never baptized. Ipswich is some four miles from Akenham, and as there is neither a cemetery nor chapel graveyard nearer, application was made to the incumbent to have it buried in the consecrated ground of the parish church. Mr Drury, on learning that the child had not been baptized, positively and peremptorily refused it burial in the consecrated ground, but gave permission for it to be buried behind the church in unconsecrated ground reserved for still-born infants, on condition that no religious service was performed within the graveyard. He very sternly refused to bury it himself, and insisted that no one should officiate in the church in his stead. Very naturally, the sorrowing parents did not wish to have their beloved child buried like a dog, and their kind-hearted employer, Mr Gooding, at once undertook to arrange for a short service being held before the interment, immediately in front of the church gate, in a meadow occupied by Mr J. A. Smith of Rise Hall. On Thursday Mr Gooding had an interview with the Rev. Wickham Tozer, of Ipswich, who readily consented to bury the child at 5.30 on Friday afternoon. Some ten or fifteen minutes before that hour Mr Tozer arrived at the church in company with Mr Gooding, and Mr Smith, who is churchwarden. The incumbent was pacing the graveyard, attired in indescribable petticoats, and inconceivable headgear. That looked ominous. As he had refused to perform the burial service, no one expected or desired his presence. The grave was dug, and the sexton was there to discharge his duties, and that was all that was needed so far as the church officials were concerned. The funeral was rather behind its time, and both of the reverend gentlemen must have felt there was something threatening in the air, for they paced up and down their respective paths, the one inside and the other outside the church boundaries, with a defiant air that reminded us of two game birds pluming themselves for a brush.

The movements of Mr Gooding and the churchwarden also indicated uneasiness, but the passive sexton sat like a monument on the corner of an horizontal tombstone. At length the humble procession arrived, and with it a few sympathizing neighbours, and possibly a few who may have been animated by no other motive than a desire to witness a scene. Altogether there may have been about thirty persons present. Before the corpse had been lifted from the cart in which it had been conveyed to the church, the sexton, who had evidently been primed for the occasion, went up to the father of the child and presented the clergyman's compliments and his request that the corpse might be immediately conveyed to the grave, and they could hold any service they chose after it was buried, in the meadow outside the yard. Of course, the vital point with this poor man's minister was that, the child not having been baptized, it was a sin to give it Christian burial, and, so far as it was in his power to prevent it, no religious service should be performed over it, either by himself or anyone else. As to what might be done after the body was in the grave, that would not affect his priestly scruples an atom. No notice whatever was taken of the incumbent's request either by the father or his friends. No bier could be procured, and the coffin was placed on the ground immediately in front of the churchyard gate. The friends gathered round it, and Mr Tozer commenced reading appropriate passages of scripture. The incumbent, in his saintly garb, but with a visage which scarcely matched, left the church door, sailed majestically up the path, came out of the gate, and stood about an arm's length to the left of Mr Tozer, facing the mourners. The situation at this point was painfully exciting. We dared hardly think of what might happen. Involuntarily we looked at the physique of the reverend gentlemen, and, in spite of the occasion, we could not resist the impulse to estimate their comparative strength and their powers of endurance. Of Mr Drury's courage in confronting the party alone there could be no question, and we also felt sure that, although Mr Tozer had always been kindly disposed towards Churchmen, he was rather a formidable defender of his own party when necessity impelled him to it. Conflict between these two champions of the faith we felt there must be either in the form of words or blows. Happily, our worst fears were not realized, but the following serious altercations which lasted for ten or more minutes, will prove that our apprehensions were not altogether groundless.

Incumbent: 'The time for this funeral was five o'clock, it is now more than half-past five, and I request you to convey the remains to the grave at once.'

The minister continued reading, and no one paid the least attention to Mr Drury's request.

With a face as rigid as steel, his lips firmly fixed at one end of the mouth and slightly curved in an upward direction at the other, expressive of disgust, the incumbent said:

'I have been waiting over half an hour, and it is not reasonable that you should keep me here until you are pleased to finish these proceedings.' No one attempting to reply, he continued: 'Why cannot you take the coffin to the grave, and then come here and hold what service you please?'

The reason for the interruption will be easily apparent to our readers. It was not so much Mr Drury's hurry as his repugnance to a religious service of any kind being held over an unbaptized child. Mr Tozer still took no notice of the obstruction, but continued quietly reading portions of scripture.

Incumbent: 'I must again request you to defer this service until after the remains have been interred.'

Mr Gooding: 'Pray, sir, do be quiet; the service will not last many minutes.'

Incumbent: 'Don't tell me to be quiet, I have a duty to perform and I shall do it. I must teach my parishioners that these proceedings are wrong.'

Mr Tozer moved slightly towards Mr Drury and said: 'I respect you as a gentleman and I would not willingly offend your religious convictions or your conscientious scruples, but do let me beg of you to be quiet for a few moments; we shall not be long.'

Incumbent: 'What has that got to do with it?'

Mr Tozer: 'Oh, I supposed you were a gentleman, a Christian, and a minister of Christ.'

Incumbent: 'I don't see what religious convictions or scruples have to do with it.'

Mr Tozer: 'Well, I have no wish to hold a discussion with you, but I appeal to your manhood, and beg you not to torture the feelings of these poor people at a time like this.'

Incumbent: 'That is all nonsense; manhood and feelings have nothing whatever to do with it, your proceedings are altogether wrong and I must teach my parishioners that I cannot sanction them.'

Mr Tozer: 'Well, sir, I thought if you were not a gentleman or a Christian, you might possibly be a man. I am sorry to have been mistaken.'

Incumbent: 'I suppose you call that Christian?'

Mr Tozer: 'Very, and for that reason I fear you are incapable of appreciating it. You have a very priestly garb and I suppose you take that as equivalent to being one, but you are destitute of the spirit of your Master, and you have not even a spark of humanity in you or you could not be capable of this conduct.'

Incumbent: 'I don't see what humanity has to do with it. That child (pointing to the coffin on the ground with his umbrella) has not been baptized, and it is, therefore, not a Christian, and I object to its being buried as such.'

The secret of Mr Drury's interference was now disclosed, and it produced an instantaneous effect upon Mr Tozer. As quick as thought he drew himself up to his full height (close upon six feet), and brought his right arm dangerously near to Mr Drury's head, and, with his eyes flashing fire, and his voice trembling with emotion, he said – 'If it were not for harrowing the feelings of these poor people, I would very soon silence your brutal speech. Though decked in the garb of a priest and holding the office of a minister, you are a disgrace to humanity.'

Incumbent: 'Don't shake your fist in my face.'

Mr Tozer: 'I was not shaking my fist in your face but you justly deserve to be made to feel it.'

Incumbent: 'And you call that Christian?'

Mr Tozer: 'Perfectly.'

Incumbent: 'You are a Baptist, and yet you can come here and perform a service over a child that has not been baptized, and is not, therefore, a Christian?'

Mr Tozer: 'I have no desire to hold a controversy with a man so destitute of the commonest feelings of humanity as you are, and if this were not a funeral I would very soon bundle you out of the meadow.'

Incumbent: 'This is a public path, and I have as good a right to be here as you have.'

Mr Tozer: 'Just so much and no more. We have carefully avoided everything that could reasonably wound your religious scruples, and we came here because it is a public footway; and you have no right to interfere with us.'

Incumbent: 'I have the right to teach my parishioners that it is wrong to perform funeral rites of a Christian form over the remains of an unbaptized child.'

The father of the child: 'Come, Mr Drury, I shall have something to say to you if you don't allow the gentleman to go on with the service.'

The mother, seeing her husband was becoming angry, and fearing the consequence, said: 'Never mind the parson, Mr Tozer; go on with the service.'

Incumbent: 'I have been waiting here more than half an hour, and it is unreasonable for you to expect me to remain while you conduct this unwarrantable ceremony.'

Mr Gooding: 'Allow me to remind you, sir, that you refused to perform any service yourself; after that you were not asked to be present, and no one wishes you to remain.'

Incumbent: 'How could I perform a service over a child that was not a Christian?'

Mr Tozer: 'Don't repeat that, sir, if you do you may have cause to regret it. The sooner you take yourself off this public highway the better.'

Incumbent: 'If you do not at once take the remains to the grave, I shall lock the gate and go.'

Mr Tozer: 'No one asked you to come, and no one wishes you to stay.'

Incumbent: 'I shall certainly lock the gate and leave.'

Mr Tozer: 'Go to heaven if you like; it would be a happy deliverance for the world if you and all your priestly tribe were there; though I fear you will stand a poor chance of getting there. Take yourself away from us, and I don't care where you go.'

The Incumbent locked the gate and went – not to heaven, but to Claydon, which, so far as the rectory and the adjoining nunnery are concerned, is a very different place.

After this sad episode, Mr Tozer concluded the service in peace and quietness. Mr Gooding and Mr Smith were equal to the emergency, and very soon made a way to the grave. There, in solemn silence, the poor innocent child's remains, over which this hard and unseemly battle of words had been fought, were deposited. The party then returned to the gate, and the usual burial service was read, and the ceremony concluded.*

* The article ended with a short editorial paragraph:
   We have thus, as far as it was possible, endeavoured to give an accurate description of what we cannot but call a discreditable burial scandal. We leave the facts to tell their own tale, reminding our readers that this staunch upholder of ecclesiastical law is already under admonition from his own bishop for lawless proceedings in his own church.

2 'A Burial Scandal'

Pasted quite close to it, printed a day later (August 27th) by the *Suffolk Chronicle*, was an account that was similar in almost every respect. Entitled 'A Burial Scandal', it forthrightly attacked the Rev. Drury, making much of the fact that he was under a 'monition' from his bishop, that he commonly misused his appointment in the Protestant church to promulgate his Romanist leanings and practices, and that the general 'firmness' of his attention to the letter of the ecclesiastical law had been carried to a point of gross distaste and inhumanity over the burial of Joseph Ramsey. 'Firm Father George' was the editor's characterization. Another newspaper had entered the fray.

The details of the report were so much the same as not to need repetition, but there was one peculiarity. The entire report was written as though it was a descriptive account from an eyewitness.

Half-past five on Friday afternoon was the time fixed for the burial service on the meadow-path over the little coffin, almost under the shadow of the parish church . . .* Mr Tozer was there a little before time, and so were Mr Gooding and Mr Churchwarden Smith. Firm Father George was there, too, on sentry duty in the churchyard. Public allusion has been made to the Father's 'indescribable petticoats', but such phraseology is flat profanity – we prefer to say he was attired in peculiar toggery . . . Except for the solemnity of the occasion, there was something comical in the scene. The rumbling cart bringing the little coffin and corpse had not yet arrived; and there in the churchyard was the firm Father, with funeral step, tramping backwards and forwards, and there over the hedge or wall, whichever it is, was the heretical pastor, also on the war path . . . As might be expected, the sexton, who was also at hand, was as cool as a cucumber, and made a seat of a tombstone on consecrated ground, which we submit firm Father George ought not to have permitted, because tombstones were not

---

* In quotations from newspaper material, short deletions (of a few words or so) are indicated by . . . within the text, and more substantial cuts (of a paragraph or more), by a clear break of three centred points. Also, for the sake of readability, I have broken long columns of solidly compressed newsprint into appropriate paragraphs.

made for sextons to rest their weary limbs upon. Eventually the rumbling cart with the little coffin and the little corpse reached the spot, and the faithful sexton was soon on the move . . .

So the account went on, complaining of the absence of a bier for the coffin, and the subsequent disgraceful behaviour of the 'Firm Father' in disrupting the service in the meadow.

The scene was saddening. It was more than that, it was a disgrace to the Church which keeps up these burial scenes.

But then, at the very end of the piece was a small, inconspicuous note; a strange final qualification.

We learn that it was by an oversight we were not advised of this burial, and, therefore, a reporter from this office did not attend. A report of the scene was furnished to our daily contemporary by one who was on the spot, and of that report we have availed ourselves in writing the above.

Quite obviously, the source of this *(Suffolk Chronicle)* report was exactly the same as that of the *East Anglian Daily Times*.
Was there more in this 'reporting' than met the eye?

3 *Letters to the Editor; 'Bosh and Bunkum'*

On the same day, in the *East Anglian Daily Times,* the 'Protestant Churchwarden', Mr J. A. Smith, felt obliged to substantiate all the details which had been reported about the deplorable state of Akenham church – and so started a correspondence which was to last far longer than he, or anyone else, could then have supposed.

To the Editor

Sir, – My attention has been drawn to the report of a burial in the parish churchyard of Akenham, which appeared in your issue of this morning, wherein the unclean and dilapidated state of the church and its surroundings was referred to.

I have been requested to state that the parishioners are in no way responsible for these things. The rector holds the keys of both church and graveyard, and although he has been frequently appealed to by successive churchwardens for the keys, or – as I suggested to him – duplicate keys of the same, he has taken no notice, and I am obliged to confess that in this matter he appears to be supported by law, but surely the parishioners have a *right of entry*. I hold office because there is no other qualified person in the parish who will take it. Owing to the locks there has been no legal vestry meeting for many years; fortunately no one has objected to the rates or unpleasant consequences would have ensued. Having received many complaints from both clergymen, landowners, farmers and labourers, who have an interest in the church or churchyard, I beg to repeat my assertion that the parishioners are quite prepared to maintain the church in decent order and repair, provided they have the key. In fact, no one ought to undertake the office of churchwarden unless he is both able and willing to provide or collect funds for the maintenance or repair of the sacred edifice.

With reference to the recent burial which occurred within a short distance of my residence, permit me to say that I was present simply as a spectator who had a mind to 'see fair'. I had not the slightest suspicion that the proceedings were being reported, or I would have taken note of what was said. However, as far as my memory serves me, the graphic report which appeared in your paper was correct. No doubt the rector acted quite legally in refusing to bury an unbaptized child, and I am anxious that while on the one hand, the laws of the Church of England and of the land shall be respected *within*, on the other hand the conscientious convictions of respectable labourers shall not be needlessly trampled upon or uncharitably outraged *without*. And all parishioners (working men as well as others), having paid the customary fees, shall be allowed to bury their dead decently and in order. Although the relations between priest and people here are somewhat strained, I hope there will be no repetition of such a discreditable scene as that which occurred on Friday last.

On behalf of the parishioners I beg to disclaim any responsibility for the present disgraceful state of the church and its surroundings.

A PROTESTANT CHURCHWARDEN

At the same time, and in the same paper, an 'Ipswich Vicar' voiced a different view. Issues such as those of political expediency, Church property, and the provision of 'cemeteries' came creeping in. Had some sort of plot been hatched? Was the burial of a child being *used* in some way?

BOSH AND BUNKUM

Sir, – I have just read your account of the scene at Akenham. If Mr Tozer was conducting a burial service *outside* the churchyard, I do not think Dr Drury had any right to interfere with him, and his zeal was perhaps greater than his discretion. On the other hand, it must be remembered that the law of the land forbids a Dissenting minister officiating in a consecrated churchyard, and it equally forbids a clergyman reading the burial service over any unbaptised person, infant or adult. Nothing could induce a Baptist minister to baptise a child, however much the parents might wish him to do so. I much doubt if a Baptist minister would allow me to baptise a child in his chapel. Why should it be more uncharitable to refuse to bury the child than to refuse to baptise the child?

Baptism is a sacrament ordained by Christ himself. The overwhelming majority of Christians in all ages and in all lands, think that all children should be baptised, and some have even thought that the child's future happiness will be less if it dies unbaptised. The Baptist parent refused to have his child baptised, and no one is offended; no one calls him a monster; no one interferes with his schismatical liberty. A burial service, though very proper, is a mere human invention – a matter of Church orders. There is no command in Scripture for it. No one, not Mr Drury himself, thinks it necessary to salvation. But while such great liberty is allowed by the press and by the public in the refusal of baptism, why is such a tremendous outcry made when a clergyman refuses the burial service? If the greater thing may be omitted without scandal, why not the less? If baptism may very properly be denied an infant on principle, why not burial? Why may not the Church clergyman have at least as much liberty as the Baptist father or mother? The law and the practice of the clergy now are exactly what both have been for centuries past. Why then 'those weeps'? as poor Artemus Ward would say. Why, my dear sir, they are for a political purpose. They are bosh and bunkum. They are a capital means of throwing dirt at the clergy, raising a prejudice among the ignorant against the Church, and preparing the way for the robbery and confiscation of all Church property. The lesson is, that lovers of peace and haters of humbug should do all they can to procure speedily village cemeteries.

Yours, etc.,
AN IPSWICH VICAR

4 *Editorial: a hard rejoinder*

I went then to the Ipswich Reference Library to see whether Mr Thurston's cuttings were full versions of the newspaper reports; wondering, at the same time, whether *other* local papers had had anything to say. It turned out that the incident, and the *East Anglian*'s and the *Suffolk Chronicle*'s reports of it, had received – on the self-same day – a hard counter-blast from the *Ipswich Journal*. This was the editorial for August 27th.

EDITORIAL

The Rev. Wickham Tozer has created what his party delight to call a burial scandal. Let us hope they have relieved themselves of some of the venom which at times threatens to split them. The reverend gentleman intruded his ministrations to the very gate of Akenham churchyard in order to read a service over the body of a child of Baptist parents. By loitering in this way for an unwarrantable time, they drew down upon themselves an expostulation from the incumbent of the parish. Here were the materials for a scene or a scandal, and we find this the Dissenting gentleman made the most of them after the manner of his kind. In fact, the Dissenting minister was imitating the boys of Donnybrook Fair, 'Who'll tread on the tail o' me coat?'

When we learn that the child's parents are Baptists we are somewhat surprised to find them assisting at such an unseemly scene. They have of their own free will declined one rite of the Church, yet they appear to have hungered for another, and to have felt it a grievance that their unbaptized child could only be interred in unconsecrated ground. This, however, is an inconsistency which may be pardoned in people who are presumably less well informed or less able to reason correctly than is Mr Tozer. That gentleman aided and abetted these poor people in their onslaught upon the Church; and he also made a great parade of their injured feelings. Who, in all fairness, hurt the feelings of the parents in this case? They knew, as well as they could know anything, that they had cut the child off from the chance of burial with the rites of the Church. Why, then, should they hesitate to accept the consequences of their own deliberate act?

Mr Tozer no doubt makes out that the Church of England is a

34

national church and as such open to everyone. We have never questioned, indeed we are proud of the national character of the Church of England, but surely even Mr Tozer will admit that such an institution must be governed by certain rules in the interests of decency and order. Suppose a company of Shakers or Mormons had made their appearance with a similar demand to exercise the right of sepulture in the churchyard, would they not have stood in precisely the same position as was occupied by Mr Tozer and the unbaptized child of Baptist parents? As such, would they not have had the same right to enter the churchyard; and will not the same argument which Mr Tozer would use for his own admission apply to these, and to even more eccentric and heterodox bodies of people? But these people who besieged Akenham Church only went as far as the gate. What they did, or wished to do there, we do not see – unless they wished to create a disturbance. If that was their object they succeeded admirably. To push the service over the dead child as near as possible to the church must have been the object of going to the churchyard gate. If these people were so tender about the church and its consecrated ground, why did they withdraw the child from all ministrations? If they were merely anxious that a service should be read over the body, that could surely have been done in their own cottage. If, however, designing politicians sought to trade upon the affair and to create a scene which would read well in the papers, what better plan could have been devised than to go to the church gate and insult the incumbent by loitering there, while they carried on a service which on the other side of the hedge would have been an infraction of the law? The political Dissenters must be hard pressed for a sensation if they are driven to arrest children's corpses by the wayside and over them create scenes which would be ridiculous were it not painful and blasphemous.

Again, the idea of a political plot was raised. *Everyone*, it seemed, might be prepared to use the death of a two-year-old child for their own ends.

5 'This Indecent Brawl'

The influence of the Ipswich articles immediately became widespread. Versions and reports of them were copied in many other journals – large and small, of limited and of great significance – far afield. The number of 'letters to the editor' from variously distant correspondents began to increase. On August 28th in the *East Anglian Daily Times* the Disestablishment issue was very clearly raised by one 'London Correspondent'.

The graphic description of the scandalous scene at a funeral at Akenham on Friday last, copied from your paper by some of the London journals, has attracted a large measure of attention. It is a nice plum for the Liberationists and will be made the most of by them during their ensuing campaign in the provinces in favour of the Burials Bill. But people who have no sympathy whatever with the aims and aspirations of the Liberation Society, speak of the impertinent and vulgar conduct of the clergyman with great disgust. I have heard the subject referred to by a great number of persons of all political and theological creeds, not one of whom has attempted in any way to palliate or excuse the behaviour of the rector of Claydon. I don't know that I ever heard of Mr Drury before in my life, but the probabilities are that his name will become familiar throughout the country in connection with this indecent brawl, and he may reckon upon seeing some rather unpleasant things said of him. The officers of the Liberation Society are about to open a campaign against the Established Churches of England and Scotland. They are moving heaven and earth to get the Liberal leaders to take up the question in an authoritative manner, and are trying to persuade them that a cry for the disestablishment and disendowment of the English Church is one that will carry them again to power, as was the case with the Irish Church. I do not think they will be successful in this, for the chiefs of the Liberal Party prefer to have a more definite expression of public opinion on the subject before they take it up. I have reason for thinking that, on principle, many of them are not averse to taking this step, but they hesitate to take the responsibility of leading an attack upon an institution built upon so many sacred traditions. Meanwhile, the intolerant and unseemly conduct of such members of the Church as the rector of Claydon, is doing the work of the Liberation Society with much more effect than Mr Carvell Williams and his coadjutors will ever be able, with all their assiduity and eloquence, to do. A few more such scandals over the burial of an innocent child, and public opinion will soon become ripe enough to warrant a master mind assuming the responsibility of leading it.

Some correspondents began to discover colourful skeletons in the Rev. Drury's cupboard. The long tales (later richly embroidered) of red-hot pokers, the abduction of innocent village daughters, the admonitions of bishops, and the like, now began.

Sir,
    Reading the account headed as above of the passage of arms between the Rev. George Drury and the Rev. Wickham Tozer, in your edition today, I made it my business to call upon a friend who lived for many years within a quarter of a mile of the former gentleman's vicarage, and from him I learned that he (the Rev. George Drury) was about the year 1862 convicted and fined £5, or two months' imprisonment, at the Needham Market Petty Sessions (Sir George Broke-Middleton, chairman), for striking a labourer by the name of Abraham Watkins over the head with a red-hot poker, simply because the said Abraham Watkins called out at the end of the service, 'No Popery – no confessional!' Any ordinary man would have thought the Rev. George Drury would after that have tried all within him lay to avoid figuring in another disgraceful affair before the public.
                    I remain, yours respectfully,
                                        W. B. FREEMAN
17 *Elm Road, Camden Square, London, August* 26th, 1878

And though this was only two days after the first article appeared, replies to earlier correspondents were already coming in.

Dear Sir – The letter of your correspondent 'An Ipswich Vicar' upon the above subject is a somewhat extraordinary one. He begins by saying that if the Rev. Tozer was conducting a burial service outside the sacred and hallowed precincts of the consecrated churchyard, the Rev. Mr Drury permitted his zeal to outrun his discretion when he interrupted him; and then goes on to state two facts which are well and generally known, viz., that it is a fundamental principle with Baptists not to have any person baptized till he or she has attained such years of discretion as to fully comprehend the nature of the ceremony, and next, that a Church of England clergyman is not permitted to read the burial service over an unbaptized child. Now, it is an incontestable fact that the service was being conducted outside the churchyard boundary, and in reply to 'An Ipswich Vicar's' enquiry – why so great an outcry is made when a clergyman refuses the burial service, while the greatest liberty exists upon the subject of baptism – I may state that the outcry in the present case is not against Mr Drury's refusal to accord Christian burial, but against his unmannerly interruption of a plain service at a spot where admittedly his jurisdiction did not extend. After reading your description of the neglected and disreputable condition of the church, I was not at all surprised to read the explanations of 'the Protestant Churchwarden' in your issue of today. Mr Drury appears to be one of those who

> 'Dres't in a little brief authority,
> Play such fantastic tricks before high heaven,
> As make the angels weep.'

It is arbitrary conduct in persistently keeping the keys of the church and of the graveyard from the churchwardens and others, and allowing the sacred edifice to fall into a disgraceful state of filth and dilapidation would appear to be characteristic of the man; and few will be surprised to hear that such a person is already under a monition from his bishop. His disregard of all feelings of decency and humanity on this occasion has evoked a widespread feeling of indignation and disgust, and I shall not be surprised if, as some gentleman observed to your London correspondent on Monday, Mr Drury more than divides the honours of carrying the Burials Bier with Mr Osborne Morgan, its promoter. With all respect to its clerical author, I must pronounce the apologetical portion of 'An Ipswich Vicar's' letter utterly destitute of good logic and of sound reasoning, while his deduction that the present outcry is raised for political aims and objects, and was arrayed for that end (for that is what he practically states), is as unwarranted as it is absurd.

I am, dear sir, Yours obediently,

A LAY READER

Colchester, August 27th, 1878

The suggestion that the funeral was a religious and political plot was already being derided.

Even so, one letter-writer, wishing to take issue with the 'special'

who had made the initial report, had clearly caught a faint smell
of journalistic impropriety.

Sir, – Will you do me the favour to ask your 'special' who went down
to do the tragic at Akenham to give the public the reason for his
assumption that the ground behind the church is UNCONSECRATED.
Stripped of its padding, the account amounts to this, that the Rev.
Drury did his duty – and a very painful duty to him, I am sure. This is
not a question of cassock or no cassock, biretta or no biretta, but the
clergy of every party – and laymen too – should support the man who
acted as the law directs him. The Baptists played me a worse trick a
few years ago in Essex. But I forbear. They were all heartily ashamed
of themselves. If a Baptist minister has a 'locus standi' in a corner of a
churchyard he has an undoubted right to occupy the pulpit – when not
otherwise engaged. The conduct of these agitators reminds one of the
bully of years gone at school who in helping himself to a new boy's
property would say, 'What's yours is mine, what's mine is my own.'
Excuse this brief notice of so serious a question. Time presses.
                    Yours faithfully,
                                        W. H. FREEMAN
Reepham, Norwich

Opinions were obviously divided. But more – much more – was
to come.

6 *A pre-concerted plot?*

With every day that followed, the volume of correspondence increased. The trickle became a flood. Press reports, 'Opinions from the Press', began to come in from journals all over the country. The correspondents began to fight. The arguments turned and turned upon themselves. The invisible volcano began to rumble and reveal the hidden pressures and heat which it contained. Surrounded by the quiet booklined walls of the reference library, with gentle portraits of Crabbe, Edward Fitzgerald and other Suffolk poets hung here and there, I became completely absorbed in this controversy of a hundred years ago. This was a story about which one had not to do too much guessing. The people who had been at the heart of it told it in their own words – the very words with which they had spontaneously attacked each other at the time. To read these worn, discoloured pages was to see and hear this ongoing controversy of the late nineteenth century as vividly as if one was a contemporary spectator. The issue was alive. The actors fought with each other under your very nose.

Here – still on only the fourth day of the dispute (August 29th) – are some examples of letters and press reports from the *East Anglian Daily Times*; some blaming Firm Father Drury, some blaming the Rev. Wickham Tozer, some blaming both.

THE AKENHAM BURIAL SCANDAL
Correspondence

Sir, – I have read with great pain your account of the 'Burial Scandal' at Akenham. I agree with you it has been a 'scandal', but I do not agree with you and some of your correspondents, in leaving the scandal at the door of the Rev. George Drury, the rector of Claydon, but on the contrary hold the Rev. (?) Wickham Tozer, the Independent minister of Ipswich, responsible for the disedifying scene which occurred . . .

. . . what are the simple facts? A child dies, the unbaptized offspring of schismatical and heretical parents in the eyes of the rector, and every member of the Church of England. The parents apply to have the child buried in the churchyard. The rector at once grants permission to have the tiny corpse interred within the sacred precincts, and allotted it a portion of that ground reserved for the unbaptized offspring of his own flock – the very spot where a child of his own would have been interred had it died without baptism. He could not in law and conscience permit it to be buried in any other part. So far so good. The parents appear to have agreed to this, and a grave was dug in this spot.

Next, as to the refusal of the rector to permit a service to be celebrated by an alien clergyman, by one whose validity of holy orders is totally ignored by the Church – who is regarded by it as a rebellious child and a teacher of error, the rector could no more permit him to officiate within the grounds than he could inside the church. And here I may ask what right have Dissenters to claim burial in Church of England churchyards? During life they repudiate the Church and its teachings; they are its deadly and uncompromising foes; they do their utmost to encompass its ruin – then why in death claim re-admission, as it were, into its bosom? If they worship in tabernacles of their own during life, and renounce all connection with the Church, why not provide themselves with a plot of ground wherein to bury their dead, and not outrage the religious feelings of orthodox and sincere members of the Church of England, by endeavouring to intrude themselves into the consecrated portion reserved solely for the faithful members of that Church? It is a monstrous piece of impertinent, intolerant, and, I may add, illogical aggression.

Thirdly, and lastly, as to the charge against the rector of unseemly conduct at the burial of the child. I conceive this charge (especially as regards unseemly language) comes home to Mr Tozer with irresistible force. An hour, five o'clock p.m., was appointed at which the burial was to take place, and the rector was present to see that no invasion of the rights of the Church would occur; for Dissenters, on more than one occasion, have endeavoured to celebrate their services in consecrated ground when they could do so with impunity. It is evident the whole affair was a preconcerted plot, on the part of the Dissenters, to create for their own purposes a 'scandal'.

. . .

Again, I repeat, it is Mr Tozer and not the rector of Claydon that has caused the scandal. He had no business to intrude as he did, and the conduct of the rector will meet the approval of hundreds of thousands of faithful members of the grand old Church of England, who are faithful to its hallowed teachings and sacred traditions.

I am, Sir, your obedient servant,

Ipswich, *August 28th*, 1878   AN IPSWICH LAYMAN

The skeletons in Rev. Drury's cupboard, though entertaining, and fated to become much more so in court, were not thought relevant to the present issue by some, and the question of the 'consecration' of the burial ground was continually aired.

Sir, – What, in the name of common sense, can the Rev. W. B. Freeman imagine that the antecedents of the Rev. G. Drury can bring to bear upon the real points of this storm in a teacup at Akenham, raised by the Rev. W. Tozer and his Baptist friends? The still-born corner – as some choose to misrepresent the part of the churchyard behind the church to be – is just as much consecrated ground as any other part of the same, or the pulpit even. We clergy, High and Low, ought to rally round a man who simply does his duty in holding the position of trustee and guardian of the freehold entrusted to his keeping.

Yours faithfully,

Reepham, Norwich   W. H. FREEMAN

Sir, – Can your Norwich correspondent prove that the ground behind Akenham Church is consecrated? If so, why did not his friend, Mr Drury, comply with the request of the sorrowing parents, and allow their child to be buried at the spot selected by them?

Also what ecclesiastical law permits of a priest stepping off consecrated ground into a meadow, and there like a tyrant interrupting the proceedings of a religious service?

Yours faithfully,

AN OBSERVER

Sir, – A discussion is taking place in your columns about the 'Akenham Burial Scandal'.

Being an admirer of the old fashioned English plan of 'calling a spade a spade', I have no hesitation in adopting the word scandal as the right word in the right place, but who was it a scandal upon? It appears to me that both the gentlemen were in fault, the Rev. Father Drury because he interfered outside his churchyard gates, and Mr Tozer because he allowed his temper to get the upper hand of himself.

I protest against making this unseemly squabble between people (who at any rate are *supposed* to be Christians) into a political or party question. It is not very edifying to us outsiders to see ministers of the Gospel defying each other to mortal combat or to a passage of arms, but I have yet to be convinced that the question of disestablishment is involved in the matter (as your London correspondent supposes).

It is simply a matter of religious opinion. The law of the Church of England forbids a clergyman to bury an unbaptized person, but a dissenter, having no ecclesiastical law for his guidance, is simply 'a law unto himself', but even he is amenable to the statute which forbids any unauthorized minister to perform any service in either the churches or churchyards of England.

Therefore Mr Drury was right in refusing to read the Burial Service over an unbaptized person, and also in excluding Mr Tozer from the churchyard.

Yours faithfully,

Ipswich, August 28th, 1878 H.H.

One thing that is quite clear, and should be said – to give full credit to the *East Anglian* – is that the paper was ready to publish letters of all shades of opinion, whether or not they were favourable to its own interpretation of the case. And here are two reports sent to the *East Anglian* which show that equally hot eruptions were breaking out elsewhere.

Press Reports

Selections from the *Daily Chronicle* were as follows:

If the Christian religion depended for its vitality upon such ministers as Mr Drury, it would become a byeword, to be scorned by every section of the community. . . Mr Osborne Morgan has found an unexpected and powerful coadjutor; for we believe Mr Drury's conduct will have more effect with the people of England in promoting the passing of the Burials Bill than all the speeches that Mr Morgan ever delivered. The English people will not allow their tenderest feelings to be trampled upon, and their dearest associations to be outraged, by 'ordained' men who disgrace the Church to which they belong, and bring discredit upon the Christian religion.

'Straight' writes to us lamenting the 'many queer things transacted by our clergymen (not parsons, they lived in the good old times) of the present day'. He always thought 'that a clergyman should be meek, kind-hearted, bending, and forgiving; something like Him we read of, but on the contrary, we find them very pugilistic, and more mortal than most of us, if we touch either their pockets or their rights . . .'

'A lover of humanity, if only to a dog,' sends a very strongly worded letter in reprobation of Mr Drury's conduct, expressing his astonishment that correspondents should be found 'encouraging such a monster'. He suggests disestablishment as the only remedy for such scenes, and concludes with the expression of a wish that Mr Tozer had 'exercised a little muscular Christianity'.

'Muscular Christianity . . .' a new category within the faith! Similarly, the editor of the *Christian World* sent Wilson (the editor of the *East Anglian Daily Times*) an advance proof of an article he was to publish later in the week. The title was as striking as some of the prose. The repulsive wings of vampires now flapped above the scene. The macabre made its entry.

A Pestilent Priest

The demon of discord is still haunting the tomb. The vampire of superstition flaps its repulsive wings over the¹ graves of the un-christened. The dead babes of Baptists are consigned to the devil by the priests. The ecclesiastical jugglers failed to handle them, and their souls perish! No drops of consecrated water fell upon their innocent foreheads, and endless fire is their only portion! These pestilent priests dare to tell us that He who loved all the little ones on earth will spurn them from paradise unless they go in by the Pharisees' door. The 'burial scandals' of the Ritualists are becoming a national dis-grace. Week by week the same tale of their disgusting inhumanity comes to us from the rural districts, and the Evangelicals look on and will do nothing to uphold the honour of the Church and of religion. It will presently be found that an outraged people will take the law into their own hands, and by some act of violence against such an anglican priest as George Drury, of Claydon, create a public opinion strong enough to force Parliament to put an end, once and for ever, to such sickening scenes as the inhabitants of Akenham witnessed last Friday . . .

Bad as all these burial scandals are, there has, perhaps, rarely been one so bad as this; for when Mr Drury refused to inter the child, no one complained. The grave was dug and the sexton paid for his work; and the Independent minister of Ipswich – who, curiously enough, has written strongly in defence of an Established Church, as against the extreme Liberationists – would have endeavoured to soothe the be-reaved parents, and call forth devout thoughts and holy resolves in the minds and hearts of the sympathizing neighbours, and no unpleasant-ness would have occurred. But he chose to sacrifice the gentleman, and even the man, and became a mere heartless priest, than whom there is no viler creature on the face of the earth. 'What has humanity to do with it?' asked he, when rebuked by the friends of the sorrowing parents for his cruel words; and truly humanity was far enough from having aught to do with his conduct in the case. The very lowest type of ordinary humanity would be dismayed, or become angry, at the scene witnessed in that Akenham meadow, whither came this pretended minister of Christ, for the single and gratuitous purpose of irritating the living and insulting the dead. One can almost fancy that only toad-stools will henceforth spring up where stood this priest uttering his maledictions over that tiny coffin, laid down there on the bare earth for want of the parish bier, which the charity of the parish church, in the person of its ruler had refused. It had nothing to bestow, in that hour of pain, but curses.

7 *The larger press*

Confusions were obviously creeping into the argument – not to speak of 'interested' interpretations – and, on August 30th, the editor of the *East Anglian Daily Times* issued a short but clear statement:

THE AKENHAM BURIAL SCANDAL

In order that correspondents may clearly comprehend the facts of the case, we may point out that the service held by Mr Tozer, which Mr Drury interrupted, took place entirely outside the churchyard, and not in a corner of it, as some of our correspondents appear to imagine. We thought our report was clear on this point, but repeat the facts in order that no mistake may occur.

But the correspondence had gained its own momentum. Nothing could now stop the flow, the forcefulness, the twists and turns of its arguments. The letters continued and increased in number. Here is a selection of them, separated only by the dates on which they closely followed each other.

August 30th

Sir, – I am ashamed to find that there can be found anybody to defend Mr Drury's conduct. I know well enough that had the dead child happened to be the 'remains' of a peer instead of one in humble life, this insult to the dead and to the living would never have happened.

I was baptized in the Church of England, brought up in the Church, have had all my family christened in the nave of the Church, but I am ashamed of the Church; and I am right heartily proud that Ipswich possesses a Wickham Tozer – a gentleman whom I have never seen to the best of my knowledge.

The insolent pretentiousness of a good many 'priests' in the Church of England calls up in one's mind this plain historical fact. There is not a man among them but who is every whit just as much a *schismatic* dissenter and *heretic* as the Reverend Wickham Tozer.

If these 'priests' were Romanists there would be, at least, some consistency in their nonsensical arrogance. To interfere in such an out-

rageous fashion with a funeral service *outside* the churchyard, excites
the deepest indignation against the offender in the mind of

Yours, etc.,

FULL AND FREE LIBERTY

Sir, – The letters signed 'An Ipswich Layman' and 'W. H. Freeman',
in today's issue of the *Daily Times* are both lacking that very 'common
sense', which would enable their authors to discern the conduct of the
Romish rector of Claydon in its true light.

The law breaker was not Mr Tozer, but Mr Drury; the latter refused to bury the child, and the parents desiring to have the usual service over the remains, Mr Tozer consented; no one wished to break
the law, by entering the graveyard to hold the service, but they availed
themselves of the public path adjacent for the solemn ceremony; this
was perfectly legal, and it is just here that the eccentric rector himself
broke the peace by so actively interfering. He had no more right to act
as he did, than to enter and preach in the Nonconformist chapel at
Claydon.

If the reverend father had kept silent in the graveyard during the
short service, no scandal would have occurred; but he did not, and the
discredit of scandal is his alone.

Mr Tozer truly used strong words (none too strong), but the inhumanity of the rector was the cause.

It is a marvel so much forbearance was manifested. A good thrashing
would probably have taught the reverend father to mind his own
business for the future.

Yours faithfully,

Ipswich, August 29th, 1878   H.

Sir, – I have much reason to be thankful to you and for the course
affairs have taken since I ventured upon letter writing. I merely wish
to ensure a fair hearing of the case, Tozer *v.* Drury, and to show that
the defendant had those who feel for him, out of Suffolk as well as in
Suffolk.

'Observer' may be your special correspondent. He does not, however, say so, but at present, as far as I have noticed, the undiscovered
'special' has not given us any reasons for calling the part of the churchyard behind the church *unconsecrated*. Not knowing Akenham I cannot
tell but that the village green may come close up on that side, if it be
on that side at all.

I am quite content to drop the discussion thus, without pressing the 'special' too closely. Most men, if they wrote in error, would have the candour to say so.

It seems to me that this *enfant terrible* which Mr Tozer – I beg pardon, the Reverend W. Tozer – hoped to bring forth out of the womb of this Akenham scandal is stillborn, and I am glad to assist, with all charity, at its interment.

When will Christian Churches of later origin than the Church of England treat their elder sister with a little more respect, and cease to grudge her these emoluments – a sort of dower – which were settled upon her before even they, the younger sisters, were born?

I hope to see Mr Special in print among 'letters from Correspondents'.

Yours very sincerely,

Reepham, Norwich   W. H. FREEMAN

Dear Sir, – I notice in the *Echo* tonight that the Rev. Francis H. Maude has had the effrontery to crib a letter which appeared in your paper on Tuesday, signed 'An Ipswich Vicar', and to insert it in your London contemporary, just altering, evidently for the sake of appearances, the last few lines. The 'Ipswich Vicar', whose letter has thus been manipulated, will be all the more annoyed because Mr Maude has persistently spelt baptized with an 's'. Such actions are a type of the morality of the High Church party.

Yours truly,

Asylum Road, August 29th, 1878   H. WALKER

'Muscular Christianity', 'Good Thrashings', charges of 'cribbing', and of grossly improper spelling . . . In good Queen Victoria's golden days the Christian gentlemen were beginning to show their true character, their true mettle. Their eyes became more contused; the saliva began to flow under their carefully trimmed mustaches . . . And the morning and the evening were only the fifth day!

August 31st

The sixth day dawned with a crop of new letters treading very hard on the heels of the old. The idea of a plot was again hotly repudiated – by the faithful 'Protestant Churchwarden'.

Sir, – Since you published my letter, disclaiming, on behalf of the parishioners, any responsibility for the disgraceful state of the parish church and graveyard, I have received a quantity of correspondence on the subject, and it appears that both the London and provincial press having taken the late burial case up, this little hamlet has gained a most unenviable notoriety.

I have neither the time nor inclination to notice all the wild statements that have been made reflecting on the parishioners, but I cannot allow one or two most unjust charges to pass unanswered. They are so ridiculous that unless coming from the clergy they would have been incredible and unworthy of notice. On the other hand, it seems to me to be very unfair towards Mr Drury to bring up the red-hot poker incident. After being buried in oblivion for sixteen years, it might well have been dropped. But 'An Ipswich vicar' and certain other clergymen are actually trying to persuade the public that the late scene was raised for political aims and objects, and was arranged for that end. Another one says that doubtless the poor child's death was anxiously awaited for weeks and the scene prearranged. These charges are not only ridiculous, but would be libellous if only the perpetrators of the alleged outrage were named.

Probably, the next absurd idea advanced will be that the whole correspondence was arranged to enable schoolmasters to settle the question whether the word baptize should be spelt with an 's' or a 'z', as 'An Ipswich Vicar' would have it. Allow me to inform him and others that the late sad scene was quite spontaneous. Politics had nothing to do with it, or certainly Mr Tozer, who, I am told, has written a book in defence of the Established Church, would not have been there.

No inhabitant of this parish need sacrifice a Baptist two-year-old or deposit his body on a meadow to create a scene. For instance, a passage of arms occurred in the church on the 19th of March last, at which, if exposed, the late burial case would sink into insignificance. But I willingly spare your readers and those highly respected clergymen who were concerned therein the infliction of an exposure, only hinting at it to show how absurd and unjust are the charges which 'An Ipswich Vicar' and others have made against this rural parish with respect to the recent interment.

I am, sir, yours truly,
THE PROTESTANT CHURCHWARDEN

Akenham, Ipswich, August 30th, 1878

It also became clear that questionable behaviour over burial

ceremonies in the Church of England was by no means confined to Firm Father Drury.

Sir, – I have read with the greatest pain the letters in your paper bearing on the above case, and especially those of clergymen justifying the unfeeling and arbitrary conduct of the rector of Claydon. The childish letters of the Rev. W. H. Freeman, who complains of some conduct of the Baptists which he does not designate or describe, compells me to state what occurred in my own case, not from a Baptist minister, but from a rector of the Church of England.

Some time ago I had occasion to complain of the conduct of the said rector, who was far from being the mild, charitable Christian minister we were of old supposed to meet with. The merits (or demerits) of that I can leave. Now comes the miserable sequel. It pleased Providence to take my son away about a fortnight ago. I applied at the rectory of my own parish (adjoining that of the rector indicated above), and as he was from home his lady kindly took great pains to obtain the said neighbouring rector to bury my son. He consented to do so, and lest he should forget, he was again reminded of it the evening before the funeral. We went to the graveyard, and then had to wait for forty minutes (not, mark, while a religious service was going on, but because the rector had forgotten it). I do not say that private pique had anything to do with this wretched delay over the corpse of my child; but it took place, and that not by a 'schismatic' or 'heretic', but by a regularly ordained rector of the Church of England.

I am, Sir,

August 29th, 1878   A DISGUSTED LAYMAN

A reply from the Rev. Francis Maude showed plainly that if touchy about burials, he was also extremely touchy about attacks on his spelling. But he took up the question of the identity of the reporter at the Akenham burial.

Sir, – One is never astonished at anything a madman may do; but I am very much astonished that you should have inserted in your paper today the letter of H. Walker, of Asylum Road. You know very well that I am the 'Ipswich Vicar' whose letter appeared in your Tuesday's paper; and, knowing that, it was unjust and uncourteous to me to insert that vile slander. One can only pity the unfortunate writer; but I think you were to blame – if you will allow me to say so. The poor fellow, I suppose, is a patient at the Asylum, and probably a near relative of the late notorious Hookey Walker. It is a curious circumstance that both your paper and the *Echo* made me spell baptize with *s* instead of *z*. I certainly used *z* in both letters. A friend has pointed out to me this morning that in Chambers's Dictionary, which is good and recent, the verb is spelt with an *s*. But this is an innovation on the old established spelling, and I am bold to say quite unauthorized. Dr Johnson, Walker (no relation of your insane correspondent), Ash, Bailey, Dyche, Blackie's Imperial Dictionary, and Fullerton's Imperial Lexicon, and others too, all spell the verb with a *z*, and so do the Bible and Prayer-book.

This post has brought me a long and courteous note from a gentleman at Sydenham, in reply to my letter in the *Echo*. I refer to one of his objections, because it has been mentioned in Ipswich. He argues that a burial service at the grave is a matter of *necessity*. This I entirely deny. In Scotland the best and most pious Presbyterians have long been buried without any service at the grave. So have, in recent years, various persons in England and on the Continent. Our catechism teaches us that Baptism is 'generally necessary to salvation'; but there is no necessity, moral or religious, for a service at the grave. During recent discussions about the Burials Bill, it was by some strongly urged, both in and out of Parliament, that all services at the grave should be discontinued, both by Churchmen and Dissenters. If Mr Tozer and the friends of the deceased child had held a service in their chapel, or in a private house, there would have been no commotion. If they think their prayers would have been more acceptable to God, and more beneficial to themselves, at the open grave, then their superstition is as great as that of mediaeval or of pagan times. I presume they do not believe in prayers for the dead.

One remark more. I have here and elsewhere buried more than a thousand persons. I never saw a reporter at a funeral. Akenham is an out-of-the-way little place. How came your reporter there? Was he not invited? Does not that invitation show that something was planned and expected – that it was in the interest of certain parties that there should be a scene, and that it should be made the most of?

I am, yours, &c.,

August 30th, 1878   FRANCIS H. MAUDE

Sir, – The letter signed 'H. Walker, Asylum Road', must have been written by the well-known Hookey Walker, who must now be an unfortunate inmate of our Borough Asylum. On this hypothesis alone is it possible to account for the stupidity and spite of the writer. He must otherwise have known that Mr Maude is 'An Ipswich Vicar', and is too able a writer to need to crib another man's production to palm it off as his own. The probability was, therefore, as was the fact, that the two letters respectively signed 'An Ipswich Vicar' and 'Francis H. Maude', were written by one and the same person. To me, this seems the common sense, as it is the only charitable, inference. With this fact within your own knowledge, Mr Editor, I am surprised at your not inserting the unfortunate H. Walker's 'derangement of epithets', as Mrs Malaprop would say, in your waste paper basket, rather than in your columns.

I make no remark on the great case of 'Tozer *v.* Drury', for I have not yet read a report of it, but from what I hear it seems to be something like a 'tempest in a teapot'.

Yours faithfully,

Ipswich, August 30th, 1878   A.H.A.

Some letters to other papers were also sent along to the *East Anglian.* **Mr John Howe, for example, of 122 Clifton Street, Finsbury, had written in this way to the** *Echo*:

Sir, – It is, no doubt, a difficult matter to argue coolly and in a friendly spirit on those subjects which touch us nearly; and I could not help thinking, on reading the letter from the Rev. Francis H. Maude, vicar of Holy Trinity, Ipswich, that he had been somewhat carried away by the exuberance of his own animosity against those who think somewhat differently to himself on matters pertaining to death and burial.

It was in a very strange manner that the reverend gentleman descanted upon comparative values of the Burial Service and the Order for Baptism, reminding one somewhat forcibly of the first gravedigger's *nonchalant* answer to Hamlet's strange query. Thus: –

'*Hamlet:* How long will a man lie i' the earth ere he rot?'

'*1st Gravedigger:* Faith, if he be not rotten before he die (as we have many pocky corses now-a-days that will scarce hold the lying in), he will last you some eight year or nine year; a tanner will last you nine year.'

So long as these burning questions are argued in this spirit, we can never either respect or listen peaceably to our opponents.

In my own parish, in Yorkshire, I have known the afflicted relations and friends left waiting with the corse of their loved one for hours at the churchyard gates while their spiritual leaders were arguing this matter of expediency among themselves. To treat this question in a

cold-hearted way will be to add another pang, in many instances, to
the heavy affliction of death; and such terms as 'bunkum' and 'bosh'
will only make the tears flow faster, and the iron sink deeper into our
souls. I am no sceptic, and God grant I never may be; but I have little
faith in the sincerity of those who would wrangle about matters of
expediency in the house of mourning and in God's acre.

The reverend gentleman says: – 'These questions are a capital means
of throwing dirt at the clergy, raising a prejudice amongst the ignorant
against the Church, and preparing the way for the robbery and confiscation of all Church property.' It is a touching sight, and one which
well accounts for 'these weeps', to see a Church clergyman with his
pockets full of the chattels of holy Mother Church, shaking his fist at
the approaching despoilers.

And press reports now came from *weekly* papers.

Methodist Recorder:

The tendency of such an act of cruelty and bigotry is obvious, and
no one can be more disgusted and pained by such proceedings than
the enlightened and charitable ministers and members of the Church
of England – and we rejoice to think they are by no means few – who
feel that the intolerance of which the above is a sample, is infinitely
more damaging to the establishment which they love than the most
determined attacks of its avowed enemies.

Methodist:

Surely the disgraceful altercation over the burial of an unbaptized
child at Claydon last week will help the cause of those who are trying
to throw open parish grave-grounds to the clergy of all churches, and
to secure for Englishmen about as much freedom as to the burial of
their dead as Turks, Papists, and Russians allow to strangers. At
present an unmanly, unchristian parson of the dominant sect can insult
his fellow-countryman in the style reported this week, because the law
is on his side making him almost absolute master of public ground.

Baptist:

We have had a nice little crop of burial scandals lately, as though
the Church, seeing the power gradually slipping from her palsied
hands, had resolved to signalize her extinction as a department of the
state by the greatest wrong-headed perverseness that even priests
could display. Perhaps, however, the climax has been reached during

the last few days. The *East Anglian Daily Times* not only describes the disgraceful episode in detail, but speaks of the incumbent as 'pacing the graveyard in undescribable petticoats and inconceivable headgear'.

Norfolk News:

We are indebted to the *East Anglian Daily Times* for a graphic representation, with particulars only too faithfully given, of a deplorable scene at Akenham, near Ipswich, on the occasion of the burial of an infant . . . The proceedings as reported are scandalous in the extreme . . . The church is answerable for the insult and the wrong, inasmuch as Parliament, at the instance of churchmen, would remove the ugly anomaly without hesitation . . . We see that even in distant Argyllshire the shameful state of the English burial law was made a topic at the hustings; and though it did not directly affect the Scotch, their love of liberty compelled sympathy for their southern brethren. At every hustings at the next general election, the cry for equality at the grave will be raised with pertinacity; and if the odious distinctions which now distress and affront the Nonconformists are not gotten rid of before, their doom will assuredly be sealed then.

Whether political in intention or not, the burial of Joseph Ramsey in this small Suffolk village was now – and after only one short week of press exposure – affecting the results of elections in Scotland! But one letter which appeared in the *Suffolk Chronicle* at the very end of August (31st) deserves the final place in this opening week's exchange. 'Red herrings' were now blasted away from the path of clear argument and truth.

Trailing the Red Herring

Sir, – I see the Rev. F. H. Maude comes out in a London Evening Paper on the 'Drury' case, and the reverend gentleman referring to the gross outrage and insult offered to the dead and to the living by his brother priest of Claydon and Akenham, used the terms 'humbug', 'bosh', 'bunkum', etc., and strongly denounces this 'tremendous outcry' as to what *he* chooses to call a 'political' affair got up for the purpose of 'throwing dirt at the Clergy' and with a kind of curious buffoonery, the 'Reverend Francis H. Maude, vicar of Holy Trinity', proceeds to drag in Artemus Ward, and – horrors! – over this sad episode, says this cold 'reverend' cynic, 'Why these weeps?'

Why trail the red herring across the scent by asking such a preposterous question as Mr Maude asks about the 'burial service'? The question which has excited our hatred of the very name of priest is the priestly indecency outside the priestly domain.

Who complained of Mr Drury's refusal to read the burial service? Nobody! But with a most preposterous air of injured innocence Mr Maude asks, 'Why may not the church clergyman have at least as much liberty as the Baptist parent or the Baptist minister?' This is foreign to the question, but with some minds it may have the effect of the 'red herring' trailed across the scent; but 'lovers of peace and haters of humbug', as Mr Maude puts it, are not so easily befooled.

I am, Sir, etc.

ONE OF THE HATERS OF HUMBUG

8 Enter 'Our Agricultural Correspondent'

One thing pleasant to find among the journalists of those days was that, though all had their specific jobs within the paper, they were by no means cribb'd, cabin'd or confined by any 'specialist', 'professional' borderlines. The 'Agricultural Correspondent' of the *Suffolk Chronicle* (August 31st) had no difficulty whatever in turning from fields and crops; corn, turnips and cows; to graveyards.

From 'Our Agricultural Correspondent'

. . . From speaking of the ingathering of the harvest, the transition is easy to speak of the work of the busiest of all reapers – Death . . . With . . . chastened sorrow we think also of the sadder side of death, the gathering of the body to the grave.

Our thoughts have been turned in this direction by reading that strange tale . . . of the burial scene at Akenham. Scandalous, indeed, it was, and repugnant we are sure to the feelings of every right-minded person. To you who dwell in towns provided with cemeteries these burial scandals do not come home as they do to us in the country. . . When the presence of death is in any household there is sorrow enough. When loved ones are borne to the grave, what is more natural than that prayer should be offered and consolation spoken by the minister under whom the family attended? We cannot find it in our heart to sympathize with the law of our church, which, in some cases, as in this at Akenham, forbids the holding of *any* service at all at the grave, and in others forbids the ministry of those whose presence the bereaved family desire . . . Neither can we understand the feelings of those who say there is . . . no grievance worth speaking of at all. Would they like to have to bury their own children in enforced silence? or to have to lay them in ground supposed to be in some way comparatively cursed, or at least unblessed? Probably dissenters, with all their faults, have much the same feelings as other people.

To a Christian man it is an additional offensiveness in the present state of the law that it is the poor who are chiefly affected by it. Dissent prevails most amongst the poor, and in country villages the parish churchyard is the only available burying place for those whose means will not allow them to carry their dead to a distant place. There is a Baptist congregation in the village where we live, and when it has happened to some of these well-meaning, if misguided, people to lose a young child, we have seen them holding their service in the road, because the law forbids prayer being offered or consolation spoken within the hallowed precincts of the graveyard. We have turned away from the sight with indignation and shame; and we know other of our fellow church-going neighbours have done the same. Who is it that upholds the present offensive law? Why is it that it is not repealed? Every Englishman has right of burial in the graveyard his country has provided for him. Why is not the law altered so as to allow Christian burial and suitable burial in *all* cases? Why?

Ask the clergy of our church. They – we regret to say – are the great obstacles to the change which their more liberal congregations would gladly welcome. Why it is that the lay element of the church is more sympathizing and tolerant than the clerical is a problem too deep for us to solve. We sincerely regret that it is so . . . If our parsons would for one Sunday sit in the pew and let us laymen occupy their pulpits we would like to take our text in the Book of Genesis, that we might commend to our reverend friends the beautiful spirit breathed in the answer of the children of Seth to the dissenter of their day, 'In the choice of our sepulchres bury thy dead; none of us shall withhold from thee his sepulchre, but that thou mayest bury thy dead.'

Surely a better spirit this, than that which would interrupt a funeral service with unseemly intrusion, or lock the graveyard in the face of a corpse, or . . . continue a law which causes unnecessary pain to numbers of bereaved households in rural England, in the hour of their extreme sorrow.

. . .

I am only a plain layman and not competent therefore to give a trustworthy opinion as against my mother church. But I confess to you . . . that the thought will sometimes cross my mind when I think of these things, 'Are our clergy really sure that the baptism they administer will improve the children's chance for Heaven?' I have at times fallen into still lower depths, and have caught myself asking, 'Whether our catechism does not put a soul-deceiving untruth into our children's mouths?' Then plunging headlong into the mire of unbelief, I ask myself, 'If in the darkest midnight of pagan times there ever was a more ridiculous threadbare superstition than this of the soul-saving efficacy of a few drops of water applied to an unconscious child?' If there is, I declare from my inmost conscience I do not know where to find the record of it. Most fitly do those who teach such 'old wives' fables' elect to clothe themselves in petticoats.

9 'A Visit to Father Drury's Domain'

Meanwhile the *Suffolk Chronicle* had sent one of their 'representatives' to look at the conditions of the churches in the Rev. Drury's 'domain'. Nothing speaks more powerfully than first-hand evidence. This is from their report on August 31st:

A VISIT TO FATHER DRURY'S DOMAIN

Now that Akenham church has been brought before the public there will probably be more pilgrims thither, for it is within reach of a pleasant ramble from Ipswich. Just as Englishmen in Brussels are in duty bound to spend a day at Waterloo, in remembrance of the famous battle fought and won so long ago, some, we doubt not, will feel an interest in gazing upon the now most famous country church and the footpath where Father Drury vindicated his church's exclusiveness, and Mr Tozer the cause of outraged parental grief. St Mary's Church, at Akenham – perhaps we ought to say the church of Notre Dame or of the B. V. M. – is certainly very prettily situated. Its tower is to be seen among the trees to the right of the Norwich Road just before one reaches a weather-worn milestone, which, after careful search, will reveal the fact that Ipswich once lay three miles behind. Between the road and the church is a pretty valley through which runs a by-road leading from the Norwich Road to the Henley Road, and on the other side of that road is Rise Hall, the residence of Mr J. A. Smith. The drive up to Rise Hall leads through a kind of park, prettily wooded and undulating, and when the 'rise' has been climbed, and the hall is passed, the church is seen behind it. It stands in the centre of a square churchyard, the entrance to which – by the gate at which the wordy battle was fought out over the child's coffin – is from one of the Rise Hall meadows. The iron gate, rather rusty, was locked when we paid our visit – as it was left by the reverend father on the memorable day – and the side gate, through which, we believe, the little coffin was carried to the grave, was also fastened with padlock and chain. The churchyard path presented the appearance of being but little used. There were but few graves and fewer tombstones, and the eye soon picked out that which was spoken of as the resting place of the weary sexton. Going round to the side, we saw from the hedge, amongst a number of tiny graves behind the church, a small space uncovered by turf, which we presumed marked the resting place of the 'unbaptized'. Whether this portion be consecrated or not we cannot say; we can say the grass appeared to grow as green there as elsewhere, and there was no difference between it and the rest of the churchyard, except its comparative obscurity behind the church.

The church is rather large, apparently, for so small a population. It consists of nave and chancel, tower, and south aisle. The nave and tower are built of rubble work, the tower having a flint 'parapet', and they have apparently been restored or rebuilt within recent years. The aisle is of red brick, and the chancel walls are plaster, and are rapidly going into decay, that end of the building having rather a forlorn appearance.

So much for the exterior, what about the inside? We cannot tell. There were some cottages near; perhaps the sexton and the keys could be found up was a natural conclusion. We make the attempt and learn at the first cottage, of some children who were apparently left at home while their elders were out harvesting, that the keys are at Mr Drury's. Trying again on seeing someone of more mature age, we find the children quite accurate. We inquire for clerk or sexton – we are told there is none. Mr Smith may have a key but it isn't at all likely. He is not churchwarden, we hear – for there is none; in fact there's nobody but the clergyman has to do with the church, and it is not often there's service. What do the people do, we ask? Well, there are not many of them. A few go to Claydon, many of them go to Whitton, and some – shall we publish it? – go to chapel. Such is the substance of a conversation which is closed as it was begun with the remark – 'I don't think you'll get the keys anywhere but at Mr Drury's, sir.' The Akenham people seem, therefore, to have very few opportunities of going to church, and to have no very great anxiety to embrace those opportunities. 'Ho, every one that thirsteth' is the scripture cry, but at Akenham locked gates and a fence, in which all the gaps are carefully mended, bar the way to the spring, and there is some suspicion that even when these are removed the spring itself is of doubtful quality. Hence, the parish church, the church of the nation but especially the church of the poor man, is deserted, the rust disfigures her closed gates, and the grass grows on the pathway to her doors. And yet 'tis said the Establishment is a guarantee that the religious needs of every portion of the country shall be met!

We forego the visit to the interior of Akenham church, not even jumping the churchyard fence in order to peep in at the windows, and the morning being fine and pleasant take our way across the fields – following the direction indicated by our friend who told us of the whereabouts of the keys – to Claydon Church. We do not ask for the Akenham keys; we are not sure we should get them, we might be suspected of heresy, and we are quite sure we do not wish to have a second journey to Claydon with the keys. We find things not quite so exclusive here. The churchyard gate swings open at the touch; we stroll around amongst the graves – more numerous than at Akenham. We notice that of the Claydon centenarian – Mrs Morphew, after the record of her age, 106, being the text, 'My days are as an hand breadth', and several others bearing well-known names. There is no sign of Catholic doctrine here, unless it be the repeated inscription '*Domine miserere*' round one grave, and one begins to feel curious as to the interior of the church. We approach the door, study the lists of gun licence holders and so on, and finally lift the latch, when the door swings open. There is no one inside, and our entry only disturbs an unfortunate sparrow which has found its way in – perhaps through a broken window in the nave, which is the only neglected part of the building – and, puzzled to make its way out, flies madly against one window after the other. We pity and reflect – are there any sparrows of larger growth under like circumstances in the village?

The church is cruciform in shape, with chancel, nave and north and south transepts. To the chancel attention is at once attracted. It is raised a step above the nave, and separated from it by a screen of open panelled tracery, not very elaborate, but painted white and red, with faded gilt shafts supporting the pointed arches in the tracery. Above the screen is a large crucifix, on each side of which is a female figure. Within the screen we find the altar raised three steps above the floor of the chancel, the walls are diapered, and an ecclesiastical chandelier suspended from the roof contains a number of candles. On the lowermost step of the altar are two large candlesticks about three feet high, with partially burnt candles in them; and on the raised part at the back of the altar, which we believe is known as the super-altar, are half a dozen candles, and the same number of vases of flowers arranged alternately. In the centre is a large wooden cross, on one arm of which the aforesaid sparrow for a short time perched with unconscious irreverence.

This is not the only altar in the church, however. At the east side of the north transept is another, but less gorgeous one. It is seen through an arch piercing the east wall of the transept, corresponding to one which communicates with the organ chamber from the south transept and appears to consist simply of a table placed against the wall, and covered with white cloth, with a kind of step at the back on which two candles and a pair of vases with flowers were placed. The 'lady altar', as we suppose it to be, looked in fact rather forlorn after the more elaborate arrangement in the chancel.

The chancel and transepts are in good repair, and the hand of the carver and decorator is seen both in wood and stone, but the nave is rather dilapidated, one window falling almost to pieces, and presents a marked contrast to the more highly honoured portions of the edifice.

Whether or not what was to be seen at Claydon was at all to be taken as a specimen of what the interior of Akenham church is, we are unable to say. There are few parishes, probably, where the like is to be seen, and Protestant churchmen in Claydon may well wonder at the long suffering patience of their bishop.

10 'A Request for Suspended Judgment': 'Justitia'

On the same day (August 31st), the *Ipswich Journal* came back into the fray, carrying a letter from a very distinguished participant indeed. This pointed an accusing finger – much more directly and forcefully than before – at the author of the initial report: the obscure 'Mr Special'. What was the true story of this 'report'?

THE AKENHAM SCENE:
REQUEST FOR SUSPENDED JUDGMENT

We publish today a letter from a correspondent who requests the public to suspend judgment on the recent scene at Akenham church until something may be heard and known of the other side of the case. Our correspondent is needlessly anxious. We apprehend that if the scene reported in a contemporary is attentively read, certain features will be discerned which will stamp it as a disgrace to all who concocted the mess known as the 'Burial Scandal'.

There is a one-sided appearance in the report which causes us to regret very much that our contemporary, the *Suffolk Chronicle*, should have been left out in the cold when the list of invitations was issued to the press. For ourselves, of course, we do not expect to be honoured whenever the word is passed amongst the political Dissenters to get up a 'Burial Scandal'. We can very well understand that a representative of the *Ipswich Journal* is not wanted whenever the lawless spirits of the Political 'Dissenting tribe' determine to lay siege to a churchyard. But we are a little scandalized to find that so honest, trustworthy and outspoken an organ of the Dissenters as is the *Suffolk Chronicle* was not entrusted to the work of reporting the scandal at Akenham. What does it mean? How is it that a paper which blows hot and cold, which now and then signalizes its love for Dissent by writing an article in opposition to Dissenters, and which professedly is 'everything by turns and nothing long', was chosen to report the 'Burial Scandal', when the honest old Puritan *Chronicle* was kept in the dark as to the time and place of the little comedy? Was it that the uncompromising honesty of principle and the undeviating professional accuracy of the Puritans' representative were feared? But the *Suffolk Chronicle* tells us that by an accidental delay the invitation to be present at the Akenham performance did not reach them.

In one sense this is an explanation to be preferred to that which we suggest. If the intention was to invite two papers to report the scene, which the Rev. Wickham Tozer and a few friends got up to assist Mr Osborne Morgan next session, it was a better resolve than to determine to get up a scene and to have their own report carefully prepared and printed. But from the lofty standpoint which the Dissenters pretend to occupy, how humiliating it is to see them reduced to the extremity of manufacturing scenes – or as they prefer to call them 'scandals' – and inviting the press to witness the little graveside comedies.

If we take the explanation of the *Suffolk Chronicle* as correct, then we see at once into the process of manufacture of this 'scandal'. The Rev. Wickham Tozer issued his cards of invitation to certain friends to attend at Akenham church, and witness his bearding of the lion in his den – in other words, the Rev. George Drury, who might naturally be expected then to defend his churchyard from the desecration of what was from beginning to end no more than a political demonstration. Of course not a word is said of this in the report of the proceedings which was furnished to our daily contemporary. It is then made to appear as much as possible that the burial of the poor child was the main business of the day. The intention of political demonstration is kept very much in the background. Still the political demonstration was made to prosper marvellously. The sighs and sobs of the parents are only brought in to give point and emphasis to the well-prepared and better-rehearsed arguments of the Rev. Wickham Tozer. The printed argument reads very much like those illustrating conversations which are published now and then in the propaganda of total abstinence, in which the man who defends the drinking of beer is condemned to utter defeat in the argument, no matter how well he may start.

Then, again, what a curious motley of attendance there was. For the funeral of a child in the secluded churchyard at Akenham there was a very remarkable assemblage. Surely the gentlemen whose names occur do not make it a point to attend the funerals at Akenham. But if people are told beforehand that the Rev. Wickham Tozer and a few others intend to try to force their way into the churchyard and to make of the burial of a labourer's child a political demonstration in favour of throwing open the graveyards of the Established Church to Dissenting ministers, we can quite understand their presence, and by the note which the *Suffolk Chronicle* appended to its account of the scene on Tuesday, we see clearly enough that this scene at Akenham had been as carefully arranged as though a public meeting had been announced with seats prepared, and a table and other accommodation for the press and the public.

We put it to Englishmen everywhere whether there be not something in such a proceeding which is to their minds odious beyond the power of expression. The cowardice of artfully contriving a scene, the report of which should be entirely under the control of the promoters of the meeting, deserves scorn and contempt of all men. If the Rev. Wickham Tozer desires to agitate for the possession of the churchyards, there is nothing to prevent his doing so, only let him do it openly and in a manly and straightforward manner. His party – we presume that he would claim to be ranked as a Puritan – have never loved the theatre. When, therefore, he quits the pulpit and platform – which we are quite willing to believe he adorns – to arrange these little graveside comedies, he is straying as far from the traditions of his party in a matter of form as he wandered in principle from the example and precepts of his great Master.

Well . . . ? certainly new grounds for thought were raised here Who *was* the author of the report? And how was the large number attending the funeral to be explained? No one could say that farm labourers were held in high public regard. Infantile mortality was common. Stillborn babies were buried on banks or in ditches. Why the concern on this one occasion?

The letter to which the editor referred was this:

The Akenham Scene

Sir, – An article appears in the *East Anglian Times* of today, headed 'Burial Scandal at Akenham', and as the contents (which are more or less false throughout) will probably become the subject of judicial investigation, will you allow me, through the medium of your columns, to request the public to suspend judgment?

My reason for thus troubling you, instead of writing to the newspaper in which the article appears, is that experience leads me to fear that reply, whether commentative or defensive, to an attack made thereon may not obtain free and unaltered admission. I trust, therefore, you will, of your courtesy, insert this in an early impression, and the more especially as I shall not trouble you again on the subject.

3

The writer of the article being (perhaps prudently) anonymous, I simply subscribe myself

Your obedient servant

August 26th, 1878   JUSTITIA

A little later, it was caustically said that this correspondent 'knew the Rev. Drury's mind very well'. But can there be any doubt at all that Firm Father Drury had approached the lists himself? For the first time, and after only one week, the smell of legal proceedings wafted over the scene. Where would this incident lead? How far would it go?

11 *An editorial offer – with no result*

With Monday morning of the second week, however (September 2nd), the time seemed to have come to close the matter. The fire of the disturbance seemed to have burned itself out. The editor who had started and fanned the blaze (i.e. the editor of the *East Anglian Daily Times*) now felt that it was dying, and that it should perhaps be extinguished. Not, however, without a final offer to the chief combatants on the Akenham meadow that a last word from both of them could be heard if they wished:

THE AKENHAM BURIAL CASE

We have received further letters on this subject, but it has now been thoroughly discussed, and, as far as we are concerned, the correspondence must end, unless the principal actors – the Rev. G. Drury and the Rev. Wickham Tozer – desire to address the public through our columns. We observe, in a letter to the *Ipswich Journal*, that a writer who appears to know Mr Drury's mind, expresses his apprehension that any reply to an attack made in the *Daily Times* might not obtain 'free and unaltered admission'. Mr Drury has many times been allowed to address the public at length through our columns when, as his friend states, no other Suffolk paper was open to him. He is at perfect liberty to avail himself again of the privilege, and, having been vehemently attacked, we will promise him that any letter shall appear unabridged and unaltered.

A letter was, in fact, submitted by Mr Tozer, but nothing was forthcoming from Rev. Drury,* so that neither were published. The matter seemed completely dead.

But . . . not quite!

* *See* pp. 230–31.

Clearly there was still a lively curiosity about the Rev. George Drury himself. What sort of a man was he? Was the conduct of his services as bad as had been said? How – as a matter of usual practice – did he conduct the affairs of his churches? Was he a monster? Was he incapable? Inefficient? Or genuinely a man of meticulous principle – and, within the rubric of the Church's regulations – a man of warmth and humanity?

Someone was sent to see. On Tuesday, September 3rd, in a special supplement of the *Suffolk Chronicle* this report appeared. It became clear that Joseph Ramsey was not the only child with whom Drury had dealt in this manner. Burial scandals were perhaps the rule rather than the exception.

SUNDAY MORNING SERVICE, AKENHAM

On Sunday when the rector of Claydon made his way across the fields to Akenham church he found that for once his walk thither had not been in vain. The congregation was there, and in rather large proportions, it being one advantage of the uncertainty prevailing as to the service that the congregation is bound to put in an appearance first and wait for the parson, instead of *vice versa*. The hour of service was also unknown to some, and this ensured punctuality. By somewhere about half-past ten, therefore, there were one or two arrivals, and later on twos and threes came up the hill, till at last when Mr Drury came, precisely at eleven, with the keys of churchyard and church, there was quite an unusual muster in Mr Smith's meadow.

Some others, apparently, had visited the church during the week, and these clearly had not waited for the opening of the gate but had gone over the hedge, for it was broken down in several places. The gates, however, still remained locked, although the side gate has customarily been unfastened, as it was found after Mr Drury left on the occasion of the recent funeral. There are several little graves behind the church, and it seems that the newest is not the only one which has sad associations in connection with the burial law, for we hear of one little coffin interred there in a manner which does not appear to have been thought unseemly at Akenham, and gives some idea of what may possibly have been desired on this occasion. In that case there was no service over the grave of the departed little one, not even a dissenting minister on the footpath outside to speak the word of consolation and of hope, but in the darkness of an autumn morning, by the feeble light of a friendly lantern, the father himself laid the little coffin in the grave, and filled in the earth which covered it out of his sight. The infant was the child of a labourer named Noller, then living in the parish. Noller had had the misfortune to lose several children by death, and this was taken from him almost as soon as it had been given – at the age of a very few weeks. It had not been baptized; Mr Drury, therefore declined to conduct the burial service, but a grave was prepared at the back of the church for the interment, and one afternoon Mr Drury attended to witness the silent burial. The father came with the corpse of his little one, but he was unprepared with a certificate, and Mr Drury thereupon said he could not allow the child to be buried till one was procured. The result was that Noller left the coffin at the tumble-down, dilapidated dwelling at the back of the church, which it seems is the glebe house, and trudged off to a parish at some considerable distance to get this certificate, getting home again towards midnight. The next morning, we suppose before going to work, at any rate while it was yet dark, he went again to the glebe house, took the coffin, and, accompanied by another labourer who held the lantern, acted as parson, clerk and sexton at the burial of his own child.

In other cases, we learn, infants have been baptized by Mr Drury in cases of illness at their parents' houses, but in these cases although he has read the burial service at the grave, the corpse has not been allowed to be taken into the church – a distinction the merits of which it is not easy to discern.

We leave, however, the consideration of these tiny graves in the back of the churchyard. Mr Drury having arrived opened the gate and church door, and entered the church, his congregation following. Twenty-one they were in all, including the policeman, who, as this was not his parish church, presumably came to see fair, and three others entered half-way through the service. Most were evidently strangers; the few natives whom we saw outside apparently preferring to keep there, for one told us he had not been inside the church door for many years, and the strangers cast their eyes round the church, as they entered. We had been asked if we had brought a duster with us, and truly it would not be undesirable to carry one in the pocket when one visits Akenham church. The porch floor was covered with dirt and dust, probably driven in through the open lattice gate, and a birch broom stood in the corner as if reproachfully saying, 'Please use me', while inside the church smelt damp and unpleasant; the benches, more especially on the book-rests were covered with dust, cobwebs adorned the handy corners of the building, while the 'altar' on which were a cross and two candles, one of which leaned respectfully to the cross in the centre, shared the general air of decay and shabbiness.

The service commenced at once, Mr Drury and the clerk sharing the reading, which was got through apparently as quickly as possible. The reverend gentleman cannot be congratulated on his abilities as a reader, being both rapid and indistinct, so much so that in the least familiar portions of the service it was difficult to comprehend what was being said, and there was a good deal to remind one of a sulky boy compelled to read as a task. There was no singing, and the whole service, including the sermon, was over in about fifty minutes.

Mr Drury, who before commencing his sermon crossed himself and repeated the formula, 'In the name of the Father, and of the Son, and of the Holy Ghost, Amen', took his text from the gospel for the day, Luke xviii., 10, 'Two men went up into the temple to pray, the one a Pharisee and the other a publican.' Almighty God, he said, had promised often to hear and answer those who had recourse to Him in His holy temple, but many persons, notwithstanding, went to church and asked His assistance, both in their spiritual and temporal concerns, who went away unhelped. He spoke of the privileges which God bestowed on the ancient temple of Jerusalem, and the equal privilege which he bestowed on our temples now, by His presence in the Blessed Sacrament; and proceeded to enquire in the light of the parable before him why with all these privileges some should go to God in His church and yet be unblessed, leaving the church in a worse condition than they went to it. One reason, he said, was that men did not pay that respect to the house of God which was due to it, and made no difference between the church and other places of public concourse. The heathen and infidel nations, he said, had always shown a respect and veneration for their temples which might cause Christians to blush, for Christian churches were not the tabernacles of images, but of the true God. That our Saviour taught the duty of reverence for God's house Mr Drury further showed by referring to the narrative of his cleansing the temple of the buyers and sellers, but notwithstanding this, he said, in the church, which was the house of God, people set snares to catch souls, there they pleased men of the world, there they became stones of stumbling and rocks of offence. Men went to church not to worship, but to see and to be seen; they went not only without reverence but without thought, and those who had the greatest need to pray neglected prayer most. It was very evident that the faith of many people in England was very small, or they would act differently towards the church which was the dwelling place of God, and he commended to his hearers the duty of reverence for the church and its services.

We hope the large congregation did not embarrass the reverend gentleman, but it occurred to us that he seemed as if he were not preaching the sermon he had before him. Our idea was rather confirmed than otherwise, when in the afternoon at Claydon we found the reverend gentleman preaching from another text – Luke xiv., 11, 'For whosoever exalted himself shall be abased; and he that humbleth himself shall be exalted', a sermon which throughout had reference to the Pharisee and the publican, a parable which occurs in a different connection. There was nothing in either sermon bearing upon recent occurrences, unless it were a remark as to Pharisees of the present day who followed their own desires instead of the commandments of God, who when told to do such and such things excused themselves by saying that those things did not commend themselves to their ideas, and who when told that the Church prescribed such and such things refused to hear the Church.

One or two nuns from the convent attended service at Claydon in the afternoon, one of them bringing several children from the convent school, who, with herself, bowed before the altar as they passed. The nuns we heard well spoken of in the parish for kindliness and generosity, and we hear also that their present quarters being now too small, other accommodation is being enquired for in the village.

Letters persisted a little longer. One is worth noting, coming from an irate gentleman whose eyes were obviously focused with a more serious concern on Scotland.

THE AKENHAM BURIAL SCANDAL

Sir, – Have you observed that your irascible contemporary, the *Ipswich Journal*, was so highly indignant at the absence of your reporter from this very edifying scene that the result of the Scotch election, in which the Liberal candidate was returned by a majority of 355, was altogether unnoticed in last Saturday's impression? Kindly avoid for the future to insert any fact that might produce a similar effect, and oblige.

AN IPSWICH JOURNAL READER

13 'Vile, monstrous law'

On September 7th, the *Suffolk Chronicle*, too, decided to make its final editorial comment, but the more important point was that the last letters to the editor revealed what lay at the centre of the matter:

THE ENGLISH BURIAL LAW

Sir, – It is a sad sight to see a little coffin carried mournfully and slowly down a churchyard path to the lowly spot where the small remains are to be laid in their last resting place. How many homes in England contain some silently eloquent, sad memento – a little dress, or tiny baby shoe, or toy – that recalls with touching pathos, the playful merriment, or sorrowful, pining sickness that has finished in a scene like this!

And such should surely be a scene of peace! Hatred, and strife, and anger, can have no lodgment here; the kinship of the world should by this painful touch of nature be felt by all her sons. But no! It is at such a scene that man who has a higher guide than nature, who is bound by our loving Saviour's law to solace and to bless, has his work of mercy stopped by England's Burial Law, by which he is directed with pharisaical bigotry (a sin more vehemently denounced by that loving Lord than any other) to withhold the solace he should impart; and with that pharisaical cold disdain to say of the remains of the little one, who is all angel now, 'stand aside, I am holier than thou'. Vile, monstrous law! Foul blot and stain on fair England's statute book! If the sorrowing father and mother, doomed to watch in helpless misery the coming of the messenger that changes the sad little plaintive face, and according to the awful words sends the little life away, do not believe in infant baptism or earthly sponsors, and, I say it respectfully, many do not – if they believe that only Jesus could be sponsor for that little child, and that their Bible teaches that the mighty sacrifice, which made the firm earth shake, hid the bright sun, and made the heavens turn dark, was all the salvation he needed, – if they believe that until a conscious age made him feel and mourn his sin, and as they hoped confess it by believer's baptism, confess *it*, and his humble trust for the pardon of it, to the mighty sacrifice, the mighty Saviour, – if they refused any baptism in infancy, believing it was never meant to save the soul – this is the consequence. This minister of this same Saviour, with his man-made dogma of salvation, is by England's law not only bound to refuse to the mourners around the child's grave the comfort of those words of hope in a glorious resurrection, but is also bound by that law – branded with the cursed bigotry of persecution – to refuse to allow another to administer that consolation. This is Christian England's burial law!

And by this burning shame and scandal, this unspeakable law that refuses, excepting by an implicated curse, to bury the innocent child, its minister is bound in solemn mockery to read those same beautiful words of hope over the blackest, unrepenting profligate that ever walked God's earth! Nay, more, the boldest scoffing infidel, if he have been baptized in infancy, can claim what is denied to innocence – a so-called Christian burial.

Will Englishmen continue coolly to allow such a vile abomination? Englishmen who look upon their fellow men in Russia as semi-barbarians, who hope to teach the pagan Turk to live a better life, who send missionaries to every heathen clime, and who with Imperial pride govern the dusky millions in tropical India? More than *semi*-barbarian, worse than the Pagan Turk, blinder and blacker than the idolatrous Hindoo, neither lips have language, nor has any language words, fit to denounce a law that, in a Christian land, bans with an implied curse the poor little innocent, dead child – one of those of whom our Saviour said, 'Of such is the kingdom of heaven', and whose spirit doubtless rejoices now in the worship of its glorified Redeemer.

This is not written for political purposes; the writer gets the credit from his closest friends of being a strong Conservative. But not to conserve a law like this! It is not written to foster or increase the difference between church and dissent; few men regret that more, or its cause. How often, Sir, does the Dissenter's heart mourn that when, hushed all around from the noise of man's toil, the still air is filled with the sweet music of the Sabbath bells, he cannot answer to their sacred call, and go together with his family, his neighbours, and his friends to the hallowed fane, and all together bow to the great Father! Though this cannot be, Christian men, dissenters or not, love the English Church so far as it, in their belief, is the church of their Lord. And though denouncing this law, no word ought ever to be breathed against those numberless noble-hearted ministers and members of that Church – men and gentle women too – who, like their beloved Master, strive by helping those in trouble, sympathizing with those who mourn, and rejoicing with them that do rejoice, and by their self-denying lives prove themselves servants of Him, who remembered not Himself, but was a glorious embodiment of self-sacrificing love.

And if that church contain as others do those who make broad their phylacteries, enlarge the borders of their garments, love the uppermost seats in the highest rooms, and to be called by great names, denounce them not. They have their consciences, their bibles, and their God. And by His grace, charity is fain to hope they may learn humility. At all events poor frail man has enough himself for which to bow in penitence, without railing at his fellow men.

But when a hideous wrong like this blazes up at our very doors, causing two men who should be meek and loving, and full of the charity that suffereth long and is kind, to stand like two animals at bay, spectacles to the world of a spirit of all uncharitableness – though naturally shrinking from publicity – man's thoughts are stirred within him, and if silent he brands himself as recreant to religion, humanity, and truth. With all respect and tenderness for the conscientious scruples of others, if any church wishes for such a law simply for its own members (however much to be regretted), let no one outside interfere, but in mercy forbear the tyranny that forces such a law upon the nation at large.

I am, Sir, &c.,

Rushmere, September 5th   JOHN SKEET

In all this, too, there was at least one man who had – in a considered way – changed sides.

THE AKENHAM BURIAL SCANDAL

Sir, – Many thanks to your Agricultural Correspondent for his openness with Dissenters; but running through the whole of that part of his letter which treats of the late Burial Scandal at Akenham, I feel something like conviction that the writer is, if he do not know it, *a Dissenter*. For first, he says (manfully too!) 'It is true many of our bishops and clergy say that the grievance of Dissenters in country parishes is only a sentimental grievance – if a grievance at all, but so do not say the laity.' Of course then the laity *dissent* from the bishops and clergy if language be language. Secondly, he asks: 'Is not the ample bosom of our church wide enough for all?' Why, sir, the bosom of 'our' church is too narrow to receive even your generous Agricultural Correspondent's conscientious views. There are indeed many signs of discontent with the Church of England's ritual in his letter. I hope all your readers will carefully read that letter again and try to profit by it.

I am glad that our friend can see no *sin* in being a *Dissenter*, if he could he would be a sinner for *dissenting* from his parson and the bishops and clergy generally as to the value of a few drops of water sprinkled on a child (by sometimes a vicious man in holy orders), though I hope from my very soul that every godly clergyman believes that this regeneration by water is an insult to his God, and also 'a soul-deceiving untruth'.

Thank God for our God-fearing clergy, but oh! how many of those monsters of ritualism in the church there are!

I commend that reference to your readers, Gen. xxiii, 6–12,* especially verse 11.

I am, Sir, &c.

A CONSCIENTIOUS 'DISSENTER' THOUGH

ONCE A 'CHURCHMAN'

September 2nd, 1878

---

* The passage in Genesis to which the Conscientious Dissenter refers is this. (It is extended by the inclusion of two earlier verses.)

Abraham came to mourn for Sarah, and to weep for her.

And Abraham stood up before his dead . . . saying, I am a stranger and a sojourner with you: give me a possession of a burying place with you, that I may bury my dead out of my sight.

And the children of Heth answered Abraham, saying unto him, Hear us, my lord: though art a mighty prince among us: in the choice of our sepulchres bury thy dead; none of us shall withhold from thee his sepulchre, but that thou mayest bury thy dead.

And Abraham stood up, and bowed himself to the people of the land. . . And he communed with them, saying, If it be your mind that I should bury my dead out of my sight; hear me, and intreat for me to Ephron the son of Zohar, that he may give me the cave of Machpelah, which he hath, which is at the end of his field; for as much money as it is worth he shall give it me for a possession of a burying place among you.

And Ephron dwelt among the children of Heth: and Ephron the Hittite answered Abraham in the audience of the children of Heth, even of all that went in at the gate of his city, saying, Nay, my lord, hear me: the field I give it thee; in the presence of the sons of my people give I it thee: bury thy dead.

And Abraham bowed down himself before the people of the land.

14 *'The Law of Burials': 'A Poor Vicar'*

The last letter of all in this sudden eruption of feelings in 1878 also dwelt on the law, but brought in, graphically, another underlying problem. The discussion had been in terms of the character of clergymen, the situation between the Church of England and Dissenters – especially when a High Church man ruled matters by the letter of the law. But . . . the nation of the living was growing, and so too was the nation of the dead. Where were these new dead to lie? Were they to be buried among the bones of earlier generations – broken, disturbed, disinterred to make way for them – whilst an obdurate Church retained its hold on cherished rights and property? Or were some new *sanitary* arrangements needed now? A 'poor vicar' posed these questions in the *East Anglian Daily Times* on September 10th:

THE LAW OF BURIALS

Sir, – As I pointed out in your columns of June, 1877, the burials difficulty is extending itself to the newly consecrated graveyards – the modern cemeteries – as witness a letter in your paper today from an Independent preacher at Ipswich, who, by the way, in his ignorance of history, calls the Church of England a sect, forgetting the origin of his own denomination not quite three centuries ago. He asks if it is illegal for a Nonconformist minister to officiate on the consecrated side of a cemetery and 'what penalty would be incurred by a gentleman so acting?' The natural answer to the latter question seems to be that no gentleman would do such a thing. But how comes it to pass that such anxiety is manifested (real or feigned) over the burial of the recently dead, and so dreadfully little regard is paid in village churchyards to the remains of prior generations? In a churchyard which is within walking distance from Ipswich (I am speaking on good authority, though not myself an eyewitness), to bury a clergyman's wife in 1849, seven bodies were cut away, and to a bury a young man two months ago, twenty skulls were dug up, and bones unnumbered. How long are scenes of this sort to last? The burial question which most needs settlement is this – when are our churchyards to be closed and to give way to village

76

cemeteries over which no bishop ever pronounced consecration, and
in which clergymen shall not be obliged to bury with a religious service
the parochial riff-raff, or the unbeliever, and Baptists may be able to
inter with rites satisfactory to themselves unbaptized infants, and
Romanists to use their own ceremonial, no man making them afraid?
The Queen in Council, on the representation of the Secretary of State,
may order the discontinuance of burials in any burial ground except
in joint stock cemeteries. And when a parish churchyard is closed, the
churchwardens must call a vestry to appoint a burial board. Two or
more parishes may write for the purpose. No burial ground so provided can be opened within one hundred yards of any dwelling house,
except by permission. Part is to be consecrated and part unconsecrated (16 and 17 Vict., c 134), and chapels may be built thereon for
Churchmen and Dissenters (15 and 16 Vict., c 85). What is wanted is
the abolition of the latter power, to which point I would invite the
attention of Liberationists, and the repeal of all Acts authorizing
the consecration of parish cemeteries. Allow clergymen to bury in the
grounds so provided as well as anyone else, and do not punish anyone
for declining to officiate, and legalize what is at present, to put it
mildly, an offence against the law of trespass, a misdemeanour, and,
therefore, for a minister of the Gospel ungentlemanly, by throwing
open the consecrated part of our present cemeteries to persons at
present excluded from officiating therein. It must not be inferred from
what I have written, that unconsecrated graveyards are necessarily
free from unseemly disregard of the sanctity of the dead. I remember a
disgraceful case at Manchester a few years ago, and I learn from the
Kidderminster Sun that a broker, who recently bought an old Baptist
graveyard there, demurred to taking the gravestones as fixtures at a
valuation, and that they have, therefore, been removed, and, incredible
as it may seem, bones are said to have been taken out of the graves and
sold to a marine store dealer.

Truly yours,

September 7th, 1878   A POOR VICAR

Under the talk – about priest and parson, High Church, Low
Church and Dissenter; about birettas and indescribable petticoats; about cobwebs, sparrows and dead birds in sacred buildings; about Church regulations and Divine intentions – lay this
sheer material problem of numbers of dead and acres of land
for their disposal. The situation, apart from its unbending
arithmetic, had become ugly, distasteful, macabre. When do

the dead deserve respect? Only when freshly dead? May the ancient be cut into pieces to make way for the modern? Is time a gradation of respect among the dead? These basic problems, these basic questions, remained and grew whilst the churches chattered.

But the Akenham Burial Case itself seemed dead and buried now, after two weeks of irate, explosive journalism. The articles, the exchanges of press reports, the letters to editors, ceased. Quiet returned to East Suffolk. However, the silence in the autumn of 1878 was an illusion.

Firm Father Drury was a man of strong will. Mr Thurston's Black Book had later chapters of this story to disclose.

ACTION IN COURT

1 *The Akenham Burial Case*

TRIAL OF THE ACTION FOR LIBEL

DRURY v. WILSON

COURT OF COMMON PLEAS, WESTMINSTER

Six months later, at the beginning of March 1879, the noise of controversy sounded again – and loudly; this time not only in remote villages in East Anglia, round about Ipswich, but in the heart of London, where parliamentarians and all the leading papers of the country were able to focus attention upon it. Now the Akenham Burial Scandal became, in real earnest, the Akenham Burial Case. Indeed, almost a test case, though this was the verdict of a jury, and not the ruling of a judge. The 'legal proceedings' hinted at earlier by Justitia had now assumed a definite form. Firm Father Drury had sued Mr Frederick William Wilson (editor and proprietor of the *East Anglian Daily Times*) for libel; and the trial of the action took place in the Court of Common Pleas, Westminster.

The trial raised and examined again (but now closely) all those points that had been matters only of conjecture six months before, clarifying them all by evidence. Very early in the proceedings, the author of the original article was identified. The skeletons in the Reverend Drury's cupboard were all taken out and given a public airing. The story gathered substance. The framework of supposition was filled out by fact. But the report of the trial speaks most directly and vividly for itself.

2 *Case for the Plaintiff** *

(i) *Opening Statement*

This libel case came before Mr Justice Grove and a special jury this morning.

Mr Day, Q.C., Mr Merewether, Q.C., M.P., and Mr Poyser appeared for the plaintiff; Serjeant Parry, Mr Bulwer, Q.C., M.P., and Mr K. E. Digby appeared for the defendant.

Mr Poyser: Gentlemen of the jury, the plaintiff in this case is the Rev. George Drury, rector of Claydon and Akenham, in the county of Suffolk. The defendant is the editor and publisher of the *East Anglian Daily Times*, a newspaper published at Ipswich in the said county. In the statement of claim the plaintiff states that on or about the 26th of August, 1878, the defendant published certain libels concerning him and his office as rector of the parishes of Akenham and Claydon. The statement of claim also goes on to say that on or about August 29th, 1878, the defendant in the said newspaper published certain other libels concerning him in his capacity of rector of Akenham. Then the plaintiff claims damages from the defendant. In his statement of defence, the defendant admits that he printed and published the newspaper containing the paragraphs as set out. He says the paragraphs were true: he also says they were matters of public interest, and that the statements and comments did not exceed the bounds of fair and legitimate criticism. Upon this statement of defence the plaintiff, in his reply, joins issue, and these are the issues you have to try.

Mr Day: May it please your Lordship, gentlemen of the jury, I may say in this case, not as a matter of form as sometimes may be said by counsel in introducing an action of libel in respect of personal character to a jury, that I am sorry such a case should be tried in a public court of justice. In this case I do say so unfeignedly and most sincerely, meaning what I say. It is painful enough to have to try in public courts of justices questions which affect personal character and personal character only; but it is painful in the extreme to any person, I think of proper sentiment to have to try not merely questions affecting personal character, but to find mixed up with them questions which

* From *East Anglian Daily Times*, March 8th, 1879. For the brief provisional report given by the *Ipswich Journal* on the same date see Appendix 1, p. 257.

touch the deepest interests of the human heart. We shall have here introduced to your attention, I am afraid – to judge from the defence set upon this record – questions which agitate the religious world, and may be said to disturb the feelings of many individuals. We shall have these questions raised, not, I believe, for the genuine and honest purpose of establishing a defence to this action, which is brought simply to clear the character of the plaintiff, but we shall have this defence set up for by purposes, and for purposes of fostering and fomenting religious and political agitation which ought not, as I venture humbly to think, to be introduced to the consideration of juries or to be dealt with in courts of justice. This action is brought by the Rev. George Drury, the rector of the parishes of Claydon and Akenham, in the county of Suffolk, to clear his character from gross imputations cast upon him by the defendant, who is the editor of the newspaper known as the *East Anglian Daily Times* – a daily paper, published, I believe, at Ipswich, and circulated throughout the county of Suffolk; and the libel that has been published on this gentleman is a libel which arises out of circumstances that occurred at the funeral of a little child, I think some two years old – the child of some poor labouring people in the parish of Akenham. I cannot help thinking, and I rather think it will be a conclusion to which you yourselves will speedily come, that the funeral of this child was not dealt with as funerals should be – as a painful occasion when parents carry their lost child to the grave, and there part with child and leave it under circumstances most solemn; but the occasion was taken advantage of by persons other than those poor persons, for the purpose of making an ostentatious display that would have the effect of worrying and disturbing the clergyman on the one hand, and of fostering and aiding an agitation which is very rife now for throwing open the burial grounds to the ministrations of others than the Church ministers. You are aware that for some years past a considerable agitation has been developed throughout the country on behalf of some of the Dissenting denominations to procure admission for their ministers to the churchyards, so that their ministers, and not the ministers of the Established Church in this country, should perform over their dead the burial service. No doubt, gentlemen, it was thought by those who promoted the scene that took place at Akenham churchyard on the occasion to which I call your attention, that a favourable opportunity presented itself of irritating and causing pain to the minister of the parish, and also of getting an opportunity, if possible of exciting still further, and fanning still further, the public flame of agitation which exists in certain districts in this country, particularly where there are many Dissenters. The parish of Akenham is a parish in which, I believe, there are few, if any, persons who may be termed members of the Church of England. It is a parish in which the farmers are, I believe, members of the various Dissenting communities, and as the employers of labour are, I think I may say, all Dissenters, it may be said that the labourers, not unnaturally, are also members of Dissenting communities, and you will find in this particular parish there are now very few persons that for many years have been members of the Church of England. I am obliged to call your attention to that because you will see the force of the libel is, as it were, an attack upon the character of my client, as though that were the cause of the comparatively neglected state in which the church is found. On the occasion of this child's funeral, communication was made to Mr Drury; the father, I believe, called on him, and requested that an arrangement should be made for the funeral of the child, and that arrangement was made, and the Rev. Mr Drury was prepared to discharge his duty according to the ritual of the Church of England. It would seem, however, that this was not exactly what was desired – I would not say by the parents of the child, because really I acquit them of all blame in this matter. The body of their unfortunate child has been made a stalking horse for other persons, and for agitators who desire to make something out of the opportunity which they naturally thought would be presented to them. They knew very well that the Rev. Mr Drury was not only a clergyman of the Church of England, but was a gentleman who had filled this living for a great number of years, and was very well known to be a strict adherent to the ritual of the Church of England, a person, who, as I understand it, adheres to the various provisions contained in the ordinances of the Church of England, and in the Prayer Book of the Church of England, and it was known perfectly well that he would neither do, nor allow to be done, that which the law of the Church of England prohibited. Now, gentlemen, it is not for us here in a court of justice to consider what ought to be the law: it is not for us in a court of justice to consider whether the Church of England should be established or Dissenters should be established, or whether Independents should be established, or whether Baptists should be established or not, or whether anybody should be established – whether there should be a general disestablishment or disendowment. Those are all questions upon which you may each of you entertain private opinions, but in a court of justice you have nothing in the world to do with them. You might as well consider whether the law as to larceny should be maintained. We have here, in a court of justice, simply to administer the law as the law is, and to deal with the cases which come before us in accordance with the law which regulates and binds us and our proceedings, and therefore I trust we shall have no attempt made during this case to discuss what the clergyman ought to have done under some different state of the law or different circumstances. He, as a minister of the Established Church, was not only entitled to obey its laws and provisions, but he was bound to obey its laws and provisions, and those persons who made use of this opportunity for the purpose of fanning this political agitation about the opening of the churchyards knew perfectly well that the Rev. Mr Drury was a clergyman on whom they could thoroughly rely to afford them the desired opportunity, because they knew perfectly well he would not sanction or allow anything in the nature of any ministration by what I may term foreign ministers in this churchyard. He was perfectly willing to provide for this child's funeral in accordance with the rules and regulations of the Church of England. He told the father, who applied to him to appoint a day for the burial of the child, with the approbation, and, I think, at the instance of the father, that he would appoint five o'clock on the Thursday afternoon. Nothing whatever was said on that occasion with reference to the circumstances of the funeral, or the character of the funeral, or anything of the kind. The Rev. Mr Drury had no further communication with the father from that day, until the day when the body of the child was brought to the graveyard for interment. At that time I believe the Rev. Mr Drury had no precise knowledge either of the denomination to which the parents belonged, or as to whether the child had or had not been baptized, but it undoubtedly did come to his knowledge in the course of the week, and that I believe from a communication which the father had with the clerk, a man of the name of Waterman – who will, I believe, be called as a witness before you – that the child was a child of parents of the Baptist persuasion, and that he had not been baptized. The Rev. Mr Drury, who was well acquainted with the provisions of his Prayer-book, was aware that the funeral service of the Church of England could not be performed over that child, because I find by a rubric in the Prayer-book, with which I dare say you may be more familiar than I am, 'Here it is to be noted that the office ensuing is not to be used for any that die unbaptized or excommunicate, or have laid violent hands upon themselves.' Therefore this office is not to be used for persons that die unbaptized. Now, gentlemen, as I said before, it may occur to the minds of many people, 'Why should it not be used upon persons unbaptized, why should it not be used for persons who dissent altogether, or if they had lived would have dissented from everything connected with the Church of England?' We have nothing to do with that. It is part of the law of the land, because it is a part of the ritual of the Church established by the law, that this office is not to be used in respect of persons who die unbaptized. The Church of England considers that baptism is an initiatory rite into this Church, and persons who have not entered this Church are not persons entitled to claim the ministrations of the Church. Whether it is wise, whether it is reasonable, whether it is what you would do, is utterly immaterial – we have nothing to do with it. It is the law of the Church of England, and persons who are not members of the Church of England would seem to have little reason to complain that they cannot have the benefit of the Church of England services, and probably the parents of this child had no wish to have the services of the Church of England, or any sort of advantage derived from the Church of England. As I said before, this is not a struggle of the parents, but the struggle of political parsons, who desire to make political capital out of the circumstances of the burial of this little infant. Well, Mr Drury being made aware that this child had not been baptized, it could not be buried with the services of the Church of England. The opportunity was too good to be lost, and accordingly two or three persons connected with the parish – I think two of the largest farmers in the parish – themselves Dissenters – took an opportunity of arranging for a religious service to be performed, if not in the churchyard, yet under circumstances that should have at least as good a political effect. I do not suppose that they sought to derive any advantages, or spiritual advantage, from any funeral service, because I do not suppose that either the clergyman who performed the service, or the persons who took part in it, supposed for a moment that any prayers they might offer up either in the churchyard or outside would in any way benefit the soul of the infant or would be of any particular good, whether offered at a funeral or under any other circumstances. That prayer would be a good thing – prayer in any place would be a good thing – nobody, I trust, would doubt or deny, but I do not suppose any of these persons would have attached any particular value to prayer offered up in a churchyard or exactly outside a churchyard; but there might be considerable political advantage derived from prayer offered under such circumstances; therefore, these gentlemen determined that as the clergyman would not read the burial service of the Church of England, they at any rate would secure that there should be some religious manifestation, or really, as I ought to say, some service of some sort for some purpose or other, which you will be able, I dare say, to understand – some service should be offered up in the immediate neighbourhood of the churchyard. Accordingly, as I understand, an arrangement was made that the service should take place in a field immediately adjoining the churchyard, and two leading farmers of the parish arranged to attend the funeral themselves, not that under ordinary circumstances it is the usual fashion of the country for the leading farmers to attend the funeral of a small child two years old, the infant of one of their labourers. It would be remarked as a very extraordinary attention if the leading farmers of the parish attended a funeral of a two-year-old child – the child of one of their labourers – but you find that they did attend. They first of all secured the services of a gentleman of some dissenting denomination who resided at Ipswich. It appears that the parents were Baptists, but for some reason or other, the Baptist minister, whether from good feeling, or unwillingness to thrust himself into an agitation with which religion could have no concern, did not attend, but a gentleman of some other denomination, I believe of the Independent persuasion, the Rev. Mr Tozer, whom I shall have to introduce more particularly to your attention by-and-by, gladly availed himself of the opportunity to thrust himself into this contention, and determined to come. Now, for some reason or other, probably connected with Mr Tozer's arrangements, the funeral could not take place on the Thursday, and notice was sent to the clergyman, the Rev. Mr Drury, that the funeral must be put off till Friday, at 5 o'clock. The grave was dug, and here again Mr Drury unfortunately has given offence to the Rev. Mr Tozer. Gentlemen, it has been said, as you find in the libel which it will be my duty to read to you by-and-by, that this child was buried 'like a dog' in unconsecrated ground. Now, gentlemen, I will not say one is surprised at this case – it takes a good deal to surprise one when political and religious passions are inflamed. People then do and say such very strange things. But here we have a person who, I suppose, does not believe in priests, to judge from the language which he applies to them in his libel; who does not believe in the consecration of priests, who does not believe in the blessings of priests, complaining of a child being buried in what he is pleased to call unconsecrated ground. Does the Rev. Mr Tozer believe, do the parents believe, do any persons connected with any of these persuasions believe for a moment that any benefit is derived by any one lying in ground that has been, to use the expression which I think is used in the libels, subjected to the leger-demain of priests? If I understand rightly the practice with reference to cemeteries, which are put up now in the neighbourhood of all large towns, a particular portion is set aside to Dissenters which is not consecrated. They have the liberty to bury their people there, and they avail themselves of that liberty and opportunity of burying in ground which has not been manipulated by priests. They disavow consecrations, they disbelieve in consecrations, therefore, they could hardly have ground of complaining if this child had been buried in unconsecrated ground. But unfortunately for the Rev. Mr Tozer, this child has not been buried in unconsecrated ground at all, and so far as in the judgment of the Rev. Mr Tozer any benefit can result from lying in ground that in a remote period, 1,200, or 1,500 years ago, was consecrated, that benefit will result. There is no part of the churchyard that has been consecrated at any more recent period. It is a very old church and a very old burying ground, and it was when it was first set apart that it was consecrated, and as far as we can tell, the whole was consecrated at the same time. One part, as far as we know, is as much consecrated as another, and I am happy to relieve the Rev. Mr Tozer's mind by assuring him that so far as the happiness of the child is concerned or can be in any way promoted by lying in consecrated ground, it does lie in consecrated ground. But you may be aware that it has been the custom in burying grounds connected with the Church of England that certain parts of a churchyard are appropriated to those who have not died in what I may term communion with the Church of England. I believe the south side is generally considered the pleasanter side to lie, in the fashionable side. The north side is the side not so much sought after, and that portion of the churchyard, as I understand it, is the portion in which the persons who are unbaptized are ordinarily buried. A grave was dug for this little child in the north side of the churchyard. Gentlemen, to you or to me I suppose it would be a matter of very little interest or importance on which side of a churchyard we lay, whether the north, the south, the east, or the west. I do not suppose it affected the feelings of the Rev. Mr Tozer in the least, and as for the editor of this newspaper, I suppose he hardly knows the distinction between the points of the compass even in a churchyard. Now, gentlemen, I will read to you the libel. I am sorry to say it is a very long one, because the *East Anglian Daily Times* did not exhaust itself at a very early stage. These papers have a species of communion with one another; they send advanced proofs from one to the other. The sympathizing papers lash one another up into a violent flame, and the *East Anglian Times*, after writing as much as it could, and exhausting all its power in virulence, quotes from other papers, so as to keep the feeling as hot as possible and make things as unpleasant as possible for the Rev. Mr Drury. Before I read this libel, in order that you may appreciate it, I must state that the writer of the first libel is not the defendant at all; he is not the editor of the *East Anglian Daily Times*; the libeller, in point of law, is the publisher, but who do you suppose was the writer of the libel? A minister of the gospel, gentlemen – a minister of a Christian denomination – a gentleman who professes, I suppose, that he is a minister of peace, and is here to assist in the promotion of peace and goodwill among men. The Rev. Mr Tozer is the writer of this libel. Now you appreciate it. The libel is headed– 'Burial scandal at Akenham. Passage of arms between the Rev. George Drury and the Rev. Wickham Tozer'; and proceeds:–

'About midway between the Whitton and the Henley Roads, and about half-a-mile from both these highways, is the very small hamlet called Akenham. On rising ground and at sufficient elevation to make it observable from a considerable distance, is the parish church of Akenham. There are not half a dozen houses visible at any one point in the village, and the number of inhabitants can scarcely be more than from fifty to a hundred, and we doubt very much whether there are anything like as many as that. The church is a very comely-looking building – at a distance. If you leave the bridle way and ascend the hill on which it stands, you must immediately be painfully impressed with the fact that the sacred edifice and its surroundings are grievously neglected.'

– Then we have a description of the hamlet. The two principal farmers are Dissenters, and the labourers naturally, I think, are Dissenters, and the Dissenting parishioners take good care to have a churchwarden who is also a Dissenter, and thus you may understand that the repairs of the church would not be very well attended to – that the church would probably be a good deal neglected. The parishioners if they did not use the church would naturally say, 'Why should we clean the church, why should we do anything for the church? We do not use the church, and we do not want the church.'

'The fences are badly kept, the graveyard is a perfect wilderness, the windows of the church are broken, the porch is in a condition which our sanitary authorities would pronounce dangerous to cattle, and the whole aspect of the place gives one the impression that it can never be used for the purpose of religious services. On looking through the broken panes of glass into the building, cobwebs in profusion, dead birds, and dust and dirt in abundance, convince us that it has never been swept for months, if for years. And yet it is a structure that might be made attractive if not beautiful. It is not many years since it was restored by a generous friend at a cost of some £800. The internal fittings are modern and comfortable, and a very small outlay would make the exterior respectable.

'The incumbent of this notable village church is the Rev. George Drury, B.A., rector of the adjoining parish of Claydon. Some time during Sunday, alternately in the morning and afternoon, the incumbent might be seen taking a pleasant airing in the vicinity of the church, and if it should so happen that any pious parishioner should manifest a desire to worship by loitering about the building, the doors are opened and service is duly performed. Such a novelty as this occurs, perhaps, about half a dozen times in the course of the year, and for this laborious duty the incumbent receives the modest stipend of £266 per annum, in addition to the living at Claydon, which is worth at least £240 per annum.'

– Mr Drury will tell you that he is ready to give a service there; that he goes to the church, but it so happens that probably not more often than twice in the month does any congregation attend. Whenever there is a congregation he is there, ready and willing to discharge his duty, and it is certainly not his fault that the congregation does not come. They have their own places of worship, which they prefer.

'A few days since a working man, in the employ of Mr E. E. Gooding of Akenham Hall, lost a child who was about two years old. Both parents being Baptists, the child was never baptized. Ipswich is some four miles from Akenham, and as there is neither a cemetery nor chapel graveyard nearer, application was made to the incumbent to have it buried in the consecrated ground of the parish church. Mr Drury on learning that the child had not been baptized, positively and peremptorily refused its burial in the consecrated ground, but gave permission for it to be buried behind the church, in unconsecrated ground.'

– That, as I told you, is a mere figment of the imagination of the Rev. Mr Tozer: –

'Very sternly refused to bury it himself and insisted that no one should officiate in the church in his stead.'

– That is untrue, you will find. He attended for the purpose of burying the child, and the child would have been buried in the presence of the clergyman, certainly without using the Liturgy of the Church of England, but in every respect with perfect decency and propriety.

'Very naturally the sorrowing parents did not wish to have their beloved child buried like a dog.'

– Now, gentlemen, that is one of those expressions that mean probably little or nothing. A very distinguished man once took the opportunity of saying that his ancestors for many generations had been buried without any form of religious worship, and that he objected to that term of 'being buried like a dog'. But the term is used here for the purpose of exciting public hatred against the Rev. Mr Drury.

'And their kind-hearted employer, Mr Gooding, at once undertook to arrange for a short service being held before the interment immediately in front of the church gate, in a meadow occupied by Mr J. A. Smith of Rise Hall.'

– Now, gentlemen, if they thought that the prayer would be good even for the child who was dead, or for themselves who were alive, they might have had quiet prayer, unostentatious prayer – with which the Almighty probably would have been quite as well pleased – offered up in the cottage where the child lay. Such services are not unknown and not uncommon. They have been practised by those who believed in the efficacy and value of prayer. The persons who, perhaps, attach comparatively little importance to the prayer itself, but a great deal of importance to the political excitement which might be developed out of it, had a little service in a field immediately outside the churchyard. They sought their opportunity with a considerable amount of judgment in that respect.

'On Thursday Mr Gooding had an interview with the Rev. Wickham Tozer of Ipswich, who readily consented to bury the child at 5.30 on Friday afternoon. Some ten or 15 minutes before that time Mr Tozer arrived at the church in company with Mr Gooding and Mr Smith, who is churchwarden. The incumbent was pacing the graveyard, attired in indescribable petticoats and inconceivable headgear – that looked ominous.'

– I suppose that is considered a good joke in Ipswich – it is a sort of sneer at the dress in which the clergyman appeared. Gentlemen, I suppose you would be above criticizing the garment which a clergyman wears under one circumstance or another? At all events, you are not here to judge of that. This was meant for the vulgar of Ipswich.

'As he had refused to perform the burial service, no one expected or desired his presence. The grave was dug, and the sexton was there to discharge his duties, and that was all that was needed, so far as the church officials were concerned.'

– Mr Drury was desirous of doing what was decent and proper. He was the rector of this parish; he was the person responsible for the interment. He felt that although he could not in conscience or in law perform the funeral service in the sense of reading the service appointed by the Church of England, still, he would appear and pay his parishioners the respect of attending. Besides, gentlemen, it was his legal duty to do so. But it is also a species of moral duty which a clergyman would do wrong in neglecting. He is bound to see that persons are not buried without the necessary legal certificate of death; he is bound to register the funeral, and these instructions alone justified Mr Drury in attending. However, his presence at the funeral was not wanted. The Rev. Mr Tozer fixed half an hour later than the time appointed by the rector, possibly thinking that he would have gone away, and the coast might be clear, and perhaps the funeral might be conducted altogether in a different way.

It would have been a grand triumph if, the clergyman not being there, they could have gone in and performed the service without let or hindrance. I can quite imagine that Mr Tozer was much annoyed to find that the clergyman was there, and that they would have to perform the service in front of the churchyard, instead of in the churchyard itself. 'The funeral was rather behind its time, and both of the reverend gentlemen must have felt that there was something threatening in the air.' This is how Mr Tozer describes himself – a minister of peace: 'They passed up and down their respective paths, the one inside and the other outside the church boundaries, with a defiant air, that reminded us of two game birds pluming themselves for a brush.' Mr Tozer must know best what he felt, and that is how he described himself, as a minister of peace. 'The movements of Mr Gooding and the churchwarden also indicated uneasiness, but the passive sexton sat like a monument on the corner of a horizontal tombstone. At length the humble procession arrived, and with it a few sympathizing neighbours.' The few sympathizing neighbours were some labourers in the employ of Mr Gooding or Mr Smith, who were brought there for the purpose. I do not know whether you have had any experience in effecting a legal process. Sometimes, if you are going to do anything very violent – to turn out a person, for instance, neck and crop, or to do anything likely to cause you to fear inconvenience – you always get accompanied either by police or by other persons, to see that no breach of the peace occurs. Well, a considerable posse of labourers had been collected together in the field, ready to prevent any breach of the peace. They had been brought there on behalf of the Rev. Mr Tozer, and that may account for the comfortable and confident manner in which, like a game bird pluming himself for a brush, he was passing up and down outside the churchyard. 'And possibly a few who may have been animated by no other motive than a desire to witness a scene.' Who had anticipated a 'scene'? Had anybody given notice to the Rev. Mr Drury that the Rev. Mr Tozer was coming with a *posse comitatus* to effect a little quiet service outside the churchyard gate? What should have brought the neighbours to witness the scene if it had not been that they knew perfectly well that it had been arranged beforehand that an attempt should be made to violate the rules and laws of the church, or, at any rate, to get up an agitation that should cause pain and distress and annoyance to a clergyman, and should promote the political ends of these people? That explains why it is that Mr Tozer suggests that possibly a few came who may have been animated by no other motive than a desire to witness a scene. 'Altogether there may have been about thirty persons present.' Now, in a hamlet where there are fifty or 100 inhabitants at the outside, do you expect thirty persons to collect when a little child of two years old – the child of a labourer – is carried to the grave?

'Before the corpse had been lifted from the cart in which it had been conveyed to the church, the sexton, who had evidently been primed for the occasion, went up to the father of the child and presented the clergyman's compliments and his request that the corpse might be immediately conveyed to the grave, and they could hold any service they chose after it was buried, in the meadow outside the yard.

– You will see how much truth there is in that statement when you hear Mr Drury, who will tell you that it was only when he found that they had come to the churchyard and would not bring the body in that he went to the gate. The usual practice is in country churchyards for the clergyman to go to the gate of the churchyard to receive the body and accompany it to the grave. He found they would not bring it in. They were more than half an hour late, and they began to read some portion of Scripture over the body of the child, and after keeping him waiting for some time, he suggested whether it would not be convenient to let the child be buried, and then continue the reading afterwards. So far there is truth in that statement. 'Of course the vital point with this poor man's minister was that the child not having been baptized, it was a sin to give it Christian burial.' It would have been sin, no doubt, in the sense of being an offence against the law, and a violation of his duties as a clergyman. 'And so far as it was in his power to prevent it, no religious service should be performed over it either by him or by anybody else. As to what might be done after the body was in the grave that would not affect his priestly scruples an atom. No notice was taken of the incumbent's request either by the father or his friends.' Mr Drury suggested that they might as well bury the child at once instead of delaying the matter as they were doing. Probably it would have been better for them if he had remained perfectly quiet in the church, or in the porch until they had completed the service. Although that might have taken goodness knows how long, at any rate it would have defeated the object which these persons had; but, unfortunately Mr Drury felt that they were trifling with him and ridiculing him, and there was no knowing when the service might conclude. As far as he could judge their object was not to do anything to benefit the child, but to harass and annoy him. I suppose they were determined to exhaust his patience, and not let the child be buried until he had gone way. 'No bier could be procured, and the coffin was placed on the ground immediately in front of the churchyard gate.' You know whether it is usual to have a bier for the burial of little infants of two years. Biers are not used except for the convenience of resting the coffins of persons of some age and weight, and you know that in the case of children of two years old a bier is never used at all. 'The friends gathered round it, and Mr Tozer commenced reading appropriate passages of Scripture.' Of course there being no ritual service it was impossible to say when this would end. If there had been a ritual it might have been known, but Mr Drury probably thought, rightly or wrongly, that Mr Tozer would read on until he had retired or gone away.

'The incumbent, in his saintly garb but with a visage which scarcely matched, left the church door, sailed majestically up the path, came out of the gate, and stood about an arm's length to the left of Mr Tozer, facing the mourners. The situation at this point was painfully exciting.'

I believe what did take place was this. The clergyman came to the gate upon the body arriving in the usual way. He then took the opportunity of telling the father that he had been informed that the child had died without baptism, and, therefore, the church service could not be read over it. He had no knowledge at that time that the father was aware that there could be no burial service.

'We dared hardly think of what might happen. Involuntarily we looked at the physique of the reverend gentlemen, and in spite of the occasion we could not resist the impulse to estimate their comparative strength and their powers of endurance. [This a minister of the Gospel.] Of Mr Drury's courage in confronting the party alone there could be no question, and we also felt sure that although Mr Tozer had always been kindly disposed towards Churchmen, he was rather a formidable defender of his own party when necessity compelled him to it. Conflict between these two champions of the faith we felt there might be either in the form of words or blows. Happily, our worst fears were not realized, but the following serious altercations, which lasted for ten or more minutes, will prove that our apprehensions were not altogether groundless.'

– Now comes the dialogue, which Mr Tozer sets out *verbatim et literatim*. Anybody would have supposed that this had been done by a shorthand writer. Ordinarily, one places implicit reliance upon a shorthand writer, because in the discharge of his duties he is not actuated by any passion or prejudice, and his notes are without colouring. But this is Mr Tozer's own version of what took place.

Incumbent: 'The time for this funeral was at 5 o'clock; it is now more than half-past 5 o'clock, and I request you to convey the remains to the grave at once.'

– Mr Drury will tell you how garbled this is, and what little truth there is in the fabrication of this dialogue. 'The minister continued reading, and no one paid the least attention to Mr Drury's request.' It was not such an unreasonable request after all. Even a parson is entitled to some consideration. If you say five o'clock and the people do not come until half-past five, and then wish to keep you waiting a little longer, while they read 'appropriate passages of scripture', it is certainly rather trying. As far as I know, there is no limit to appropriate passages of Scripture, for all Scripture is instructive, and written for our profit and advantage.

With a face as rigid as steel, his lips firmly fixed at one end of the mouth, and slightly curved in an upward direction at the other, expressive of disgust, the incumbent said: 'I have been waiting over half and hour, and it is not reasonable that you should keep me waiting here until you are pleased to finish these proceedings.' No one attempting to reply, he continued: 'Why cannot you take the coffin to the grave, and then come here and hold what service you please?"

The reason for the interruption will be easily apparent to our readers. It was not so much Mr Drury's hurry as the repugnance to a religious service of any kind being held over an unbaptized child.

– Now, Mr Drury was there simply to protect the decency of the churchyard, to see that the child was buried in the regular and usual way, and to assist himself at the funeral. He had no desire at all that the friends of the child should not pray over it, or read, or do anything they liked, but he thought it was unreasonable of them to detain him, not for the purpose of benefiting the child, but to harry and worry him, the parson.

Mr Tozer still took no notice of the obstruction, but continued quietly reading portions of Scripture.

Incumbent: 'I must again request you to defer this service until after the remains have been interred.'

Mr Gooding: 'Pray, sir, do be quiet; the service will not last many minutes.'

Incumbent: 'Don't tell me to be quiet; I have a duty to perform and I shall do it. I must teach my parishioners that these proceedings are wrong.'

'Mr Tozer moved slightly towards Mr Drury, and said, "I respect you as a gentleman, and I would not willingly offend your religious convictions, or your conscientious scruples, but do let me beg of you to be quiet for a few moments; we shall not be long."'

Incumbent: 'What has that got to do with it?'

Mr Tozer: 'Oh I supposed you were a gentleman, a Christian, and a minister of Christ.'

Incumbent: 'I don't see what religious convictions or scruples have to do with it.'

Mr Tozer: 'Well, I have no wish to hold a discussion with you, but I appeal to your manhood, and beg you not to torture the feelings of these poor people at a time like this.'

Incumbent: 'That is all nonsense; manhood and feelings have nothing whatever to do with it. Your proceedings are altogether wrong, and I must teach my parishioners that I cannot sanction them.'

Mr Tozer: 'Well, sir, I thought if you were not a gentleman, or a Christian, you might possibly be a man; I am sorry to have been mistaken.'

Incumbent: 'I suppose you call that Christian?'

Mr Tozer: 'Very; and for that reason, I fear you are incapable of appreciating it. You have a very priestly garb, and I suppose you take that as equivalent to being one, but you are destitute of the spirit of your Master, and you have not even a spark of humanity in you, or you could not be capable of this conduct.'

Incumbent: 'I don't see what humanity has to do with it. That child (pointing to the coffin on the ground with his umbrella) has not been baptized, and it is, therefore, not a Christian, and I object to its being buried as such.'

'The secret of Mr Drury's interference was now disclosed, and it produced an instantaneous effect upon Mr Tozer. As quick as thought he drew himself up to his full height (close upon six feet), and brought his right arm dangerously near to Mr Drury's head, and with his eyes flashing fire, and his voice trembling with emotion, he said, "If it were

not for harrowing the feelings of these poor people, I would very soon
silence your brutal speech. Though decked in the garb of a priest and
holding the office of a minister, you are a disgrace to humanity.""

Incumbent: 'Don't shake your fist in my face.'

Mr Tozer: 'I was not shaking my fist in your face, but you justly
deserve to be made to feel it.'

Incumbent: 'And you call that Christian?'

Mr Tozer: 'Perfectly.'

Incumbent: 'You are a Baptist, and yet you can come here and perform a service over a child that has not been baptized, and is not,
therefore, a Christian.'

Mr Tozer: 'I have no desire to hold a controversy with a man so
destitute of the commonest feelings of humanity as you are, and if
this were not a funeral I would very soon bundle you out of the
meadow.'

Incumbent: 'This is a public path, and I have as good a right to be
here as you have.'

Mr Tozer: 'Just so much and no more. We have carefully avoided
everything that could reasonably wound your religious scruples, and
we came here because it is a public footpath; and you have no right to
interfere with us.'

Incumbent: 'I have the right to teach my parishioners that it is
wrong to perform funeral rites of a Christian form over the remains
of an unbaptized child.'

The father of the child: 'Come, Mr Drury, I shall have something
to say to you, if you don't allow the gentleman to go on with the
service.'

The mother seeing her husband was becoming angry, and fearing
the consequence, said, 'Never mind the parson. Mr Tozer, go on with
the service.'

Incumbent: 'I have been waiting here more than half an hour, and
it is unreasonable for you to expect me to remain while you conduct
this unwarrantable ceremony.'

Mr Gooding: 'Allow me to remind you, sir, that you refused to
perform any service yourself; after that you were not asked to be
present, and no one wishes you to remain.'

Incumbent: 'How could I perform a service over a child that was
not a Christian?'

Mr Tozer: 'Don't repeat that, sir; if you do you may have cause to
regret it. The sooner you take yourself off this public highway the
better.'

4

Incumbent: 'If you do not at once take the remains to the grave, I shall lock the gate and go.'

Mr Tozer: 'No one asked you to come, and no one wishes you to stay.'

Incumbent: 'I shall certainly lock the gate and leave.'

Mr Tozer: 'Go to heaven if you like; it would be a happy deliverance for the world if you and all your priestly tribe were there; though I fear you will stand a poor chance of getting there. Take yourself away from us, and I don't care where you go.'

The incumbent locked the gate and went – not to heaven – but to Claydon, which, so far as the rectory and the adjoining nunnery are concerned, is a very different place.

– Now I must call your attention to that passage, because it has caused great pain to Mr Drury and to other persons and has subjected him to an enormous amount of obloquy and ribaldry. Mr Drury is a married man with a family of several children residing with him. I do not suppose that there is any imputation of any sort cast upon his moral character, which is thoroughly unimpeachable. In the neighbourhood of the rectory certain ladies have settled down who prefer to live together, and the place, for aught I know, may be called a nunnery, but it was a pity to mention them in this way. Suppose there are ladies who like to live together, to live a life of charity and good works to other people – probably many of them had not the opportunity, to which many women look forward, of getting married, and they had settled down in this way. I do not know there is any particular harm in it; and if they choose to devote themselves to religious exercises that perhaps, is as well as devoting themselves to the vulgar frivolities very often indulged in in the world. They may indulge also in works of charity to their neighbours, and I am not aware that there is any great mischief in that. But is it not a pity they are introduced to the public in this way? Not merely are they held up to the ridicule of the public, but to the vulgar ribaldry of the persons who read papers of this sort. You will find that Mr Drury has been subjected to the utmost possible annoyance by the filthy ribald postcards, with which he has been inundated by persons who have read this article. I say that ladies ought not to be introduced into matters of this kind, with which they have no concern.

Mr Serjeant Parry: I should like to remind my learned friend that the statement in his claim does not insinuate anything of this kind. It says that 'On or about August 26th, 1878, the defendant maliciously printed and published in the defendant's said newspaper of the plaintiff, and of him as clerk in Holy Orders and rector as aforesaid, and with respect to his conduct in such office, and otherwise and of him and his conduct with reference to the burial and intended burial of a child the words following.' There is no innuendo or statement that those words were ever intended to convey the idea of personal immorality as against Mr Drury. I call attention to that because I shall show that the words were never so intended.

Mr Justice Grove: They may not have been, but I do not see how I can stop Mr Day. Part of the question for the jury will be whether this is libellous – in fact I do not know whether that is traversed.

Mr Serjeant Parry: My friend has gone further. He has said something about ribald postcards, which is entirely new to me.

Mr Justice Grove: That may be a question of admissibility of evidence. If Mr Day tenders them it may be a doubtful question whether they can be received, but I do not think that I can stop Mr Day in stating what he pleases. But is there no possibility of preventing this matter going further? I do not wish to express – and at present I do not entertain any opinion as to which side is right or wrong – but what good can this trial do either to the parties or to the public? It will only lead to a further publication of a very sad scene. I do not wish to avoid the pain of trying such a case myself, but I really had not read the declaration before coming into court. It is a very sad thing. I do not see any good that can arise either to the cause of morality or religion by having a personal inquiry of this sort, in which personal animosity exists, carried on to the painful end, whatever it may be. I will say no more.

Mr Day: I shall have something to say before I sit down with regard to your Lordship's observations.

Mr Justice Grove: With regard to this particular phrase, whatever interpretation different people may put upon it, it would be difficult to avoid saying that it is a very strong phrase, 'Not to Heaven, but to a very different place.' I cannot say that Mr Day is not justified in making a comment on that.

Mr Day: I am sorry that my friend has called attention to this matter. I shall now have to do something more than comment upon it. At first I only intended to say that it was a pity that the character of these respectable ladies should be ever referred to; or that their very existence should be mentioned in a matter with which they had no earthly concern. What had these ladies to do with the Akenham Burial Scandal, or with anything of the kind? I merely said that it was bad taste to refer to them in connection with such a matter, because it was calculated at any rate to bring them into ridicule, and that was probably the object. But a newspaper, circulating as this paper does, desiring to bring women into ridicule must know perfectly well that it is likely to expose these women to ribald jokes, and to expose Mr Drury to that which he has had to undergo – namely, these offensive and ribald communications made to him in a most ostentatious and public manner in the form of postcards. I have here a document from Birkett and Bantoft, who describe themselves as solicitors to the defendant. It is a notice to produce, served upon my client, Mr Drury; and among the documents which he is called upon to produce are fifty-one letters and postcards and newspaper cuttings sent anonymously and received by the plaintiff by post. They have actually challenged us to bring these newspapers and postcards into court, and, gentlemen, they shall be in court.

Mr Serjeant Parry: I was not aware of any such notice, and I disclaim it utterly. I am responsible for the conduct of this case in court. If any error has been committed by improperly giving notice of anything of that kind, of course my friend has a right to avail himself of it to any extent he pleases; but I disclaim it, and I shall call for nothing of the kind.

Mr Justice Grove: I have no doubt you will do everything properly, but you see this is forwarded to the plaintiff's attorney. It is the act of the defendant, and I cannot stop Mr Day. It may be that if the defendant had consulted you earlier it would not have happened.

Mr Serjeant Parry: This notice refers to things that were mentioned by the plaintiff in his affidavit of documents; and hence it was that the notice was given, and for no other reason. I think that ought to be stated to the jury.

Mr Day: I am delighted to have it stated. Let me tell you, gentlemen, what an affidavit of discovery is. A judge makes an order that you shall, upon oath, declare every document that you have in your possession relating in any way to the matters in dispute. My client would have disobeyed that order and made a false affidavit, and subjected himself to the penalties of perjury if he had not disclosed all these documents. Then the other side look at them – inspect them, as it is termed – and having inspected them, they tell him to produce such documents as they think will answer their purpose. Accordingly, they give him notice to produce fifty-one letters, newspaper cuttings, and postcards sent anonymously to the plaintiff by post. What is the object of that? Simply in the blind malice of their hearts, in the feeling of animosity they entertain towards my client, they were desirous, for the purpose of injuring him, to bring before the jury all these vile aspersions cast upon him by anonymous slanderers. They had seen them, and thought it would answer their purpose to have them produced in court. They thought it would pain and shame my client, a clergyman of the Church of England, to have produced in a court of justice these filthy, ribald communications; and, therefore, they thought they would take the opportunity of parading them before the jury. My client has brought them here. It may be, or it may not be, competent for me to produce them; at any rate it is competent for my friend to produce them. The case is in his hands. He will never forget what is due to himself as an advocate and a gentleman; and, above all, Serjeant Parry never forgets what is due to his client, even if it is against his own wishes, for an advocate is bound to protect a client even against himself; therefore he will never allow this case to be conducted upon the lines upon which it was defended up to the time when it got into his hands. Now, the case is in the hands of an advocate who never forgets what is due to himself and his profession, so that I do not suppose you will be troubled with these things; but, at any rate, I am entitled to comment upon the malice of such proceedings. The defendant justifies what has been said upon the ground that it is matter of public interest, and that he was entitled to discuss it, so long as he discussed it without malice. I shew you the course which has been taken and the way in which the case has been defended up to the moment when it got into my friends' hands; and you will judge for yourselves how much foundation there is for the suggestion that this was a *bona fide* discussion of a matter of public interest. They have not limited themselves to these matters; but they have actually ransacked the life of Mr Drury as far back as 1864, and given him notice to produce certain correspondence which took place between him and his bishop with reference to some services performed, I believe, in the Church of Claydon. There is a section of the Church which will not be very popular at the present time; but, as I said, we are not here, and you are not here, as High Church or Low Church, or Dissenters, or any other denomination. You are here merely as jurymen, and you are to set aside all your prejudices of one kind or another: you are here simply to administer justice as English jurymen, and you have nothing to do with squabbles and disputes as to ritual or liturgy between the Bishop of Norwich and Mr Drury; yet, in the malice of their hearts, they have gone into those things, and they have given us notice to produce four letters written in 1864. Then there are other letters by Mr Conder (a private person, whose name I here offer for the first time), written in 1863. These letters are referred to in their notice to admit. They say that we have got letters from Mr Conder and they call upon us to produce them. This shows the malicious character of these proceedings, and their determination at any cost or risk to harass and ruin Mr Drury in the estimation of all whose opinion is worth having. Mr Drury's character has been at stake in this enquiry, and I feel confident that it will issue forth from it unscathed. I will now proceed with the reading of the libel: –

'After this sad episode, Mr Tozer concluded the service in peace and quietness. Mr Gooding and Mr Smith were equal to the emergency, and very soon made a way to the grave. There, in solemn silence, the poor innocent child's remains, over which this hard and unseemly battle of words had been fought, were deposited. The party then returned to the gate, and the usual Burial Service was read, and the ceremony concluded. We have thus, as far as it was possible, endeavoured to give an accurate description of what we cannot but call a discreditable burial scandal. We leave the facts to tell their own tale, reminding our readers that this staunch upholder of Ecclesiastical Law is already under admonition from his own bishop for lawless proceedings in his own church.'

– I should say that this libel came out the day after the funeral. It was in the very handwriting of the Rev. Mr Tozer, and it was handed into the editorial box by a messenger of Mr Tozer. The paper was published on August 26th, and three days afterwards on the 29th, the editor was able to announce to his readers that the article was producing the desired effect, that the conflagration was rapidly extending. An article from the *Daily Chronicle* is transferred bodily to the columns of the *East Anglian Daily Times*, and it begins thus: –

If the Christian religion depended for its vitality upon such ministers as Mr Drury, it would become a bye-word to be scorned by every section of the community. We cannot suppose that this incident will remain unnoticed by Mr Drury's diocesan. The Bishop should be hurled from his episcopal throne if he did not visit Mr Drury's conduct with the severest reprobation. We fear that he can do nothing further. The rector of Claydon was, we imagine, within his legal right in the course which he pursued, but the incident shows how necessary it is that the law should be altered. Mr Osborne Morgan has found an unexpected and powerful coadjutor; for we believe Mr Drury's conduct will have more effect with the people of England in promoting the passing of the Burials Bill than all the speeches that Mr Morgan ever delivered. The English people will not allow their tenderest feelings to be trampled upon, and their dearest associations to be outraged by 'ordained' men who disgrace the Church to which they belong and bring discredit upon the Christian religion.

'Straight' writes to us lamenting the 'many queer things transacted by our clergymen (not parsons, they lived in the good old times) of the present day'. He always thought 'that a clergyman should be meek, kind hearted, bending and forgiving, something like Him we read of, but on the contrary, we find them very pugilistic and more mortal than most of us, if we touch either their pockets or their rights.' In conclusion he says: 'Let the dead rest, and let us have more simple-minded, kind-hearted, old-fashioned parsons, and less of the new-fashioned cant.'

'Lover of Humanity, if only to a dog', sends a very strongly worded letter in reprobation of Mr Drury's conduct, expressing his astonishment that correspondents should be found 'encouraging such a monster'. He suggests disestablishment as the only remedy for such scenes, and concludes with the expression of a wish that Mr Tozer had 'exercised a little muscular Christianity'.

– That must have been very gratifying to Mr Tozer's feelings, seeing that he has described himself as being 6 ft. high and very powerful. This discloses the object of all this scene, which was to promote the success of the Burials Bill agitation, for they say it would be better than all the speeches ever delivered. Their object was not to secure any comfort to the relatives of the child, but simply to get up a scene for the furtherance of political ends. Then we have this statement: – 'The editor of the *Christian World* favours us with an advance proof of one article to appear in this week's edition in relation to the Akenham case.' You see the kindness of these people who are engaged in violent agitation in sending advance proofs to one another. It is headed 'A Pestilent Priest', and is as follows: –

'The demon of discord is still haunting the tomb. The vampire of superstitition flaps its repulsive wings over the graves of the unchristened. The dead babes of Baptists are consigned to the devil by the priests. The ecclesiastical jugglers failed to handle them, and their souls perished! No drops of consecrated water fell upon their innocent foreheads, and endless fire is their only portion! These pestilent priests dare to tell us that He who loved all the little ones on earth will spurn them from paradise unless they go in by the Pharisees' door. The "burial scandals" of the Ritualists are becoming a national disgrace. Week by week the same tale of their disgusting inhumanity comes to us from the rural districts, and the Evangelicals look on and will do nothing to uphold the honour of the Church and of religion. It will

presently be found that an outraged people will take the law into their
own hands, and by some act of violence against such an Anglican priest
as George Drury, of Claydon, create a public opinion strong enough
to force Parliament to put an end, once and for ever, to such sickening
scenes as the inhabitants of Akenham witnessed last Friday.'

– Here is an invitation to outrage, to take the law into their own
hands, and act with violence towards an Anglican priest – to tar and
feather him as it were. A public opinion is to be created by ill-treating,
massacring, or brutally ill-using the Rev. George Drury, of Claydon,
so that when he has been thoroughly thrashed either by Mr Tozer
(who says he is six feet high), or by some people who had come there
to see that there was no breach of the peace, and when he has been left
dead, or half-dead, Parliament will interfere and say, 'We will have disestablishment.' 'A story like that recorded elsewhere ought to aid in
bringing priestism into contempt, and putting another nail into the
coffin of State Churches, which alone makes such outrages possible.'
That is, a church exists, and it has its own regulations, but persons who
do not like to comply with them are to violate them. 'The pretensions
of these mountebank Ritualists to be the delegates of heaven for the
manufacture of Christians by sprinkling water upon babies.' Why that
should be connected with Ritualists I do not know. Ritualism is a term
that does not go more than a quarter of a century back. High Churchmen and Protestants were earlier, but Ritualists were hardly known
before. Baptism, however, was recognized at the time that the Prayer-
book was instituted. I will not go farther back than that lest I should
get into the regions of controversy; Baptism, at any rate, was acknowledged in the reign of Queen Elizabeth, and I think I am right in saying
in the time of James I. Long before the time of the Ritualists, when the
Prayer-book was composed, Baptism was adopted as an initiatory rite
in the Church of England.

'The pretensions of these mountebank Ritualists to be the delegates
of Heaven for the manufacturing of Christians by sprinkling water
upon babes could be treated with mere scorn and loathing were it not
for their relations to the civil power. Herein lies the mischief and the
misery – they are invested with authority to refuse Christian burial in
the national churchyards, to all who die without having been submitted to a rite – meant to be of spiritual significance – which these
men would impose upon people as an act of legerdemain, entrusted to
their hands to perform. Till this jurisdiction over the graveyards is
taken away from them, there will be no assured peace for Nonconformists in the agricultural part of England. The parish of Akenham,

near Ipswich, has only a small population, less than an hundred inhabitants, and Mr Geo. Drury, priest, takes £266 a year out of the tithes –
nearly all paid by Nonconformist farmers – for walking up occasionally
to the church on a Sunday afternoon, to see if any of them would like
him to read the service of the Prayer-book to them; and if none of them
care enough about his ministrations to be there, he goes back to Claydon, of which he is rector, and where he keeps a colony of nuns.'

Well, I think they might go some distance before they could find a
better service than that in the Prayer-book; still it is said that if they
do not care about it he goes back to Claydon, where he keeps a colony
of nuns. Why these ladies are again introduced one does not exactly
see. Women are at any rate entitled to be treated with consideration.
If there is a quarrel in which women can be fairly introduced, let them
be introduced; but if there is nothing to do with women in a quarrel,
what object can there be for introducing them into matters of which
they have no concern?

'There is at present no Dissenting place of worship in the parish,
nor very near it, so that Lord Selborne's "educated gentleman" has had
an uninterrupted opportunity of training up the handful of labourers
and their wives and children in the "sweetness and light" of the Gospel.
And this is the result – absolute spiritual destitution, or worse, so far
as the State Church is concerned; and when bereavement falls upon
the homes of those parishioners who happen to have come under the
quickening influence of the Baptists of Ipswich or of Witnesham, they
are insulted by their incumbent, and treated as dogs or swine. One can
only hope that every man and woman in Akenham will keep as far
from this hireling as possible, and that means will be devised by the
Nonconformists of Ipswich, either from Burlington Road, or Stoke, or
Tacket Street, or St Nicholas, to establish at least one Sunday service
in this unfortunate district of Suffolk.'

– This seems to have been written by some gentleman who has considerable knowledge of the locality, because I do not suppose that any
of you have heard of Burlington Road, or Stoke, or Tacket Street, or
St Nicholas in Ipswich. The article was probably written by some
gentleman of Ipswich, and by and by if Mr Tozer comes we shall
ascertain what hand he had in suggesting that means should be devised
by the Nonconformists of Tacket Street to establish at least one Sunday service in this unfortunate district of Suffolk.

'Bad as all these burial scandals are, there has, perhaps, rarely been
one so bad as this: for when Mr Drury refused to inter the child, no
one complained. The grave was dug, and the sexton paid for his work;

and the Independent minister of Ipswich – who, curiously enough, has written strongly in defence of an Established Church as against the extreme Liberationists – would have endeavoured to soothe the bereaved parents, and call forth devout thoughts and holy resolves in the minds and hearts of the sympathizing neighbours, and no unpleasantness would have occurred. But he chose to sacrifice the gentleman, and even the man, and became a mere heartless priest, than whom there is no viler creature on the face of the earth. "What has humanity to do with it?" asked he, when rebuked by the friends of the sorrowing parents for his cruel words; and truly humanity was far enough from having aught to do with his conduct in the case. The very lowest type of ordinary humanity would be dismayed, or become angry, at the scene witnessed in that Akenham meadow, whither came this pretended minister of Christ, for the single and gratuitous purpose of irritating the living and insulting the dead. One can almost fancy that only toadstools will henceforth spring up where stood this priest uttering his maledictions over that tiny coffin, laid down there on the bare earth for want of the parish bier, which the charity of the parish church, in the person of its ruler, had refused. It had nothing to bestow, in that hour of pain, but curses.'

– Nobody ever dreamed of having a bier for the interment of such a child, and this was simply put to hold Mr Drury up to public execration just as they spoke of a priest uttering his maledictions. 'Malediction' is a fine word of many syllables; it might be shortened into 'cursing'. Mr Drury will tell you that nothing of the sort ever took place. He had no intention of saying anything to hurt anybody's feelings, but he was there simply in discharge of his duty. He had no notion of any scene being got up, and when you have heard him examined and cross-examined, I think you will be of opinion that he never said one word which could justify even in the remotest degree the suggestion that he had stood uttering maledictions over the tiny coffin. There is not a scintilla of foundation for even the wickedest imagination to suggest that Mr Drury had uttered maledictions of any kind or sort. He was there to discharge his duty, and he discharged it with all courtesy, until these people, who had come there prepared to make a scene, treated him in the way you have heard. My learned friend says that my client has not complained of the postcards. In technical language, he says that 'by reason of the premises the plaintiff has been brought into great disrepute and has suffered much ignominy and disgrace amongst his parishioners and others, and his efficiency and character as a clergyman have been seriously impaired and lowered'. He will show you that he has been subjected to great ignominy and disgrace, that he has been cruelly treated by certain persons – not his own parishioners – persons from a distance who have read these things, and who believe that he is a man who took the opportunity of this child's death to utter maledictions over the coffin and curse it as it was lying before him. He has been compelled to come here to clear his character. He is an unwilling plaintiff; he has no desire to subject himself, in his religious capacity as a minister of the Established Church, to a public inquiry in a court of justice; he feels that this is not a convenient tribunal to discuss the administration of the service of the church; but he feels also that his character has been publicly outraged, not on one, but on many occasions. Newspapers throughout the country have been induced to send advance copies and their articles have been reproduced in order to secure attention to this charge. Mr Drury has been made a victim of the malice of these persons, who are seeking to promote their political ends, and also their, I will not call them religious, but their sectarian ends. They have spared no pains, they have gone out of the way not only to do this, but to get it done by others, and then republished the most offensive things said about him by others in their own columns. I do not suppose that either Mr Tozer or the editor can have any personal feeling against Mr Drury, but they have for their own by-ends detracted from his personal character, and tried in every possible way to hold him up to the contempt and ridicule of the whole people of England. Under these circumstances he is compelled to come into a court of justice. He has endeavoured by every means to secure redress without coming into a court of justice. He would have been anxious to accept any explanation which the paper could give, and at one time we had reason to believe that the paper would have been willing to say that it had been misinformed as to that burial, but unfortunately other counsels have prevailed and they have thought fit to pursue, even to the time of coming into court, the same course against Mr Drury, maligning him in every possible way, and at last, adding insult to injury, by adopting as their own the publication of these infamous postcards which they have called upon us to produce. You will now hear the case; it may occupy some considerable time, but I am satisfied that in the end the character of my client will be thoroughly purged from the foul aspersion which has been cast upon it.

(ii) *The Burial: Evidence: Rev. George Drury*

The Rev. George Drury, sworn, examined by Mr Merewether, said: I am the rector of Claydon and Akenham, near Ipswich, and am the plaintiff in this action. I have been rector for thirty-three years. I am a married man with a grown-up family. The rectory house is at Claydon, about a mile from Akenham church. The population of Akenham is only between sixty and eighty. Services are held at Akenham every Sunday, alternately morning and afternoon, and at Claydon there are two services in the day. I remember Ramsey coming to me, and he arranged to have the funeral upon a Thursday at five o'clock. He asked me if I would bury the child in Akenham churchyard. I said I would, and then he asked me to appoint my own time. I asked him if three o'clock would suit him, and he said if it was agreeable to me he would rather have it a little later. He suggested five o'clock and I agreed to it. I think this was on the 20th or 21st of August. It was on a Monday. At that time I was not told that it was an unbaptized child. On Thursday morning the clerk came and told me that the funeral was put off till Friday, and that the child had not been baptized. I went over to Akenham on Friday afternoon at five o'clock. The whole of the churchyard there is consecrated, and unbaptized persons have been buried on the north side from time immemorial. I believe the reason is because it is a smaller piece of ground. I never then, or at any other time, refused burial to a child in consecrated ground. I could not possibly do such a thing as that; it is against the canon: I am obliged to bury them.

But you did not positively refuse that, and give permission for it to be buried in unconsecrated ground?

No; nothing at all about it.

Did you make any condition that no religious service was to be performed within the graveyard?

No.

And did you sternly refuse to bury it yourself?

No, certainly not; I went over there on purpose.

What duty have you to perform? In ordinary cases do you meet the corpse at the churchyard gate?

Always; the funeral commences with the meeting of the corpse and the clergyman.

And then you go forward to the church, and afterwards to the grave.

At first I receive the certificate at the gate, and then I have to precede the coffin to the grave. It is then customary for the clergyman to see the coffin lowered, and earth thrown in, and then the clerk fills up the grave. After that it is my duty to register the burial. That was the duty I went to perform that afternoon in the ordinary way. The first persons who came were Mr Smith, Mr Tozer, and Mr Gooding, and they came at about five or ten minutes before half-past five.

And after that did you pace up and down?

No, no.

I believe you had on an ordinary cassock?

An ordinary cassock and priest's hat – the dress I always wear. I was waiting in the churchyard with the sexton, and the funeral procession came from the east. When they arrived at a gate leading into Mr Smith's field, instead of the cart, in which the body was, going on the road to the church gate, they took a direction towards the centre of the field. I then asked the clerk to go and bury the child at once: I did not know how long they might delay me there. I thought they were going to hold a service in the centre of the field. After the clerk left they changed their direction and came at a right angle to the church gate, and I left the church to meet them. When I was about half-way towards the gate the cart stopped. There was a boy in the cart; he pushed the coffin towards the end of the cart and it fell on the ground. Mr Gooding then took the coffin from the ground and placed it in front of the churchyard gate, where coffins are always placed at funerals. I went to the father to explain to him why there could be no service, and after doing that I told him that the child could derive no benefit from the reading of the service. The office of the 'burial of the dead' in the Prayer-book is not to be used for persons that die unbaptized. Mr Tozer came and interrupted me while I was talking to the father. I never saw Mr Tozer before. He came up and shook his fist at me within about a foot of my head, and he criticized my priestly garb. He said, 'You wear the garb of a priest, and you look like a priest.' I said as quietly as I could, 'You ought not to shake your fist at me.' That was the very first that passed between me and Mr Tozer.

You have read the libel and the statement of a long conversation before that. Is that representation accurate?

No, it is a complete romance. He put his hands down and said, 'I am not shaking my fist at you.' He then went on and said I was not a gentleman or a Christian, and he told me to go to – he stopped at 'h', and then he said – 'heaven'. *(Laughter.)* He then said he did not care where I went to provided I went away, and he wished that all that thought like me would go away too. I told him I had as much right to be there as he had. Then he said he wanted to perform a service. I told him he had no right to perform a service there. I said I did not regard him as having any authority there at all, that I would not recognize his authority. He then appealed to the feelings of the parents. I could not hear them very distinctly, but I think they both said they would like to have a service. I said nothing at all to that. Gooding then came and asked me to go away, and I asked for the certificate, which Gooding gave me. He told me that if I remained there the burial could not take place if they stopped there until eight o'clock at night. I said if I went away I should lock the church gate and take the key with me and go home. Mr Gooding then told me to lock the church gate and go. I accordingly locked the church gate, and went home to Claydon. The account given of the proceedings in the statement of claim is not correct. I did not say, 'That is all nonsense, manhood and feeling have nothing to do with it,' nor anything of the sort. I never mentioned the word 'humanity'. I did not point demonstratively or insultingly to the corpse with my umbrella. The umbrella may have been directed to it. I had an umbrella because it had been raining. I was not 'pluming myself like a game cock, preparing for a battle'. I neither felt nor expressed any objection to the service being performed by them in the field if they wished it. I have received since then fifty-one letters, postcards and newspaper cuttings sent anonymously. I sent them to Ipswich to the police office.

Cross-examined by Mr Serjeant Parry: It was on Monday that Ramsey came and asked me to bury his child. I told him to go to Waterman, the clerk, to ask him to dig the grave. Waterman did not tell me on that Monday evening that the child was unbaptized. I did not then say to Waterman, 'Then the burial service cannot be read over it.' I saw Waterman on the Thursday, and that was the first time he mentioned the child's not being baptized. Waterman is my clerk and sexton of Akenham church. I never gave him orders always to ask whether a person had been baptized or not. If he asked the question of Ramsey it would not be by my order in any way. Waterman did not say whom he had heard it from. He said to me, 'Will you read the service?' and I said, 'I cannot.' I did not receive any message on the Friday morning that the burial could not take place until half-past five o'clock. I am perfectly certain no message was left at my house. The clerk and myself both arrived at the church at the same time, at five o'clock. We remained there until the cart containing the coffin and corpse arrived. The father and mother were with the coffin. Mr Gooding, Mr Smith, and Mr Tozer came from Mr Gooding's house, which is on the right-hand side of the church, but the funeral came from the left-hand side of the church. The field I referred to is in Mr Smith's occupation.

Mr Smith is a farmer, and he is the churchwarden of Akenham?

I do not know whether he is churchwarden or not; he is said to be churchwarden.

What do you mean by you do not know whether he is church-warden?

The custom at Akenham is for the parish to appoint a churchwarden with the consent of the incumbent, but my consent was never asked; I never knew anything about it.

Does he act as churchwarden?

I suppose he does.

Is he called churchwarden? Was he elected by the parishioners?

I do not know.

You really do not know?

I do not know anything about it; I was not present.

Nobody asked whether you were present; do you mean to tell the jury you did not know that Mr Smith was the churchwarden of Aken-ham parish?

I do not know that he is; he is not the churchwarden with my consent.

Was he elected by the parishioners?

He may have been.

Do you not know that he was?

No.

You have never given your consent to it.

No.

Is that the reason why you say he is not churchwarden?

I do not know that I say exactly that he is not churchwarden, but I do not recognize him as churchwarden.

But you said he was not churchwarden?

I said he does not act as churchwarden; he does nothing.

Do you remember the bishop and rural dean visiting Akenham church in 1877?

Yes.

Was Mr Smith there as churchwarden?

Mr Smith was there.

As churchwarden?

Mr Smith was there.

What position was he in?

He was there. *(Laughter.)*

Was he treated by the bishop and rural dean as the churchwarden of the parish?

I do not know that he was.

Did not the bishop ask you to give Mr Smith the key of the church, and did not you refuse to do it because he was churchwarden?

The bishop asked me to give Mr Smith the key of the church.

Yes, that you should always give him the key when he asked for it for any purposes connected with the church. Did not the bishop, in the presence of the dean and of Mr Smith, do that? Come, Mr Drury, there were three persons present.

I do not remember.

Oh! Do you swear you do not remember?

I do positively.

That is the state of your mind now?

That is the state of my mind, honestly and truly, at the present moment. I do not at all say that the bishop does not consider Mr Smith to be churchwarden. I have no legal proof that he is; he was not elected in my presence, and I do not know that he is. I am the incumbent of the church. Mr Smith has never been to any service there. I have heard that he is a Dissenter. He has never attended any services at my church. He was there when the bishop was there. When I went to the church on that Friday I had an umbrella in my hand. It had been raining. Mr Tozer had a mackintosh on. I was dressed in my ordinary cassock – the dress I always wear in my parish.

Had you a girdle or anything tied round your waist?

Yes.

You always wear that?

Not always – generally.

Had you a robe on, a stole I think it is called, coming down to your heels?

No, you know better than that. *(Laughter.)*

No, I do not, indeed; I know nothing about it. Had you any robes on that day except what you walk about in in your parish?

No; none whatever. You mean, had I a surplice on?

I do not give the name of any particular robe. I ask you, had you any dress on but that which you walk about in in your parish?

No.

Mr Justice Grove: I do not suppose he walks about the parish with robes on. I suppose he walks about with a black frock coat.

Mr Serjeant Parry: Oh dear no; nothing of the kind. If your Lordship had seen him you would not say so. *(Laughter.) (To witness.)* You walk about with this girdle on; is not it the priestly custom to wear robes?

The dress I wear is made for me by Mr Pratt, of Tavistock Street; I gave him the order to make me a cassock, and he sent it down.

Mr Serjeant Parry: Theatrical garments are made there, I know.

No. 42, The Butter Market,
Ipswich, where Joseph
Thurston, cabinet-maker,
collected his newspaper cuttings.

The churchyard, Akenham.
'. . . his sexton reclined on a
nearby tombstone, waiting.
. . . ury marched out into the
meadow, broke up the
service . . .'

8. (a) The nunnery, Claydon.

8. (b) Back kitchen at the nunnery: the grate and window, now barred, where Drury anointed Lovely's head with hot water.

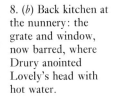

8. (c) A small stained-glass window in the wall of the nunnery chapel.

9. Portrait of Rev. Wickham Tozer.

10. 'Miserere Domine': Drury's
family vault, Claydon.

11. Portrait of Frederick Wilson, editor of the *East Anglian Daily Times*.

12. The headstone of Joseph Ramsey, erected by Mr Wilson.

Mr Justice Grove: When you walk about your parish do you wear the dress you now have on, or your cassock?

My cassock.

Mr Serjeant Parry: And a girdle, is that a rope?

It is a cord: we call it a cincture.

It is a rope.

No, it is not a rope.

It is a priestly garment.

No, I do not think it is.

Mr Justice Grove: What is the cassock? – A silk dress?

It is a long coat, buttoned up in front.

Of silk?

No, of cloth.

Mr Serjeant Parry: What does a frock coat want with a rope? That is what I ask. *(Laughter.)*

The clergyman in the adjoining parish does the same.

If he were here we should see it; you have not now on the dress you ordinarily wear?

No.

Is that a new suit you have got in honour of the occasion, made by Mr Pratt? *(Laughter.)*

Not in honour of this occasion.

Is this the first time you have worn it?

It is, nearly, I think.

Were you advised not to wear the dress you always go about in in the parish?

Advised?

By the eminent gentlemen, your solicitors – were you advised it would be better to have a new suit of clothes, and not wear the coat you generally have in your parish, with the rope round it?

No.

Were you not advised that you had better have a new suit of clothes rather than come in the ordinary dress that you wore in your parish?

Most certainly not.

That an ordinary dress of that kind might frighten us Londoners?

No, Mr Serjeant Parry. I am in the habit of wearing a cassock in my parish always. I wrote to my solicitor and said, 'Shall I go into court with my cassock?' and he said, 'Do as you always do.'

Then you bought a new suit of clothes? *(Laughter.)*

Whenever I go out of my parish I put on a coat like this, and Mr Block thought I had better do the same as I always did.

Do you mean to say that when you saw the cart coming and the coffin placed at the gate, that you went up to the father and explained to him that the burial service could not be read?

I explained to him why it could not be read. I said, 'The child has not been baptized, and therefore it has not been made a Christian.' I also told the father the reading of the service would be of no benefit to the child.

Why?

Why should it?

But I ask you why? I know nothing about this. Tell me why you told the father that the reading of the burial service could be of no benefit to the child. What do you mean by that?

No spiritual benefit.

Do you mean as regards its condition in the next world?

Yes.

That it could not go to Heaven – is that what you meant?

Not in the slightest degree.

What did you mean by no benefit?

No benefit to the child after the child was dead; the service would do it no good.

Because it had not been baptized?

I did not say that at all.

I thought you did.

No.

What! After the child was dead, and the burial service to be of no use to it?

Yes.

Did you not mean that because it was unbaptized?

I did not mean anything at all except what I have said.

Tell us why you said it.

I said it to induce the father to go on with the burial.

Have you not said you told the father, 'This child has not been baptized, and therefore has not been made a Christian, and cannot have the burial service'?

No, I did not say what for. I gave it as a reason why the burial service could not be read.

That this child had not been baptized, and therefore had not been made a Christian?

Yes.

Did you mean that the condition of the child would be altered in another world because it had not been made a Christian?

I did not mean anything about it at all.

I am now upon what you said to the father. You told him it could be of no benefit?

I will tell you what I meant, if you like. The Church of England orders that the burial service should not be used in the case of un-baptized persons, or persons who are excommunicate, and also persons who destroy themselves. The reason of that is because they are not visible actual members of the Christian family.

What are they? Heathen? Is that what you mean?

They are not visible actual members of the Christian family. They are not recognized members.

They are not recognized Christians?

Baptism admits persons into the Church, and they are known to be Christians by baptism.

And a person who is not baptized is not a Christian?

Not a recognized member of the Christian family.

Do you not believe and teach that an unbaptized person or child cannot go to Heaven in a spiritual sense?

I did not teach anything of the kind.

Do you not teach that doctrine?

No; I do not teach that doctrine.

You never have?

Never; but I teach this, that a baptized child who has not com-mitted actual sin, undoubtedly does go to Heaven, but as to a child that is not baptized I say, and I teach, nothing at all.

You do not know where it goes? *(Laughter.)*

I say nothing about it.

I ask you, do you not teach as a doctrine, which you act upon, that an unbaptized child or person cannot enter the Kingdom of Heaven?

Baptism is entrance into the Kingdom of Heaven.

Then an unbaptized person cannot enter; is that your opinion?

The Kingdom of Heaven is the Church upon earth.

Not the Church of England?

The Church.

The Catholic Church?

The Christian Church.

And do you exclude all unbaptized persons from the Christian Church?

I do not exclude any.

But do you believe they are excluded?

I do not believe anything about it; I do not say anything about it at all in my teaching.

While you were speaking to the father, do you represent that Mr Tozer came up and shook his fist in your face?

Yes; I do.

That was the first thing that happened?

That was the first time Mr Tozer interrupted me.

When you began to speak to the father was Mr Tozer reading a service, or reading something?

I heard him read something.

Apparently a service over the dead body of this child.

I cannot say what it was. He did not read, I think, above a dozen words.

Then did you go from the church gate and go towards the party, towards where he was reading?

No: I did not go near him.

You stood at the church gate?

I went to the father, and then I heard him reading.

How far was the father from the church gate?

Three or four yards.

What was he apparently reading from – a Bible?

I do not know.

Did you never enquire?

No.

You did not know anything about it?

No.

And you say that he then came and shook his fist in your face?

Yes.

You saw him with a book in his hand and heard a voice as of reading?

Yes: I saw a book in his hand.

Did you want the child to be buried without any service at all being read over it?

No.

Do you swear that?

I do. Whenever I have been asked by any Baptists to give my advice, I have always told them to have a service in their cottage.

Did you not wish that the child should be buried in your churchyard there and then without any service previously being read over it?

I did not want them to read a service while I was waiting; I wished to get home.

Is the reason you interrupted them, and spoke to the father, because you had been waiting half an hour?

I did not interrupt them.

If you say so, it will be better for the jury to judge whether you did or not. The reason you spoke to the father was because you were in a hurry, and had been kept there half an hour. Is that so? Let us understand what your reasons are.

The reason I spoke to the father was chiefly to induce him to go on with the burial.

Without having the service read?

Without, of course, having the service read.

And was that done because you had been waiting half an hour?

I had been waiting half an hour.

Was that the reason you did it?

The reason I did it was because he brought it to the churchyard to be buried.

The field is adjoining the churchyard?

No.

The path is across the field adjoining the churchyard?

No.

The reason you spoke to the father, as you tell us, was because the corpse was at the church gate?

No, the reason why I did it was because they had delayed the burial.

Had you been inconvenienced by staying there with your umbrella half an hour?

No; when they brought the corpse to the churchyard gate they ought to have buried it. Instead of burying it they put it on the ground, and went away.

Did not they read a service over it?

Mr Gooding went away.

Was not the service being read by Mr Tozer?

No.

Not at all?

Not when I went into the churchyard.

Not when you went up to speak to the father – was not he reading the service then?

I cannot exactly say whether he was or not.

But you said he was just this minute.

Mr Justice Grove: He was reading something.

Mr Serjeant Parry: I call it a service.

I think I see what you mean, but I am unable to say.

I ask you when you spoke to the father and urged him to bring the corpse into the graveyard to be buried, was not Mr Tozer reading something, and were not the people standing round the corpse listening?

I do not know whether Mr Tozer began to read before I began to speak to the father, or whether I began to speak to the father before Mr Tozer began to read. It was both within a moment.

Have not you just told us Mr Tozer was reading something when you spoke, but he had not read many words?

When I was speaking to the father.

Was not there a group of persons, including Gooding and Mr Smith, while Mr Tozer was reading, standing round that coffin with their heads uncovered listening to what he was reading?

You may call it standing round if you like. There were two persons near the coffin.

Were there not persons standing round with their hats off, listening to Mr Tozer reading?

Mr Tozer had his hat on; they all had their hats on.

That you swear? With hats on or off, were they standing round the coffin?

I do not think they were standing round the coffin, but I will explain to you how they were standing if you like.

I like nothing, you can do what you like – if you wish to explain you have a right to do it.

The coffin was on the ground, the father and the mother were on the south side of the coffin. I was on the north side of the coffin. There was an old woman by the name of Garnham on my left hand and Mr Tozer was on my right hand. There were one or two persons a little further off. Mr Smith was about six or eight yards off.

Did not you believe that they were going to perform some service over the body of the child?

I thought they were going to perform a service in the meadow, but when they came to the churchyard, then I thought they were going to bury it in the churchyard.

What did you mean by saying they had no authority to read a service?

I meant as a clergyman of the Church of England I was bound to bury the child, and that Mr Tozer was not. I was in the performance of my legal duty; Mr Tozer had no legal duty.

Is that what you mean you said to them, according to your own account, over and over again, that they had no authority to read any service – is that what you meant, because they were not members of the Church of England?

Mr Tozer had no right to interpolate a service after the priest had met the corpse at the church gate.

Then you were determined if you could to prevent a service being read; that was your object?

My object was to have the child buried.

Without a service?

Without my reading a service.

Or anybody else, if you could prevent it?

It is nothing to do with me. I had no right to allow Mr Tozer to interpolate a service.

I have asked you distinctly whether you did not intend if you possibly could to prevent a service being read over the body of that child – when you went up to the father and spoke to him what was your intention?

My intention simply was to induce the father to go on with the burial.

Without any service?

That was no business of mine. I did not do it for that reason.

(An adjournment was here made for luncheon.)

On the judge again taking his seat, the witness was not present, and some time was spent, during which the ushers of the court were calling his name in Westminster Hall.

His Lordship: I don't know if he thought his examination was finished.

Mr Serjeant Parry: Probably he has returned to Suffolk, my lord. *(Laughter.)*

When the Rev. Mr Drury at last returned to the witness-box.

His Lordship said: You have kept the court waiting nearly ten minutes; everybody has been here waiting except you.

The witness: I am very sorry, my lord.

His Lordship said: You have kept the court waiting nearly ten *(The cross-examination was then continued by Mr Serjeant Parry.)*

You said that Mr Tozer came up to you and shook his fist in your face – did you not, after speaking to the father, say to Mr Tozer, or to those people that were assembled, 'I must again request you to defer this service until after the remains have been interred'?

I have no recollection of saying that. I asked the person who was standing on my left-hand side to go on with the service.

Just answer my question, please – Did Mr Gooding say to you, 'Pray, sir, do be quiet; the service will not last many minutes'?

I do not remember his saying that.

Did you say this to him – 'Do not tell me to be quiet; I have a duty to perform, and I shall do it. I must teach my parishioners that these proceedings are wrong'?

I did not.

Before you said, 'I must again request you to defer this service' did you not say to them all, 'The time for this funeral is five o'clock; it is now more than half-past five, and I request you to convey the remains to the grave at once'?

I do not think that I said the latter part of it – not the last two or three words.

I have asked you whether you did not say, 'I must teach my parishioners that these proceedings are wrong,' and you deny it.

Altogether.

Did not Mr Tozer advance towards you and say, 'I respect you as a gentleman, and I would not willingly offend your religious convictions or your conscientious scruples today; let me beg of you to be quiet for a few moments, we shall not be long'?

No, I do not remember his saying that. He did not come to me in that way at all.

Leave out the coming; did he say that to you, whether he came to you or not?

I have no recollection of it at all.

Did you say, 'What has that got to do with it'?

Of course I did not.

Then did Mr Tozer say, 'I supposed that you were a gentleman, a Christian, and a minister of Christ'?

No, I never heard him say that at all.

Did you not say, 'I do not see what religious convictions or scruples had to do with it'?

I do not remember that.

Did Mr Tozer say, 'Well, I have no wish to hold a discussion with you; but I appeal to your manhood, and beg you not to torture the feelings of these poor people at a time like this'?

I never heard the word 'manhood' used.

Never mind about 'manhood', we will leave that out. Did he say, 'I have no wish to hold a discussion with you, but I beg you not to torture the feelings of these poor people at a time like this'?

Those are not the words; but Mr Tozer made an appeal to the people – to the father and mother.

To you – not to interfere with the father and mother?

No, he did not say that. I think he said, 'Consider the father and mother.'

To you?

The words were addressed to me, but he was addressing the father and mother by his actions.

When he begged you not to torture the feelings of those poor people, did you say, 'That is all nonsense; "manhood and feeling" have nothing whatever to do with it. Your proceedings are altogether wrong and I must teach my parishioners that I cannot sanction them'?

I did not say anything about teaching my parishioners.

But did not you say, 'That is all nonsense; "manhood and feeling" have nothing to do with it?'

I did not use the word 'manhood'.

'Feeling' has nothing to do with it?

I do not remember anything about it, at all.

Mr Justice Grove: Did you say anything of the sort?

I do not recollect it.

Mr Serjeant Parry: Will you undertake to say that you did not say it?

I swear, on my oath, I do not recollect.

You thought that the proceedings were altogether wrong?

I thought that Mr Tozer had no right to interpolate a service.

Did Mr Tozer say to you, 'Well, sir, I thought, if you were not a gentleman, or a Christian, you might possibly be a man; and I am sorry to be mistaken'?

No; I think I may say positively he did not say that, I told him his conduct was not 'Christianly'.

Did he say, 'You have not a spark of humanity in you, or you could not be capable of this conduct'?

I did not hear Mr Tozer say that.

Did you say, 'I do not see what humanity has to do with it. That child' (pointing to the coffin on the ground with your umbrella) 'has not been baptized; therefore, it is not a Christian, and I object to its being buried as such'?

I did not say that. I said, 'It had not been baptized, and, therefore, had not been "made" a Christian.'

Was not it then, and not till then, when you said that the child was not a Christian, that Mr Tozer became excited, lifted his hand, as you described, and afterwards put it down by his side?

No; it was not. He lifted his hand at the first. Mr Tozer was excited all the time.

Did you say this to him – 'You are a "Baptist" and yet you can come here and perform a service over a child that has not been baptized and is not therefore a Christian'?

I did not say those words.

Did you repeat more than once that this poor child was not a Christian?

Only once, to the best of my recollection.

Did you say, 'This is a public footpath, and I have as good a right to be here as you have'?

Yes; I said, 'This is a public road.'

Did the father say, 'Come, Mr Drury, I shall have something to say to you if you do not allow the gentleman to go on with the service'?

I did not hear him; he said something to me, but I thought he said he should like to have the service. I am quite sure the father did not say that, because he did not use so many words.

Did the mother say to her husband, in your hearing, 'Never mind the parson, Mr Tozer, go on with the service'?

No. I did not hear it. I think the mother said she should like to have a service. The mother said something, and the father said something.

Did you say, 'I have been here more than half an hour, and it is unreasonable for you to expect me to remain while you conduct this unwarrantable ceremony'?

Not the latter part of it. I told them twice, at least, that I had been waiting there.

You had received the burial fee, had you not?

I do not think that I had; the clerk had, I think.

Did not you know that your clerk had?

I supposed he had. I do not know whether he had given it to me or not.

Did Mr Gooding say this to you, 'Allow me to remind you, sir, that you refused to perform any service yourself. After that you were not asked to be present, and no one wishes you to remain'?

I cannot remember that I did hear him say that.

Did you say, 'How can I perform a service over a child that was not a Christian'?

No.

Did Mr Tozer then say, 'Do not repeat that, sir: if you do, you may have cause to regret it: the sooner you take yourself off this public highway the better'?

No; he said something about my going off the highway.

Now I will ask you about the meaning you attached to this observation of yours, that the child was not a Christian. Did you mean to insult the father and mother?

No.

You meant to console them? You are an educated man, a priest of the Church of England, a clergyman – what was the reason of your going to a labouring man, the father of this little boy, two years old, and explaining to him kindly that his child was not a Christian?

Because he not having been baptized, the service could not be read.

That was your reason?

Yes. He had not been admitted into the Christian family.

Then he was outside the Christian family?

The recognized Christian family.

The only family recognized?

The only one which is recognized by any public act.

By Act of Parliament do you mean?

No.

What do you mean by public act?

I mean that a person is made a Christian by baptism.

But what do you mean by the only Christian family that is recognized by public act?

The act of baptism. I do not mean the Act of Parliament.

That is by the sacrament of the church?

Yes.

Will you positively state that you did not call the child a heathen?

Yes; I will swear that I did not.

You meant that it was a heathen when you said it was not a Christian?

If it is not a Christian it is a heathen. But I never said so.

It is so self-evident that a child that is not a Christian must be a heathen that you might have said so?

All persons are, in common parlance, called heathen when they are born. I only meant to explain to the father why the service could not be read.

And could not benefit the child?

And could not benefit the child.

Did not you mean by that that the child could not enter?

No; I meant nothing but what I told you.

Into happiness hereafter, or into the Kingdom of Heaven?

You are trying to entangle me. I meant nothing but what I told you.

Do you believe yourself that unbaptized infants never enter the Kingdom of Heaven?

I do not say anything about it at all.

I ask you this, do you not believe that unbaptized infants never enter the Kingdom of Heaven?

I answer you truthfully, openly, and honestly, that I do not believe either one way or the other.

That is 'openly, truthfully, and honestly'?

It is an open question so far as I know anything about it – so far as the English Church has decided.

Have you never publicly stated, as a minister, or rather as a priest – if you object to the word minister – the doctrine that unbaptized children are detained in hell, where they shall never have the sight of God?

It is an open question. I do not teach one way or the other.

You considered it your duty to be at the church to receive the corpse – that is what you said?

I said it was my duty to meet the corpse at the churchyard.

Do you consider it your duty in reference to an unbaptized child or person, as well as others?

Certainly.

At the head of the Burial Service it is thus stated: 'The priest and clerks meeting the corpse at the entrance of the churchyard, and going before it, either into the church or towards the grave, shall say or sing.' Do you mean to say that you have marched before the coffin to the grave?

Yes, the 68th canon requires me to do it.

I am afraid that is not within my knowledge.

If I refuse to bury anyone except a person who is excommunicated with the greater excommunication, I subject myself to three months' suspension.

Excommunicated by whom?

By the highest ecclesiastical authority.

What ecclesiastical authority has the power of excommunicating anybody in this country?

The canon subjects me to three months' suspension if I refuse to bury.

What power in this country can excommunicate anybody?

I quote the canon to you.

Some canon gives a power to somebody to excommunicate somebody. You have told me about this canon, and I am going to be silent about it. Have you buried an unbaptized person before?

Yes.

And you have always marched with it to the grave?

That is my custom.

You really have?

Yes.

Do you sometimes throw a lump of earth into the grave of an unbaptized person?

Yes.

Have you done that and left the church suddenly at any time – have you taken up a lump of earth and thrown it into the grave where an unbaptized person was being buried, and then turned on your heels and gone out of the churchyard as soon as you could?

No, I do not think that.

Did not you do so the other day?

No.

Have you attended the burial of an unbaptized person recently?

Are you alluding to the child who was baptized about a month ago in Claydon churchyard?

Baptized?

Buried I mean.

Did you throw a lump of earth into the grave then?

A handful.

And then you left the church?

Shortly after.

My question is yes or no. Did you take up a lump of earth and throw it into the grave and then walk off?

I threw it into the grave and then walked off afterwards, but I did not do it in the way in which you are putting it.

Mr Justice Grove: It might be done in a contumelious way or in the ordinary course.

Witness: I did not do it contemptuously.

(iii) *Admonitions: Evidence: Rev. George Drury*

Mr Serjeant Parry: There is an allegation in this first article that you were under an admonition from your bishop for lawless proceedings in your own church. Is that so?

No.

Are you under a monition from the bishop?

Not for lawless proceedings.

For any proceedings, lawless or lawful?

The bishop informed me he was going to send a monition to me to remove certain ornaments from the church. That was published in the *East Anglian* last year, and it was said that I had thrown the monition on the railway, and that the monition ordered me to remove some ornaments of the church, but in the libel it says it was for lawless proceedings. The churchwardens have received the monition to remove some ornaments.

Do you know a Mr Steward?

Yes.

Did he in May, 1878, or thereabouts, come to you and serve you with a monition?

Mr Steward came to me in a meadow, and he informed me that he had a letter for me from the Bishop of Norwich, and I refused to receive any letter from the Bishop of Norwich through him, and I walked away.

Did he tell you that it was a monition?

He said a letter.

Did you say, 'I only receive those things through the post'?

No, I did not say that, I said I would not receive them from him.

Mr Steward is here. Did he say it was a monition or simply a letter?

Mr Steward said he had a letter from the bishop. He did not use the word 'monition' in my hearing.

Did you say, 'I only receive these things through the post?' Did not Mr Steward thrust the document, whatever it was, into your girdle which you then wore?

He did not, but he touched me with his hand. I do not know whether that was a service or not.

Did you square up to him to fight him? Did you double your fist at him?

I think I did.

Did you call him a rascal?

No, I did not.

That you swear?

Yes.

I ask you, did you not take that paper that was in your girdle and throw it away?

I did not.

You complain here that your character as a priest of the Church of England has been attacked, and so on, but you have been under a monition more than once from your bishop, have you not?

I have never received a monition from the bishop, unless that was a monition.

But in the courts?

I received one for performing service in an unlicensed chapel.

Was that at the instance of your bishop?

Yes.

Was that unlicensed chapel a place called the Monastery?

Yes.

What service had you performed there?

The Holy Communion.

Did you perform what you call 'mass' there?

Yes.

Was a person well known as Father Ignatius joined with you in the parish of Claydon at any time?

He lived in my house for nine months.

Was he connected with this 'Monastery'?

Yes.

I think you administered vows of poverty to him, did you not?

He took the three vows in my presence.

From you?

In my presence.

But from you, in his bedroom?

He took them in his bedroom.

From you?

I do not know 'from me'.

Was there anyone else present?

I do not think there was.

What were the three vows?

Poverty, chastity and obedience.

Do you mean to represent to the jury, sir, on your oath, that you yourself did not administer those vows to this gentleman, Father Ignatius?

Brother Ignatius he was called at that time.

Brother or Father – I do not mind which?

He told me that he wished to take vows, and he took them in my presence. I did not advise him to take the vows.

And you did not administer them?

I do not know what you mean by administering. He took vows in my presence.

Have you pleaded guilty to any proceedings, and submitted yourself to the bishop?

Submitted myself to the bishop's judgment, certainly.

I have an office copy of your submission in the Arches Court of Canterbury.

That was submitted to me by the bishop, and I submitted to it.

Now, these processions that you were prohibited from, were they processions through the streets of Norwich with monks?

No; processions through the streets of Claydon.

Were processions through the streets of Norwich complained of?

I never did engage in any processions in the streets of Norwich.

It was only in Claydon?

Only in Claydon.

The bishop complained of them, and then you promised not to repeat them; have you kept that promise?

Yes, I have.

Was Brother Ignatius a party to these processions?

He was present.

Did he preach in the pulpit at Claydon, in a monk's dress?

In his habit.

A monkish habit?

He gave evidence in court in that dress.

I do not know that that is so very bad; you have done so in yours.

In the same dress he wore in the Claydon service.

He preached in your pulpit in a monkish dress?

He did not.

I though you said he did?

He had a surplice when he preached.

Did not he wear a monkish dress in your pulpit?

Of course he wore the dress; but he wore the surplice over it.

Were processions around your church with pictures of the Virgin complained of?

I never saw any picture of the Virgin.

Was there a banner?

Oh, yes; several banners.

With an alleged portrait of the Virgin on the banner?

Not that I am aware of.

A picture on the banner, not a framed picture?

I never saw one.

You say you never saw anything like a picture of the Virgin on the banners?

There was a banner used in Claydon Church, and it is used at the present day, of Our Lady, and Our Lord, too.

Now about this question of the nunnery. I am afraid public attention has been called to this nunnery more than once, has it not?

I do not know.

I do not suggest immorality, or anything of the kind, for a moment, or believe it for a moment.

Oh, it is not what you think.

You are certainly justified in saying that. Upon one occasion, did you detain a young girl, about sixteen years of age, in this nunnery, against the wish and the will of her father?

What is the name of the young lady?

Rolfe?

Certainly not – a Miss Rolfe was admitted into our convent, but she was twenty-one years of age.

I am much obliged to you for informing me of it. Did she take vows?

Yes, she did take vows.

Did you perform Mass in that convent?

I celebrated Holy Communion in that convent.

What you call Mass?

The Prayer Book of Henry VIII, 'commonly called Mass'.

It is so called in this convent?

You may call it anything you like.

Did not the father of that young lady come to the nunnery, and request that she should be given up to him?

The father of that young lady sent her to the convent.

I ask you, did not he come to the convent and claim his child, and did you not resist it?

Dr Rolfe did come to the convent, I believe, but I did not see him.

Did he not claim her, and did not you resist the claim by force?

He did not claim her of me at all.

But were you in the nunnery at the time?

Now you are going to another question.

Were you asked whether Miss Rolfe was in the nunnery, and did not you say that she was not?

I can only answer that question by telling you what went before.

Were you asked whether the lady was in the nunnery?

I was asked whether she was in the convent.

Did you say either that she was not, or that you did not know whether she was?

That was about thirteen years ago. Some people broke into the convent.

Were you asked whether the lady was in the convent or not?

One of the persons who broke into the convent, named Lovely, said to me, 'Where is she?'

What did you say?

I said that she was not in the house, to the best of my knowledge.

I do not want to go particularly into the details of their breaking into the convent, but was she found in a closet upstairs in the nunnery, and carried away?

She was in the chapel.

In a closet I say?

I am not answering from my own knowledge, but I believe she was in the chapel.

Did you resist the persons taking her away?

Yes.

Did you pour boiling-water upon them?

No.

Had you any weapon?

You ask me questions which I cannot answer, unless I go further into matters and you won't allow me. I am very willing to answer your questions.

My question is substantially this – whether this lady was not in the nunnery, whether she was not asked for by her father, and whether her being given up was not resisted, and by you, amongst others?

I will answer you in six words, if you will allow me. Dr Rolfe allowed his daughter to come to the convent. After some time Sister Teresa was informed that her father, with some labouring men and others, were coming from Witham to break into our convent, and take her away. She was informed of that the day before. She entreated me not to let her be taken away, because she knew that her father was going to take her home and lock her up as a lunatic in a room which he had prepared.

And that is the reason you resisted?

When these persons came to the convent I was sitting in the common room, and she immediately ran out of the room, and ran to a door at the back of the house. I did not see her go out of the door, but I heard a door at the back of the house close, and I concluded that she had escaped from the house. After that I saw one of the sisters fastening up the doors and windows, and after that I heard a great noise at the back of the house. There I went and saw William Lovely, who, I believe, has broken into the house twice before, very active in breaking through the kitchen window. I wished to save Miss Rolfe as much time as I could, and I threw a basin of cold water in his face, and he ran away, and it did delay him for a little while. After that they renewed the attack with large sledge hammers on the doors and windows, and finding that I could not keep them out of the house I went upstairs. The reverend mother was ill in bed and I stood outside the door with the intention of not allowing them to go into her room.

That was a very proper thing to do.

When Lovely came up and saw me standing there, he said, 'Where is she?' I said, 'She is not in the house,' to the best of my recollection. Lovely then took hold of me by the coat collar, and another man – a blacksmith – by the arm, and pulled me away, and they went into this room where the reverend mother was, and three other sisters, and they examined the whole room, under the bed and everywhere, in the most indecent manner. Then as they went away I went away too. As I was passing the top of the stairs I saw Sister Teresa dragged out by four men, and she said, 'Oh, Father, do help me!'

Sister Teresa was Miss Rolfe?

Yes. I said, 'I am sorry to say I cannot help you. They are twenty to one.'

Was she carried away?

Yes, against her will, and she was carried to the station against her will. She was twenty-one years of age, and her father locked her up in a room at the top of the house, and she was confined as a lunatic for nearly twelve months, and when her father died he excluded her from the whole of her share of the family property.

Do not attack the memory of her father.

The reason why I would not receive that letter from Mr Steward was because he gained his influence against Miss Rolfe by the use of false affidavits.

But this is attacking Mr Steward. He will be called as a witness.

It is all one.

Whether your conduct was right or wrong, I do not seek to inquire. Was all this about the nunnery well known in the county of Norfolk and the county of Suffolk?

Well known? Why, the newspapers and farmers have been going on in this way against me for more than twenty years. This libel that you are trying now is only a specimen of what they have been doing for more than twenty years.

Was there a young girl or young woman of the name of Gardiner in the nunnery, and was she taken away by her mother?

I do not know if she was taken away by her mother.

I did not say she was taken away by her mother. I do not think she was.

I was not there.

This nunnery has been well known, as you tell me, for twenty years. Had you besides this basin of water any weapon at all in your hand?

None at all.

Nothing at all?

None whatever.

No stick of any kind?

None whatever.

Nothing that you were using? You merely used this basin of water. I ask you this: Were you ever fined for assault, or charged with assault, before the magistrates, for striking one of your parishioners with a red-hot poker?

No. There you have gone too far. There was no red-hot poker in the case. I was fined by a magistrate for assaulting a labourer in my church, but I never assaulted the man at all.

Never mind what you did. Was a gentleman of the name of Sir Geo. Broke Middleton chairman of the bench?

He was chairman.

And were you fined £5 for assaulting a parishioner in your church? I was.

Rightly or wrongly. You were perfectly innocent, no doubt.

I never assaulted him at all, but I was fined £5.

You say the red-hot poker is altogether a mistake of mine?

There was no poker in the case at all.

Was anything alleged to have been taken out of the fire by you, with which you struck the parishioner?

I did not strike him at all.

With which you were alleged to strike the parishioner. What was taken out of the fire?

A piece of wire.

Not a poker? I have gone too far.

Why do not you examine the man himself? He is alive.

Sometimes I think you yourself use very strong language to your opponents. Do not you?

I think I do. I am rather a warm temper.

Do you know an association called the Church Association?

I know the Church Association.

Have you spoken of them as a body of assassins?

A body of what?

Assassins?

I have compared them to the Ancient Order of Assassins. *(Laughter.)* But I have said that they were worse than the Assassins. *(Renewed*

laughter.) The Assassins acted openly. The Assassins acted by pre-
scription.

Have you spoken of Protestantism, as it is called, as 'poison'?

Very likely.

And preached it from the pulpit?

No.

Do you mean to say that?

I mean to say that I have never called Protestantism 'poison' from
the pulpit.

Well, was it in a lecture that you delivered?

That is very likely.

Only not from the pulpit. Where was the lecture delivered?

The lecture was delivered in the common hall at the convent.

Oh! before these nuns?

Yes, they were present, some of them.

May I ask you how many there are?

There are four at the present date.

Do you mean to say that there were persons from outside admitted
to hear this lecture, or only nuns?

There were some from the outside.

Only a few?

Not very many there.

And I think there is a lady there called the Mother Superior, is
there not?

Well, you know, this convent is a private house. It is not a public
house.

It is known as a convent, is not it? And is not there a lady called by
the inmates the 'Mother Superior'?

Yes.

Do not you address her as such?

Yes, no doubt.

Serjeant Parry: I have no more questions to ask you.

Re-examined by Mr Merewether: With regard to this convent, I suppose
it is a house like other people's?

It is a house.

And they pay rates and taxes?

It is their own house, and they pay rates and taxes. They live on their
own money. They are not dependent upon the public at all.

And unlike other people, a mob came and broke into the house? How
many were in the mob when they came?

Oh, there were a great many in the mob altogether; but there were about twenty men armed with crowbars and hammers.

They broke into these ladies' house?

They broke into the house.

And went up into the lady's room, and examined it altogether? Were any of the police about?

The magistrate had sent the police away in the morning – at least, so the people told me.

So that they had it all their own way without the constables?

They had it all their own way altogether.

Who was it pulled you away from the lady's door at which you were standing?

Lovely, and another man.

Lovely is the man whom you are charged with having assaulted?

Yes.

Where was this basin of water which you threw in his face?

That was at the back kitchen. He was getting in at the kitchen window. He had broken the glass and he was getting into the window.

I did not precisely know what my friend intended to impute to you. We had better have it straight. He asked you whether you said she was not in the house. Did you believe that she was not in the house when you said that?

I believed that she had made her escape.

Afterwards you found that she had not, but was in the chapel?

Afterwards she was found in the chapel.

Mr Serjeant Parry; I must really say, with great deference, that this is not examination-in-chief. It is putting a series of leading questions. Perhaps I ought not to object.

Mr Merewether: I am repeating your questions.

Did you honestly believe or not, when you said she was not in the house, that she was not?

I honestly believed that she had escaped by the back door, and gone into the next door premises.

You objected to her being taken away as a lunatic, I believe?

Yes.

Was she restored or not? After her father died was she let out by the Lunacy Commissioners?

No, I went to the Lunacy Commissioners, and they –

But she was let out?

She was confined nearly a year.

Then she came out again?

Yes, and then she returned to the convent of her own free will, with her mother's consent.

Her father was then dead?

Her father was dead.

I think that is all I need ask you about the convent. That was, I believe, in 1867?

Yes.

Now then comes the poker.

Mr Serjeant Parry: It was not a poker – 'a piece of wire'.

Mr Merewether: Oh, I beg pardon, a 'red-hot poker', Serjeant; you said 'boiling water'; it turned out to be a basin of cold water. You said a red-hot poker.

How long ago is the poker matter, because we will call it a 'Poker' at present. When was that?

Fourteen years ago.

Did you write an explanation of the whole of the nunnery case to the papers at the time, about Sister Teresa?

I do not know. I do not think I did.

The poker case you say was fourteen or fifteen years ago? You say that. Were you called into the church and told that there was a man there?

Yes.

Just tell us how that was?

I was in my house, and a young woman came to the house and told me that there was a drunken man in the church who refused to go away.

Had a drunken man any business in the church, to begin with?

No.

Your regular church at Claydon – Church of England church. And did you go to the church and find a man?

I went to the church, and I went to the man, and I asked him to leave the church; and I said, 'Now, Watkins, it is no use your stopping here to annoy all the people. I wish you to go away.' He pretended to be asleep.

Then I told two men who were there that I thought the best thing to do would be to put out the candles and the fire, and they went to put out the candles, and I went to put out the fire.

What did you put out the fire with?

A piece of wire that was by the stove.

Is that the 'red-hot poker' that my friend talked about?

Mr Serjeant Parry: He has told us so.

Mr Merewether: How big was the piece of wire, and how long?

Well, about half an inch thick – *(laughter)* – and about eighteen inches long, perhaps. *(After a pause.)* A quarter of an inch thick; I made a mistake, a little thicker than a pen.

Is it the thing that you scratch the fire out with?

Yes.

And you had that in your hand?

I had that in my hand, and the man was sitting close to the stove. I turned to him and asked him to leave the church. I had this piece of iron in my hand. I asked him to go away. I told him that if I put the fire out, it would be very inconvenient to all the people who were coming to the service; and he looked up and laughed, and then he snatched at the iron just above my hand, and pulled it towards himself. I think it touched his forehead, but I am not quite certain; I think it did. Then he got up and abused me very much and went away.

Then who took him to the inn where he afterwards went, where the solicitor was – the lawyer?

Well, I do not know exactly who took him to the inn. They painted his face with paint.

And you were summoned before the magistrates and fined £5.

Yes; I think I ought to have the £5 back. If the man was brought here he would tell you it was all a take in.

I should like to see the man.

Well, you will see him.

How long ago was it that you performed Mass and were summoned for it? Is that sixteen years ago?

That is about fourteen – very shortly after the poker case.

The first thing we talked about was thirteen years ago, the last fourteen; and now we are coming to one which you say is what?

About thirteen or fourteen.

All about the same time?

About thirteen years ago.

Did you communicate this submission, and what the date was, to the *Ipswich Daily Times*, or is it their own industry that has found this?

I do not know what that is. *(Referring to a paper in Mr Merewether's hand.)*

An office copy of your submission?

Oh, yes.

Were these processions in what you are pleased to call 'streets' of Claydon? How big is Claydon?

A thousand acres.

How many streets are there in it?

There is one main street.

What is the population?

Five hundred and fifty, or thereabouts.

Through these streets you walked in procession?

Yes.

I did not gather from your description of Claydon just now that Claydon was a place with very extensive streets, and the electric light, or anything of that sort.

Oh, no. It is only a country parish.

You promised to discontinue the processions and ceremonies?

In the street; yes.

I observe that you undertook to obey the bishop, which you say you have done conscientiously ever since. You never had any more processions. And you also undertook to pay all the costs to the proctor, as between proctor and client?

I had to pay all the costs.

Did you do that?

Yes; I paid him £100.

And that was in the year of grace 1864?

Yes, but I think I might say something more about that.

Well; I do not know. I should have thought that we might have been spared what we have heard about it.

(iv) *The Burial: Further Evidence: Rev. George Drury*

Merewether: Have you ever behaved in an irreverent way at a grave, as suggested?

Drury: I never have in the whole course of my life. It would be utterly repugnant to me.

Is it customary for a person to throw earth on the coffin, as you go on with the service?

Yes; it is always the custom, either for the clerk, or for the clergyman, or someone standing by. It says so in the rubric.

Mr Serjeant Parry: That is where the service is performed.

Mr Merewether: And where the service is not performed, have you always thrown earth on the grave?

Not always – generally.

And have you thereupon turned on your heel, and gone away?

No; I have done nothing which would justify that being said at all. I have no ill-will to the Dissenters at all. I am friends with them as far as I can be.

How much is your burial fee by law?

Four shillings and sixpence.

Did you accept the burial fee from this poor man?

No; I told Ramsey that I would only take half a crown of him.

And then it is suggested that, as you had had the half-crown, or the clerk had, you went away at five o'clock?

Yes.

What time was it that you think you went away?

I did not go away till after a quarter to six. I was there more than three-quarters of an hour.

As to the conversation, I understand you that some of these things you swear you did not say?

Yes.

And some you do not remember? In the first place, did it all occur, according to your recollection, in the order in which it is put in the libel?

Oh, no – altogether wrong – wrongly arranged.

I am not going to take you through it again; but, as I understand, you adhere in cross-examination to this – that the first thing the Dissenting gentleman had to do with it was, coming up to you and putting his arm on yours?

That was the first thing.

He called it putting his hand dangerously near you; you call it shaking his fist in your face?

He shook his fist like this (showing).

Was the first word that you had from him or to him?

From him.

That you are sure? That gets it two pages further on. Now, in the first place, according to your recollection – you are a gentleman of education – how do you think it was? There are two pages and a half of this. Was the conversation altogether as long as is represented here?

No, not nearly so long – not half so long.

How much more do you think there is of it, when it is put here in such fine language, than actually took place?

Not half of it. It says three times that I said something about teaching my parishioners. I never said it once, or anything like it at all.

Some of the things that are mentioned you said?

Some. I can recognize some.

And you said them at a later time – later on in the day, as it were, than he has put them here?

Yes.

And you did not say 'Nonsense'; and you did not say, 'What has humanity got to do with it?' Now about this 'Christian'. It is said that you told them that he was not a Christian but a heathen. Did you use the word 'heathen' at all?

No.

Did you say that he was not a Christian, or that he had not been made a Christian? Do you remember which you said?

I said that the child had not been baptized, and was not a Christian, or had not been made a Christian. I do not know which, it is much the same.

You were asked about children being baptized, and whether they are heathens, or whether they remain in a bad place. Has the Church left the matter thus: 'It is certain, by God's word, that children who are baptized, dying before they commit actual sin, are undoubtedly saved'?

Unquestionably – yes.

That is the way the Church has left that matter?

That is my doctrine.

And the Prayer-book has left it so?

Yes, I do not go beyond that.

You have read a good deal of theology, I suppose the divinity of the Church?

Oh, yes.

Is it a doctrine of the Church of England, or is it laid down in any canon or in any part of the Prayer-book that any further opinion upon unbaptized children is to be expressed by the Church?

I do not know whether it is expressed anywhere else.

I say, is anything further than that expressed by the Church in its canons or formularies?

It leaves the question there.

Have you ever gone beyond that?

No.

You have left it as the Church has left it?

Yes.

Now, am I right in saying that throughout the whole of the two baptismal services, and through the part of the burial service which relates to his being a Christian, it is stated that baptism receives a person into the congregation of Christ's flock?

Yes, that is what baptism does.

And when the child is baptized privately, it is simply baptized with the form of baptism and one short prayer?

Yes.

And then afterwards the minister asks certain questions as to whom he was baptized by, and who were present, and so on?

Yes.

And when those questions are answered do you rebaptize the child?

No, not if they are answered in the affirmative.

Satisfactorily. And do you say that all has been done well, and that he has been therefore received into the number of the children of Christ?

Yes.

And is that what you have throughout adhered to, not only on this occasion, but in the ministrations of your life?

Yes.

Mr Justice Grove: Well, I have got, 'I have followed the Prayer-book.'

Mr Merewether: Yes. Do you understand that there is any pre-scription here, except of order, as to what you are to do at the burial of an unbaptized person where you are not to use the office?

It says that the service is not to be read.

And you have your discretion then as to what shall be done in that case where the office is not used?

I do not think we have any discretion, but we have to bury. We have to perform the ceremony.

Can the bishop give you three months' suspension from your office and your income if you refuse to bury anybody in the churchyard?

Yes.

And did it ever enter into your head to refuse to bury the child, as stated here?

Never.

Or to bury it in unconsecrated ground?

No.

There is one thing about the dress. Had you on the dress you ordinarily wear in the parish?

Yes.

And when you go out of your parish you put on the coat you have got on now?

Mr Serjeant Parry: No.

The witness: Yes, or similar. Serjeant Parry thinks I have had a new coat made for the purpose. Let him have his joke.

Mr Merewether: But the dress you wore on this occasion was the one in which everybody in Claydon had seen you for years?

Oh yes, for years and years.

And it is not likely that anybody there would suppose that it was an extraordinary dress?

No, no one there would suppose I had put it on to insult the child except Serjeant Parry.

Did you put it on and go there for the sole purpose – the single and gratuitous purpose – of irritating the living and insulting the dead?

No, certainly not. The only reason why I went over there was to bury the child. No other reason.

Mr Merewether: I have no other question.

Mr Serjeant Parry: Will your Lordship ask him whether on the north side of the church stillborn children are buried?

Mr Justice Grove: I think somebody said so. Is that so?

I do not think there are stillborn children in the north of Claydon churchyard at all. There are twelve or fourteen graves there. They are mostly graves of children.

Mr Serjeant Parry: Unbaptized children?

I think, Mr Serjeant, that the custom for burying a stillborn child is to bury it either in a ditch or a piece of wasteland.

Mr Merewether: But as far as you know, has any stillborn child been buried there since you have been there?

No, there is no foundation whatever for the statement.

Mr Justice Grove: Is that so, that stillborn children are buried in a ditch?

My authority is the old clerk.

Mr Justice Grove remarked that he thought that the witness must be thinking of premature children.

The witness: The clergy have nothing to do with them.

(v) *Henry Waterman: Parish Clerk and Sexton*

Mr Henry Waterman, sworn, examined by Mr Poyser: I have been parish clerk and sexton at Akenham for five years. I remember in August last Ramsey coming to me about his child. He said he had been up to the Rev. Drury's and arranged for the funeral of his child to take place on the Thursday. That was on the Tuesday evening. He said that the funeral was to be at five o'clock on Thursday afternoon. He paid me my fee, which was half a crown. I afterwards found out from Mr Drury that Ramsey had fixed the time. Ramsey's wife came to me on the Wednesday afternoon and asked me if I would go to the Rev. Drury and ask him if he would oblige her by burying the child on the Friday afternoon.

Did she say anything to you about having a service there?

Yes; Mrs Ramsey told me that she had been and picked a place out for this child in front of the church, and I told her stillborn babies and unbaptized children would be at the north part of the church.

On the Friday, did Mr Drury and you go together to the church about five o'clock in the afternoon?

I overtook the reverend gentleman. *(Laughter.)*

What time did you get to the church?

As near as we could tell the time, about five minutes before or five minutes after.

How soon after that did you see Ramsey coming?

Well, I think it was half-past five or a quarter to six – very near a quarter to six.

Before that, did you see Mr Gooding, and Mr Smith, and Mr Tozer?

Yes.

Where did they come from?

They seemed to be coming from Rise Hall, which is on the right-hand side from the church.

Who lives at Rise Hall?

Mr Smith, the churchwarden.

From which side did Ramsey and the coffin come?

They came from the left-hand side from Akenham – the left of Rise Hall.

Did you see them come up to the gate of the church?

Yes.

Did they take the coffin out of the cart there?

Yes.

Did any of them go into the churchyard at all?

Yes, Mr Gooding and Mr Tozer came into the churchyard before the coffin came.

They went into the churchyard first?

Yes.

Did they go and look at the grave?

Yes.

Did they say anything about it?

Yes.

What did they say?

Mr Gooding asked me why I did not tell the gentleman where the grave was, and I told Mr Gooding I did not hear him.

Where did they set the coffin?

Very near opposite to the gate of the churchyard.

Where were you standing then?

Close by the church door.

Mr Drury was standing with you?

Yes.

Did he send you with a message to the father of the child – Ramsey?

Yes.

What did you say to Ramsey?

'The Rev. Mr Drury sent his compliments to the father of the child to have the child buried, if you please, because he had been waiting for some time, and wanted to be agoing.'

What did he say to that?

Mr Ramsey asked me to ask the Rev. Drury if he could wait a little while longer.

What did you say to that?

I told him I couldn't ask the Rev. Drury to wait any longer. He had been waiting a long while, and I thought it was hard for the gentleman to wait any longer.

Then did you go back to Mr Drury and tell him?

Mr Gooding first asked me what I wanted of him and Mr Ramsey.

Mr Gooding spoke to you while you were there?

Yes, before I could get to the father of the child.

Mr Serjeant Parry: Well, I object to that. We are not responsible for that.

Mr Poyser *(to the witness)*: Well, never mind that. You went back to Mr Drury, then?

Yes.

And after that, did you and Mr Drury go to the gate where the coffin was lying?

Yes, the Rev. Drury went to the father of the child.

Where were you then?

In the churchyard.

Near there?

Within about four or five yards.

Did you hear Mr Tozer reading or anything?

I did hear the gentleman reading of something, but I am sure I don't know what the gentleman read.

Where was Mr Drury then?

The Rev. Drury went to speak to the father of the child first.

He went to speak to the father of the child first?

Yes, after the reverend sent the message by me [*sic*].

How far was the father from the gate at that time?

Well, I should think not more than five or six yards. I should think not.

As far as across the court?

Well, I should think from here to that side of the jury, if you please, not farther *(referring to jury box)*.

You say that Mr Drury went up and spoke to the father, and then Mr Tozer began to read?

Yes.

Is that what you said before?

Yes; as soon as ever –

Mr Justice Grove: No; what he said before was that he heard Mr Tozer read some words. He did not say particularly when. Then the father was not more than five or six yards off?

The witness: No.

Mr Justice Grove: I suppose that means when Mr Tozer was reading the words. He does not say so in terms.

Mr Poyser: How long did Mr Tozer go on reading?

I really cannot say. I do not know how long he did, for there was such a to-do with the reverend gentlemen that I do not know how long he did read. *(Laughter.)*

What do you mean by 'such a to-do'?

Well, he kicked up such a row.

Are you speaking of Mr Tozer?

I am speaking of the Reverend Tozer.

Mr Serjeant Parry: You said just now 'reverend gentlemen'.

Mr Justice Grove: Did he say 'gentlemen'?

Mr Poyser: What was Mr Tozer doing when he was not reading?

Well, the Reverend Drury went to the father of this child, and asked him to have this here child buried; and during the time the Rev. Drury was talking with the father of this child, the Rev. Tozer began to read.

Then what did he do when he left off reading?

Well – abused the Rev. Drury. *(Laughter.)*

How long do you think this talk between Mr Tozer and Mr Drury lasted?

Well, I think some ten minutes or a quarter of an hour.

Some ten minutes or a quarter of an hour?

I should think so.

Did you see Mr Drury point at the coffin with his umbrella, or anything of that kind?

No, sir; I did not.

What was the first thing that you saw Mr Tozer do with regard to Mr Drury? I do not mean the first thing you heard him say.

Not in regard to speech? You mean what he did?

Yes, what he did.

Well, he bent his fist in his face. That is what he did.

Bent his fist in his face, you say.

Yes, drew his guard. I should call it so myself.

After Mr Drury had gone away, what did Mr Tozer do then?

He went on reading something over this coffin.

Yes, then what did they do?

Then went and buried it after.

How did they get in the churchyard?

They went by a private gateway.

Did you see Mr Smith go in?

Yes.

How did he go in?

Over the hedge.

He went over the hedge?

Yes.

Did you hear Mr Tozer say anything to Mr Smith?

Yes, sir.

What did he say?

Mr Tozer told Mr Smith when he was going away that he would give the Rev. Drury such a dressing for that as he never had in his life.

Cross-examined by Mr Bulwer: You say that Mr Smith went over the hedge?

Yes.

He could not get into the churchyard without? The gate was locked, was it not?

They carried the corpse through the gateway.

What made him get over the hedge?

Well, I suppose Smith thought that was the shortest way.

I suppose there was not much damage done to the hedge. You cannot hurt the hedge?

Well, gentlemen's stock have ruined it. He did not mend it.

He did not do much harm?

And he did no good.

Mr. Bulwer *(to the witness)*: You are taking stock of me pretty well.

The witness: Well, I am obliged to look at you. You are talking to me.

Ramsey came to you on the Tuesday?

The evening. Yes.

Did he tell you then that the child had not been baptized?

Yes.

I thought so. Did you ask him for that information or did he volunteer it?

I cannot say how that was, but in our conversation that did come out.

You generally consider it part of your duty, as parish clerk, to get that information –

No, I am not informed to do so.

You answered my question before I asked it.

I beg your pardon.

I wanted to know whether you consider it as part of your duty, as parish clerk, to ascertain those little particulars before speaking to Mr Drury?

No, I am not authorized to do that.

How do you mean – 'not authorized'?

I was not asked to do such a thing by the Rev. Mr Drury.

You had seen this account in the newspaper, had you, of what took place on the occasion?

I saw it before I saw it in the newspaper – heard it rather.

You saw the account in the newspaper of what was said to have taken place?

No, sir, I heard it before the newspaper was printed.

After the newspaper was printed you saw the account?

I do not know that I did.

Did not you see it, and did not Mr Drury come and ask you whether it was true, and what you knew about it?

No.

Has he spoken to you about it at all?

I do not know that the reverend gentleman ever has on this subject.

Do you mean to say that Mr Drury has not asked you about what took place this afternoon at the funeral?

The Rev. Mr Drury has not asked me about the matter today scarcely.

I mean at Akenham?

Yes, I know what you mean.

Do you mean to say that he has not said anything to you about it?

I do not think that the reverend gentleman ever uttered ten words to me since the job occurred.

He has uttered ten words to you?

I do not know that at all.

But he has talked to you about it?

I do not know.

Can you give me any information about whether he has or not? Do not fence with me.

Well, I am not looking at those gentlemen *(referring to the jury)*; I am talking to you.

I want you to look at those gentlemen.

I have nothing to do with those gentlemen; I am talking to you.

He came to you on this Tuesday evening, and in the course of the conversation it oozed out that the child had not been baptized. I presume that that was a bit of information that Mr Drury would like to know?

I do not know about that, sir.

Did you tell Mr Drury the fact that the child was not baptized?

Yes; I did.

When?

On the same evening the man told me.

You always do whenever a child comes to be buried, you always tell Mr Drury if it has not been baptized?

I am not certain about that.

Are you certain about anything? You are quite certain you did not on this occasion?

Quite.

Did Mr Ramsey want to know that night if the child could be buried?

No.

Did he go up with you to the rectory, Mr Drury's, at Claydon?

Yes.

And Mr Drury's house has a glass door, I believe?

I believe it has.

You might say it has or has not? We do not want your belief; we want to know as a fact.

It has.

You might as well say it has; and did Mr Ramsey sit outside this glass door while you spoke to Mr Drury in the hall?

Yes.

He did?

Yes. I cannot hear you if you look that way, sir; look this way, if you please.

You are hard of hearing are you?

I think I am, sir.

I wanted to know – you heard me sufficiently to be able to answer – whether there was a glass door between the place where Mr Ramsey was standing and the hall where Mr Drury was standing?

Yes.

I suppose Mr Ramsey, standing outside, could hear what passed between you and Mr Drury?

He could hear right through the door, I suppose; but if he could, he could hear better than I.

He was there?

Yes; that is quite right.

When did Mrs Ramsey come to see you?

On the Wednesday evening, the next day afterwards.

Did she come with a friend of hers?

Yes; I suppose it was a friend.

Did you know who it was?

No.

Did she want to choose a place where the child was to be buried?

She had done that before that.

When she saw you – on the same day?

Yes.

She had told you so?

Yes.

And where had she chosen the spot?

In the front of the church.

On the south side?

Yes.

Did you tell her that the child could not be buried there?

No; I did not tell her it could not be done there.

But did you say anything further?

Yes.

Did you lead her to expect it would be buried there or somewhere else?

Yes.

And did you give her the reasons why it would be buried on the north side of the church?

I did not tell her, but I thought that possibly it would.

You told her that Mr Drury said it would be buried there, being unbaptized?

Being unbaptized.

How came you to form that notion in your head. Mr Drury had not told you so?

No, but that is the custom of the country in regard to stillborn babes and unbaptized babes wherever I lived.

Did you tell her it would be buried there like a dog?

No.

Nothing of that kind?

No.

What I want to know is if they came here and said you stated what was not true?

I tell you I did not say so.

Nothing of the kind?

Nothing of the kind. I am dull of hearing, sir; would you look at me.

Mr Bulwer: That is why you were chosen parish clerk?

Witness: I do not know.

Did not this person, when she came to you to speak about this child being buried like a dog because it was unbaptized, have a conversation with you as to whether an unbaptized person could have money left him, or whether they could get it?

No; I never heard the woman mention it.

Was there any talk about it, jocular or not, as to whether an unbaptized person could inherit a fortune or money left them?

I do not remember anything of that kind.

Was there anything of the sort mentioned?

I think I mentioned that to the woman.

What did you tell her – that there was some money left her, and that she was unbaptized and would not be able to have it?

Possibly I might.

Where did you get this doctrine from, that an unbaptized person cannot inherit a fortune?

I am sure I do not know where I can get that.

That is not the custom of the country, is it?

I do not know.

You are upon your oath.

I am telling you the truth, to the best of my belief.

This is the sort of answer you are giving upon your oath?

Yes; that is quite right.

Now, Mr Drury, I suppose, was rather impatient the afternoon when the funeral took place?

I should think not.

He was in a great hurry, was not he?

No.

He was not in a hurry to get the funeral over and done with?

No.

He was not in a hurry to get it over and done with it in three-quarters of an hour?

No.

You thought he waited long enough?

Yes; and so did the reverend gentleman.

Having waited so long you thought he was quite justified in getting away?

Yes.

You were rather in a hurry?

Yes.

You knew Mr Smith was the churchwarden of Akenham parish? You were there with the bishop?

Yes, I met his lordship. I believe he told me Mr Smith was there.

Did you ever go within Akenham church?

Yes.

How often?

Perhaps twice in the month; perhaps a little oftener; I cannot say. I did not go in the week days.

Twice in the month and on a Sunday?

Probably.

Do you agree that it is all over muck or dead birds and filth and rubbish?

I do not know what you call filth. There is a little dirt and rubbish of that kind. There may be a dead bird; but it is not to be wondered at.

Are the windows broken?

Yes.

You have never cleaned it?

No.

Nor anybody else to your knowledge?

Yes.

Who?

The late clerk, about four years ago, before I came. It might have been longer. I do not know. This man Ramsey was a labourer of Mr Smith's and the child was brought there in the usual way.

And Mr Smith's house adjoins the meadow?

Yes.

And that is where Mr Tozer, who came from Ipswich, put up his horse?

That I cannot say anything about.

This gateway to the church was on the south side of the church.

Yes.

And going through the gateway, that would lead you up to the south side of the church, if you walked straight on – do you understand that?

No, I do not.

When you had got into the gate and you walked straight on would you walk up against the south side of the church?

The gateway to the church is opposite; it may be where you stand, and that was locked.

That is not very intelligible; it was on the south side of the church – the gateway was?

Yes.

And how far was the coffin laid from the gate?

About four or four and a half yards. The gate opens into the church-yard. On the other side is a meadow.

Then this gate in the churchyard is bounded by the meadow?

Yes. There is a ditch parting it. It is a hollow ditch and there is also a bank. The meadow is Mr Smith's. The bearers and the father and mother and Mr Gooding came up with the coffin, and Mr Smith was standing there. They came up to Mr Smith, and Mr Tozer, who was there too. I did not see any take their hats off when the coffin was placed upon the ground. They stood round the coffin.

Did you see Mr Tozer have a book in his hand?

Yes, or something to that effect.

You do not know a book when you see one?

I cannot say.

Did he read from it?

He read something, but I do not know what. I could not hear whether it was prayers or not. I do not know if it was from a Bible.

Was that the first thing that happened when they laid that little child upon the ground?

No.

What was?

That could not be, because I set the little child down and the Rev. Mr Drury sent me to the father.

You went and delivered Mr Drury's message to the father, and the father sent you back to Mr Drury with his answer?

Yes.

And upon that did Mr Tozer begin to read from this book?

Yes.

Now, what became of you after you delivered the message to Mr Drury?

I stood there all the time, against the gate.

Were you sitting on the tombstone, waiting for them, before they came?

No; I was standing up all the while. I never heard what language was used by the two reverend gentlemen. There was a great jangling with Mr Tozer.

Then Mr Drury said nothing at all?

Yes.

Then you mean the jangling was on both sides?

The Rev. Mr Drury answered the gentleman, no doubt.

And that you call a jangle?

I do, when they get into a fighting attitude. *(Laughter.)*

That is to say when Mr Tozer was on his guard? Now, there is only one thing more, perhaps, that it is necessary I should ask you – can you tell me how often Mr Drury has performed the service on a Sunday at Akenham church?

I cannot tell exactly.

Can you tell me within once a year or so, as near as that?

Once or twice in a month – three times on an average.

Do you mean to say that upon your oath, so that the people of Akenham may see that you said that on your oath?

I think I may.

I am not speaking since this occurrence, but before that occurrence?

That was often before this occurrence, before Mr Smith come a great deal.

Mr Justice Grove: How many times in the month do you say – once or twice?

I think so.

Mr Bulwer: What do you mean by saying before Mr Smith 'come' – before Mr Smith came to live at the farm?

Yes, I do not know how long Mr Smith was on the farm before this occurrence happened.

Do you undertake to say that it was before this –

Mr Merewether: I do not want to interrupt my learned friend; but in regard to the other point, I think Mr Drury might have been asked this question about the number of times.

Mr Justice Grove: He did say something.

Mr Merewether: He said the service he attends every other Sunday.

Mr Justice Grove: Every Sunday?

Mr Merewether: When there is no congregation he is obliged by the law to go back.

Mr Justice Grove: What he certainly said was that he performed the service there on the Sunday morning and evening alternately – a morning service this Sunday and an evening service next, and that he said happened twice a month, or something of that kind.

Mr Merewether: There were three services last month out of four, and the last was the other evening.

Mr Bulwer: My question is how often has there been a congregation there? You are a parish clerk, and you ought to be able to give us information.

Mr Justice Grove: Not a congregation, but how many people. Three is considered a congregation, you know.

Mr Bulwer: I won't put it in that form, I will put it in another form. How often has service been performed within the last half-year before this funeral?

To the best of my knowledge once or twice in a month; but I cannot say exactly, and I won't swear.

Re-examined by Mr Merewether: If no congregation comes, you say as far as you make out every other time?

Yes.

Do you know why the priest is not allowed to say the service with only you there?

I do not understand that at all.

How many church people are there in the parish altogether, do you think? Any?

I do not think there is any, sir. *(Laughter.)*

They are all Dissenters?

Yes, they treat the service like it anyhow.

There are only eighty of you altogether, and they are charged with not keeping the church clean. May I ask you what the parish pay you?

They don't pay me anything.

And they expect you to keep the church clean without any payment?

They do.

And you have not done it?

And I have not done it.

Are there any church rates? Did you ever have a church rate to pay?

No, we have no church rate.

How long have you been clerk?

For about five years.

How many burials have you had in that way?

Where do you mean?

In the churchyard?

In Akenham or Claydon – all sorts of burials in the last four years – at Akenham I mean – I should not think above two or three – three I should say.

Because you were asked this solemn question whether you were not always obliged to tell Mr Drury when children were not baptized. How many altogether, men, women, and children, baptized or unbaptized, should you say there have been?

Not above two or three – I cannot say.

Did you mention to Mr Drury what Mr Ramsey said?

Yes.

According to your impression was that the second time you mentioned the subject to him about being unbaptized?

Yes; I was obliged.

He says you mentioned it the evening before?

The same evening the woman came to me.

You told him then again about the child not being baptized?

Yes.

Mr Justice Grove: You told him twice?

I told the reverend gentleman the same night the woman told me – that was on the Tuesday – and again when it had been postponed.

Mr Justice Grove: On the Thursday?

On the Wednesday.

Mr Merewether: It was postponed from the Wednesday night; you think you told him on the Wednesday evening as well?

Yes.

Mr Merewether: My Lord, that will be the plaintiff's case subject to two or three letters which I shall put in. I shall not trouble your Lordship with them now, but I shall put them in, and any portion of them may be read in the morning. I want to insure that I shall not be precluded from putting them in.

Mr Justice Grove: No.

*

The court then adjourned till Saturday morning at 10.30.

The court was crowded throughout the day.

Among those present were Edward Packard, Esq., Sen. [members of Parliament long eminent in supporting the cause of Burial Laws reform and editors of well-known journals].

3 *A Change in Court**

At the opening of the court this morning it was stated that owing to the death of Lady Grove the court would not sit. The learned counsel engaged in the case, however, had a private consultation with the judges of the court.

After a short delay, Mr Justice Denman took his seat upon the Bench, and, addressing the jury, said: Gentlemen, since you were sitting yesterday the very sad intelligence has reached me that my brother Grove, who has been presiding at this trial, has lost his wife. Lady Grove is dead. Some arrangement has, therefore, become necessary for the continuance of this case, and I have consulted with counsel as to what would be the best course, and they have come to the conclusion that it would not be necessary that the trial, so far as it has proceeded, should be altogether abortive, and that if I will read through Mr Justice Grove's notes, and the shorthand writers' notes of the evidence so far as it has gone, I shall be in a position to go on with the case, so that you need not be obliged to begin it again. This process will take a considerable time. I could not begin the case without having an hour or two for that purpose, and that would bring us so very near to the hour at which the court adjourns on a Saturday that counsel agree with me that it would be better to resume on Monday. This arrangement will enable me to sit in the Court of Criminal Appeal, where I am due today; and it will, I think, also enable us to go on with this case in a more satisfactory way.

Mr Serjeant Parry expressed his cordial concurrence in the arrangement.

Mr. Day, Q.C., asked that the case should be fixed for half-past eleven o'clock in the morning to suit the convenience of the witnesses, who had to come from the country.

Mr Justice Denman acceded to the application, and the case was accordingly adjourned till Monday.

---

* From *East Anglian Daily Times*, March 10th, 1879.

4 *Case for the Defendant**

MONDAY, MARCH IOTH, 1879

(i) *Preliminary Questions*

Mr Justice Denman: I have read the report which appears in the *East Anglian Daily Times* of what took place the other day; it seems to be a very close one indeed, and is presumably correct. There is, however, one question which I should like to ask the clerk, Waterman, if he is still here

Mr Merewether: He is not here today.

Mr Justice Denman: I am sorry for that, but I do not know that it is of such importance as that I should require him to be sent for. It is possible the point might be agreed upon. A great deal of evidence is directed to the question as to whether the funeral was to take place at five o'clock or half-past five o'clock. The hour originally fixed was five, but the clerk does not appear to have been asked whether any hour was mentioned when the day was changed from Thursday to Friday.

Mr Serjeant Parry: I asked Mr Drury whether he did not receive a message on the morning of Friday telling him the funeral could not take place until half-past five o'clock. He said he did not receive such a message.

Mr Justice Denman: The clerk probably would be the person to take such a message, and I should like to have asked if he had any information to give upon that subject. If the case is likely to last long enough for him to be here before the evidence is completed, I think I should like to ask him one or two questions.

Mr Day: He certainly ought to have been here, and I will take care he is here before the case is over.

Mr Justice Denman: I see the plaintiff's case is concluded, subject to certain letters being put in.

Mr Day: There are one or two answers to interrogatories I should like to have read. The first is, 'In whose handwriting is the original manuscript of the report headed "Burial Scandal at Akenham", set out in the second paragraph of the plaintiff's statement of claim.' The answer states that the manuscript referred to was in the handwriting

* From *East Anglian Daily Times*, March 11th, 1879.

157

of Mr Wickham Tozer, and that there are some interlineations and alterations. I should like to call for the manuscript, so that it may appear which are the interlineations and which are not.

Mr Serjeant Parry: My friend has been furnished with the original. It consists of a number of small pieces of paper, and I will put it in; but I have a copy I can hand to your lordship.

Mr Day: Then the seventh interrogatory is, 'Were any copies of your said newspaper of the 28th of August last, or the 29th of August last, sent or forwarded by you, or by your authority, to the editors or publishers of any other newspapers?' And the answer is that, in accordance with the usual practice, when a report of public interest appeared, the defendant had sent copies to the publishers of other newspapers.

This closed the plaintiff's case.

(ii) *Opening Statement*

Mr Serjeant Parry: May it please, your lordship, gentlemen of the jury, I shall, I believe, best discharge my duty in this case, I hope to your satisfaction and the satisfaction of his lordship, if I now only detain you for a few moments stating to you the nature of the evidence that I shall call, and reserve my remarks upon the whole of the case till that time when the evidence for the plaintiff and the evidence for the defendant will be completely before you, when any remarks will come, I will not say with greater force, because I will not attach any force to them, but at all events will be better understood by you, and I shall be more able to deal with the facts as proved upon the evidence on both sides, and to contrast the evidence of the defendant with the evidence of the plaintiff, and ask you to consider upon which you will place the greatest reliance. I shall call before you the editor, and I believe also the part proprietor of this paper, Mr Wilson, who is the defendant. I shall call before you Mr Tozer, and several persons who were present at what took place in the field. I shall call before you the Rural Dean, and also the Bishop of the Diocese to speak as to the state and condition of Akenham church, and I shall also prove to you most distinctly that Mr Drury was under monition at this time for an ecclesiastical offence which he has denied. Gentlemen, I believe one of the main facts of this case for you to come to a conclusion upon will be whether the statement of what occurred near Akenham church, in the meadow where the service was held over this poor child as published in the *East Anglian Daily Times*, is or is not substantially true and correct. You are aware that Mr Drury has denied it, and with that denial I shall deal when the evidence for the defendant is before you. I shall call before you certain respectable witnesses in whom I trust you will place implicit credit, and show beyond all doubt the correctness of what has been stated, which was really, as we now understand, written by Mr Tozer. As to the various parts of the libel to which my friend has called attention, I reserve what I have to say, believing that in taking my present course I am consulting the convenience of all parties to the inquiry, and, above all, shortening it by abstaining from making a long comment now, because I shall make it more conveniently and certainly more tersely when the whole of the evidence is before you.

(iii) *Frederick William Wilson: Editor of the* East Anglian Daily Times

Mr Frederick William Wilson, examined by Mr Serjeant Parry, said: I have been editor and proprietor of the *East Anglian Daily Times* since it started in 1874. The manuscript of the alleged libel was sent to me by Mr Tozer. I did not know him personally, but I knew him by public reputation. He was minister of Nicholas Street Independent Chapel. I know he has a son who is a clergyman of the Church of England, and I also know that he has written favourably with regard to the Church of England. I received the manuscript on the Sunday following the Friday on which the funeral took place; it appeared in the newspaper on the Monday. My manager informed me that Mr Smith, the churchwarden of Akenham, had gone over the manuscript, made one or two slight corrections, and guaranteed its entire authenticity. I knew Mr Smith personally, he is a farmer at Akenham. I knew him as churchwarden of Akenham church, in consequence of the publicity which arose from the admonition to Mr Drury. I believe the report to be a correct one.

Cross-examined by Mr Day: I attend my parish church. I had a personal knowledge of Mr Smith because he happened to be a member of an Ipswich scientific society, of which I am also a member. I had not an opportunity of speaking to him personally about this proceeding. It was my manager who told me that Mr Smith had looked over the report. Mr Tozer had previously contributed a review of a theological work to my paper, but he was not an ordinary correspondent. I published an extract from the *Daily Chronicle*, on the 29th of August. That paper had not received a special copy of the *East Anglian Daily Times*. The report was copied next evening in the *Echo*, and all the papers in the country copied from the *Echo*, as I knew from the fact that the *Echo* report was slightly abridged. 'Straight' is a direct correspondent of our own. I knew at the time whom it was, but I could not tell you now. I have no personal knowledge of 'A Lover of Humanity' that I am aware of; but all correspondents have to send in their name. An exchange copy of the *Times* was sent to the *Christian World*, and they returned the compliment by sending an advance proof of an article which appeared there. I did not read that article before it was inserted in my paper; my sub-editor inserted it. He is not the same person as the manager; he is in court. I did not read the article until after it appeared in the paper. I asked someone in our office to look over the back files of papers with reference to former matters connected with Mr Drury.

The proceedings that took place in the year 1863 were all matters of great public notoriety. I am not in possession of any letters that had passed between Mr Drury and other persons. My solicitors are responsible for any description in the 'notice to admit' of all correspondence between the Bishop of Norwich and the plaintiff as far back as 1864, or with reference to Father Ignatius. Of course I provided my solicitors with information where I was able. Before I started the daily paper, I published the *Suffolk Mercury*, the *Ipswich and Colchester Times*, and *Ipswich Express*, and those papers contained references to these matters. There was no necessity to search among them for information because these were matters of notoriety. We had only to take the files down from the room to find the reports at once.

I frequently go through Claydon. I believe I went there twice during the three-quarters of a year that this action has been pending. I went there for the purpose of an afternoon ride, and have called on a Mr Moore, an old churchwarden of Mr Drury's, on one occasion. I did not call on a labourer there. There is no doubt I have taken all reasonable means of obtaining information about Mr Drury. I have been attacked, and I have endeavoured to defend myself. I hope that every method that I have adopted has been fair and legitimate. I have done my best to obtain information about Mr Drury.

Re-examined by Mr Serjeant Parry: I placed the matter in the hands of my solicitors (Messrs Birkett and Bantoft). After the action had commenced Mr Block (Mr Drury's solicitor) sent me a statement which he wished me to insert as my own in the newspaper. I made inquiries and found the statement was incorrect.

Mr Justice Denman: We must not have this. After making inquiries you refused to insert that statement.

Mr Serjeant Parry: As far as I am concerned I do not seek to have that statement in.

Mr Justice Denman: He was beginning to give hearsay evidence.

Mr Serjeant Parry: You say you had reason to believe the statement was true before you published it?

I had.

After this action was brought against you, did you again make full inquiries as to whether this statement was true or not?

I made further and full inquiries.

(iv) *Rev. Wickham Tozer*

Rev. Wickham Tozer, examined by Mr Digby: I am minister of the Congregational Church, in Nicholas Street, Ipswich. In consequence of a communication from Mr Gooding I went over to Akenham on Friday, August 28th, and arrived there a few minutes past five. I went for the purpose of performing a funeral service. I put the horse up at Mr Smith's and went direct to the meadow fronting the church. The meadow adjoins the churchyard. Mr Smith's house is possibly a hundred yards from the church gate. I went to the meadow from Mr Smith's house. Mr Gooding was with me. We went into the church-yard to see if the grave was ready for interment; then we left the churchyard again. The funeral party came up possibly ten minutes after we left the churchyard. They were all strangers to me. I was never there before, and I had not long been at Ipswich. I should think there were possibly six or eight in the cart, and the coffin also was in the cart. The cart stopped possibly within twenty yards of the church gate.

Mr Justice Denman: Do you mean on the road?

The witness: There is no road; it is a bridle path across the meadow, and on that path the corpse was put. The corpse was placed there, there being no bier. A sheet was placed on the ground and the corpse was placed on that. The relatives gathered round the corpse, forming a semi-circle. I stood in the centre, and as soon as I found they were ready I commenced reading. Is it necessary for me to state what I read?

Mr Justice Denman: Yes, you had better do so at once.

The witness: Gentlemen seem very curious about that.

Mr Justice Denman: You must not make speeches.

The witness: Pardon me, my lord; I never was in a court of justice before.

Mr Justice Denman: What were you reading, is the question.

The witness: The narrative of the death of David's child. I had been reading several minutes, when Mr Drury came out of the churchyard gate and stood near to my left hand, and addressed himself to the parents of the child. He requested them to go immediately to the grave

6

to inter the child. I went on reading. He repeated a second time his request, no notice having been taken of the first. Mr Gooding then requested him to be silent for a few moments. Mr Drury replied that he believed it his duty to be there to instruct or admonish his parishioners as to the irregularity of the proceedings at that funeral service. Up to that time I had not said or done anything to Mr Drury. I remember Mr Drury saying, 'Do not tell me to be quiet; I have a duty to perform, and I shall do it.' He told them that the service was an irregular one, and that he felt it his duty to endeavour to prevent the service being held. I then made a very earnest appeal to him. I am not prepared to state every word that I uttered on that occasion. Excited and confused as I am, I really am not in a position to state every word.

Mr Justice Denman: If anybody in the world is, you ought to be, because you very soon afterwards sent to the newspaper what purported to be an exact account of it.

The witness: My lord, you have not the right account of that, I believe – excuse my saying so. I appealed to him as a gentleman and as a Christian not to interfere with the service, and said that it would not last long, only a few moments, and I sincerely hoped that he would be quiet. I told him that I respected his religious scruples, and that I was anxious not to give offence to him. He replied that that was all nonsense, and it had nothing whatever to do with the point. I then said that I thought an appeal to his Christian feelings ought, at any rate, to have induced him to be quiet for a moment, and as my appeal to his Christianity had failed, I appealed to his manhood. He then moved towards the grave, and with his umbrella pointed to the corpse, and he said, 'That child has not been baptized; it is, therefore, not a Christian, and I object to its being buried as such.' I both did and said something then. I moved up to him a little nearer than I had been – I had not been more than two or three yards from him – but I went up to him and put my finger up in that kind of way *(stretching out his right arm and pointing with his index finger)*, and I said, 'If this were not a funeral I would silence that brutal speech of yours,' or something of that kind. He said, 'Do not shake your fist in my face.' That was the first and the last time in the course of the conversation that I made any gesture of any sort. I told him I was not shaking my fist in his face, which was true, but that he richly deserved to be made to feel it, which was also true.

Mr Justice Denman: I wish you would not comment.

The witness: Forgive me, my lord, I am sorry I did it.

Mr Justice Denman: You merely produce a laugh by it. Though you may think it clever it damages the evidence of the witness very much.

Mr Digby: Go on telling us what passed.

The witness: You will have just to lead me a little bit, for my memory gets shaken by the excitement.

Mr Justice Denman: Would you like a glass of water?

The witness: No, my lord. I am not a dry talker – *(laughter)* – I mean I never take water.

Mr Digby: Was anything said about your being a Baptist or anything of that sort?

The witness: Yes, he immediately said that I was a Baptist, and that I had come to perform a service on an unbaptized child. He again repeated that it was not a Christian, and that he objected to a service of that kind being performed over it. I am not quite sure whether it was exactly at that stage that Mr Gooding interposed. I very earnestly begged him not to repeat that statement. The language in which I expressed myself I believe was, 'Do not repeat that statement; if you do you may have cause to regret it.' I believe I said something to the effect of bowling him out of the meadow if he did. He was then outside the churchyard on the road way, or bridle path, which is a public path. Whether at that stage or not I cannot say exactly, but at one stage the father interposed and said, 'Come, Mr Drury, if you do not allow the service to proceed I shall have something to say to you.' The mother then immediately addressed herself to me, and begged me to go on with the service, and not to regard Mr Drury. 'Never mind the parson,' I believe were the words used, or, 'Never mind him.' Mr Drury told them that he had been waiting over half an hour, and he thought it was very unreasonable for him to be kept waiting longer. Mr Gooding made an appeal to him to be quiet for a few moments, as the service would not last long, and then he repeated the statement that he had a duty to perform towards his parishioners, and that he should do it. He said that the service was an unwarrantable one. Either at that stage or another, he said he had as much right to the path as any of us had, to which I replied, 'Just as much, and no more.' Then I think he made a statement to the effect that he should lock the gate and leave, if they did not proceed to the interment immediately. He was told that his presence was not sought, and that he was not wanted. Mr Gooding, I believe, told him that he was not asked to be present, and that no one wished him to remain; and I told him the sooner he did leave, the better for us. I believe Mr Gooding also said something about his resolution to have the service if he remained there till a late hour in the evening. He then repeated the statement that he should go away and lock the gate if we did not go at once and bury the child. I believe almost immediately after that he locked the gate and went away.

During the reading I had my hat on, but not during the prayer. I never take my hat off while reading the Scriptures, because it is dangerous to my life and health. When I was praying, I did take my hat off. The friends of the child were all uncovered, and the few other working men who had gathered round in the course of their passage through the field homeward and stopped to see the funeral, were also uncovered; but I cannot answer for Mr Smith or Mr Gooding, because I was not looking in their direction. After Mr Drury went I finished the service. I believe Mr Smith scaled the hedge. The coffin was taken round to the east side of the graveyard, and carried to the part in which cases of that kind are interred – the north. It was put silently into the grave. I think I had a hand in it. There was no bier, and three or four men carried the coffin on a sheet, which was the bier really. Mr Gooding and Mr Smith officiated at the interment. The burial was silently, and I hope reverently performed. We then left the churchyard by the same gate as that by which we had entered, and returned to the spot where the previous part of the service had been conducted, in the meadow. There I read the usual order of service after interment in the Church of England service. I certainly did not tell Mr Smith as I was going away that I would give the Rev. Mr Drury such a dressing for that as he had never had in his life.

I drew up the report on the evening when the event itself occurred. The circumstances under which the report was drawn up were really these. Immediately after the funeral service was concluded, Mr Gooding and Mr Smith expressed the opinion that such an outrage as had been perpetrated, in their judgment, was a matter of public interest, and ought to be made public. They made an appeal to me. They said, 'You are accustomed to literary work: will you do it?' I said it was a very disagreeable duty for me to perform, and a very difficult one, as I had been an unfortunate principal in the affair. We went into Mr Smith's house and made notes of what each remembered. Mr Smith, whom I had never seen before until that hour, and whom I did not know, made some communications to me respecting the history of the church there, which, as a stranger in the town, were new to me, and he thought that that also ought to be incorporated with the report. As I wished to be correct in anything I stated, I expressed a desire to go and see the church, as he had described it as being in a very unseemly condition; and we went to look at the place, and I took notes on what I regarded as the physical condition of the place. I then returned and took a cup of tea, and went home. Immediately on arriving home I went into my study – it had got late then – and I wrote the report that night, or very late on in the morning, and then I walked over to Akenham after having an hour's rest to see Mr Smith, to submit the report to him, and ask if it were correct. Some of the statements in that report, of course, I accepted from Mr Smith and Mr Gooding, and therefore I felt it necessary to submit what I had written to Mr Smith, because I did not pretend to remember all that had occurred. Mr Smith was not in when I called. I left word as to what my errand was, and Mr Smith called at my house in the course of the Saturday afternoon. I had then sent the report to the paper, and he went from my house, after some little conversation, to the office of the paper, and there read the report. I have read the report in the *East Anglian Daily Times*. All that is down is true, but I cannot swear that all that was said and done is really down. I could not swear to the threefold repetition of his duty.

Cross-examined by Mr Day: I have been in Ipswich for three years. I am minister of the chapel in St Nicholas Street. There are four Baptist ministers in Ipswich. The name of one of them is Mr Emery. Mr Gooding first called upon me on the Thursday. He is a Congregationalist.

Mr Day: Then he is not a member of your denomination?

The witness: Yes, he is. I am a Congregationalist.

Mr Day: Then I may take it that an Independent and a Congregationalist is the same?

The witness: One and the same. He is not a member of my congregation. I did not know him till he called. I had never seen him before. There is no minister of his denomination residing in Akenham. There is no chapel at all in that village – none nearer than at Claydon, where there is a very small chapel, but no minister. The nearest resident minister of Mr Gooding's denomination is in Ipswich, where there are four Congregational ministers. He is a member of Tacket Street Congregational Church. I really cannot quite tax my memory as to whether it was in the morning or afternoon when he called upon me, but my impression is that he called towards the middle of the day. He simply told me that a child of one of his working men had died; that the father was a Baptist; that he had been to the Baptist minister who lived opposite and asked if he would inter the child; that Mr Emery had an engagement at the same hour, and that Mrs Emery who had seen him – Mr Emery not being in – expressed a wish that he would go across the road to me as we were very friendly indeed, and said that no doubt I would be willing to perform the service for Mr Emery. On that account Mr Gooding came to me. He was quite a stranger to me. I had no communication with Mr Emery about it. I felt very great reluctance to enter into such a service. All my relatives and friends are Church people, and my son is in the church, and Bishop Tozer is a distant relative of mine, and I did not wish to enter into a controversy of this kind. Mr Gooding assured me that every precaution had been taken not to give offence to Mr Drury, and it was on that understanding alone that I ventured to undertake what I felt to be a very delicate service indeed. For a long time I expressed an unwillingness to go into it, but on his assuring me that everything had been done that could be done not to give offence to Mr Drury, I ultimately consented to go.

He told me that the arrangement was that the funeral should be conducted in a meadow, belonging to a gentleman whom I then did not know, outside the graveyard; that the service would be conducted there, and could not possibly give offence to Mr Drury. He told me there would be no attempt at a service at the graveyard. I believe he told me what time had been fixed for the funeral. I have no recollection of his telling me that it was originally appointed for the Thursday, and then changed to the Friday. I was not asked to attend on the Thursday. It was Thursday noon when he came to me. No suggestion was made to me except for the Friday. The report was drawn up by me late at night, and early in the morning, between the Friday and the Saturday, entirely in consequence of what Mr Smith and Mr Gooding suggested. I do not know what I might have thought when I got home, but it did not occur to me then to send a report to a newspaper. It did not enter into my mind to do so before Mr Smith and Mr Gooding suggested that it was a matter of public interest, and should be reported. The bulk of the report is my own composition. Mr Smith only made one or two alterations, but there had been alterations made by the sub-editor. I have written a good deal. I have been more or less connected with various periodicals for sixteen years, and have been a regular correspondent of one paper, and am also at the present time. Sixteen years ago I began on the *Sheffield Independent*. I have ever since been more or less connected with the press, and I am an author of several works. I do not own a paper myself, nor do I edit one. I know a paper called the *Monthly Record*; but that is simply a Congregational magazine limited to my own people. It is not circulated beyond my own congregation, except stray numbers. The circulation is limited entirely to my own people. Nearly all our congregation have such things. I have made passing references in the *Monthly Record* to the fact of the trial coming on.

Mr Day: How often does this *Monthly Record* come out?

The witness: Monthly. *(Great laughter.)*

Mr Day: That does not follow.

Mr Serjeant Parry: The *Fortnightly Magazine* comes out once a month.

Mr Day: You have referred occasionally to the trial coming on just to keep yourself straight and right?

Witness: 'Occasionally' perhaps may convey a wrong meaning. I think twice would be the outside, and then very shortly. To the best of my belief, at the present moment, I think I can positively swear that I have never written anything at all on the subject to any other papers since Aug., 1878.

Mr Day: I do not want to mislead you. I am not at all imputing to you that you are not answering with the utmost candour. I will tell you at once what I allude to. I believe you have written to the *Suffolk Chronicle*?

Witness: No; not at all.

Mr Day: You must be under a mistake; but, apart from that paper, have you written to any other paper on the subject?

Witness: I wrote to the *Suffolk Chronicle* to correct a report, but I have no recollection of having written to any other newspapers. I have never written to the *Christian World* on the matter.

Mr Day: You are not the 'Lover of humanity even to a dog'?

Well, I hope I am human.

You know what I refer to?

I do not exactly.

Surely you read the *East Anglian Daily Times*?

Yes.

Have you not seen there a communication from a person who signs himself that way?

Oh, yes; I remember a letter.

You have written none of these articles?

Oh dear, no; I should be sorry to disgrace myself.

Nor the article in the *Christian World*?

No.

Then you would have been sorry to have written such an article?

That is another thing. There, were, however, many letters that appeared in the *East Anglian Daily Times*, and I was asked to reply to them, and I really felt ashamed of the whole thing.

You did not write that about the 'Vampire' for the *Christian World*? Certainly, I did not.

Nor any of the other communications that have appeared in the *East Anglian Daily Times*?

None whatever; I should be very sorry to have written some of them.

You have mentioned that you did communicate with the editor of the *Suffolk Chronicle* – that was to clear yourself from some report that had got abroad. What was the report?

That I had been served with a writ by Mr Drury, and my people were in such consternation about it, and I got pestered so dreadfully that I felt it necessary to make some public explanation, or, at any rate, to say that I had not been sued.

In the communication to the *Suffolk Chronicle*, among other things, you say, 'In the estimation of many correspondents I left undone a good many things I ought to have done; but so far as I know no one has ever supposed I said or did any thing that was actionable.' Will you kindly tell me what were some of the many things that some people thought you ought to have done?

Is it worth while for me to tell you all the ribald rubbish I received? 'Ribald rubbish'. That is quite sufficient for my purpose.

A great many asked me why I didn't punch his head.

'Punch his head', there is nothing ribald in that. That is one of the prescriptions you were supplied with.

Yes.

Serjeant Parry: I apprehend if these are written documents we ought to see them.

Mr Day: I shall put it in.

Witness: I am sure you won't see my ribald letters, for I put them in the fire.

Mr Justice Denman: You ought to see this article.

Mr Day: I am going to put that in.

Mr Justice Denman: You have already examined him as to his mildness of mind, and this is to show that his mind was not so mild.

Cross-examination continued: At the time I wrote to the *Suffolk Chronicle* I of course knew that I was the author of the report. I do not believe that that report is actionable. I also wrote, 'The *East Anglian Times* is solely responsible for the publication of the undisputed facts of the case; and if Mr Drury could be infatuated enough to take proceedings against any one, it would be against the editor of that journal, and not against me.' I certainly had not the most remote idea in any way that I was just as much liable, or just as little liable as the editor of the paper. I had previously communicated with the sub-editor. I did not put it into the editor's box on Sunday morning. I do not do such things as that on a Sunday. For a minister there is a little distinction between doing a thing of that kind on a Sunday and on a week day. It was on Saturday afternoon. I never intended to convey to the minds of my congregation that I had not written the article. All my congregation and friends knew that I had written it. I never supposed that it was actionable in any way. The sentence 'The funeral was rather behind its time, and both the reverend gentlemen must have felt there was something threatening in the air, for they passed up and down their respective paths, the one inside and the other outside the church boundaries, with a defiant air that reminded us of two game birds pluming themselves for a brush', was my composition. I was writing as a reporter, ignoring Mr Tozer. Up to this time I had every reason to believe that every arrangement had been made to prevent any unpleasantness to the rector of the parish. I had a very few moments' intercourse with Mr Gooding when he came to me at first, but he fetched me on the Friday afternoon, and as we were going over in the cart he gave me some little account of this Mr Drury, of whom to that hour I had never to my knowledge heard, and when to our surprise we discovered that Mr Drury was there, Mr Gooding expressed apprehensions, and that led to the description I wrote. Coupling the fact of his being there with what Mr Gooding had previously described to me as to Mr Drury's antecedents, of course I felt apprehensive. I certainly did not expect Mr Drury to be there. Mr Gooding assured me that there was very little probability indeed of it. I never heard a hint of any intention to hold the service in the churchyard. It was to be held in the meadow, with a view of avoiding any unpleasantness. Before a word was said I fully anticipated that there would be a conflict, either in the form of words or blows, 'between these two champions of the faith'. I had heard of Mr Drury having struck people with a poker and put his fist in their face, and all the rest of it, and I thought if he began to be obstreperous in that way there might be very possibly.

Mr Day: 'Conflict between these two champions of the faith!' That is the reporter describing you as one of the champions of the faith?

Witness: That is a flower of rhetoric.

Mr Day: Your own rhetoric, grown on your own soil, in your own garden.

Witness: Yes.

Mr Day: Then you kindly described Mr Drury, 'With a face as rigid as steel, his lips firmly fixed at one end of the mouth, and slightly curved in an upward direction at the other, expressive of disgust, the incumbent said,' &c. That is another flower of rhetoric culled from the same garden?

Witness: Perfectly sober fact. I had begun reading when his face was in this contorted condition. Besides the account of the death of David's child I read, before the burial, so much of the Burial Service of the Church of England as consists of Scripture. It is a few verses of the latter part of 1 Cor. xv. Perhaps all I read before that, and that portion together, would be about twenty verses. That would probably take about five or six minutes. I had begun the service before Mr Drury came to us – probably three or four minutes before. I was in the act of reading when he came out of the graveyard. I cannot swear I had finished reading before I spoke to him, but I certainly must have very nearly done so. I did not read the whole Church of England lesson that is appointed for the burial of the dead. I read eight or ten verses from the lesson, and then thirteen or fifteen verses of the account of the death of David's child. I did not use the Church Prayer-book, but I am acquainted with it. Up to the time when I was quite a youth I was always accustomed to go to church. I used a portion of it, as I always do, after the burial. I am aware of the rubric which says, 'Here it is to be noted that the office ensuing is not to be used for any that die unbaptized, or excommunicate, or have laid violent hands upon themselves'; but I am not a Church of England minister. I quite understand that that rubric would be binding on Mr Drury, who is a clergyman of the Church of England. No one expected him to read the church service for the dead. It would not be reasonable. I read the whole of that service after the interment. After the interment, because it could not be done in the churchyard, we came back to the meadow and read what under other circumstances would have been read over the corpse, and after the interment. I read nothing else. My extempore prayer lasted probably five minutes. It was not a prayer taken from the Prayer-book. That was before the interment. The prayer had not begun before Mr Drury left. I was not aware that Mr Drury had been waiting a considerable time. I am not quite sure that I was aware that five o'clock had been appointed for him to attend. We were there a few moments after five o'clock. The corpse was there before half-past five. The report makes Mr Drury say, 'The time for this funeral was five o'clock; it is now more than half-past five, and I request you to convey the remains to the grave at once.' That is what he did say. What I state in the report is true, that Mr Drury said, 'I suppose you call that Christian,' and I said, 'Very, and for that reason I fear you are incapable of appreciating it. You have a very priestly garb, and I suppose you take that as equivalent to being one, but you are destitute of the spirit of your Master, and you have not even a spark of humanity in you, or you could not be capable of this conduct.' It was my opinion then. Of course I was very much hurt. I swear most positively that Mr Drury said, 'I don't see what humanity has to do with it. That child has not been baptized, and it is, therefore, not a Christian, and I object to its being buried as such.' That was the thing that stung my manhood. He certainly objected to a service being performed over an upbaptized child, even in the meadow. I have no recollection of his suggesting that it might have been performed before it was brought to the meadow at all, but he did suggest that we might come back and perform it after the interment.

Mr Day: Among other statements you told him he was a disgrace to humanity. That, I think, is according to your version when you drew yourself up to your full height, close upon six feet?

That is not mine.

Is that the sub-editor, or you, or Mr Smith?

The little bit about six feet is the editor's touch.

Mr Justice Denman: 'Drew himself up to his full height' is yours?

That is mine.

Mr Day: The sub-editor measured you, I suppose? *(Laughter.)* 'Brought his right arm dangerously near to Mr Drury's head.' That is yours, I am sure?

That is mine.

That is no flower of rhetoric?

No flower of rhetoric.

That is real, hard fact?

Hard fact.

'Dangerously near the rector's head.'

Very near being hard.

I fully appreciate it. It was only great self-restraint, I suppose, you mean?

I do indeed. It was under circumstances of extraordinary provocation.

I think you say you threatened him with 'bowling' him out. In the report it was 'bundling' him out. That is the same thing, I suppose – turning him out by force?

That was my feeling at the time.

'Go to Heaven, if you like.' Do you remember a painful difficulty you had in expressing that wish?

That is a mere farce.

Which is correct?

As set down. I had no wish to send Mr Drury to the other place.

'Go to heaven if you like; it would be a happy deliverance for the world if you and all your priestly tribe were there, though I fear you will stand a poor chance of getting there'?

I should think so if he could do as he did in the face of those poor parents – tell them that their poor child was not a Christian. It was that that stung me more than anything else. I have lost half a dozen children myself, and to hear it said in the face of weeping parents that the child was not a Christian, was more than I could stand as a father.

Are you aware that in the Church of England baptism is regarded as being an entry into the Christian Church?

We all believe that, as an initiatory rite.

Initiatory is, I suppose, a beginning?

Initiating them to discipleship.

Are you aware that many persons believe baptism to be an initiatory rite into the Christian Church – that when they speak of a Christian they mean one who, having been baptized, believes, &c.? Baptism is looked upon, is it not, as a condition of membership of the Christian Church?

Yes, that is so by the Baptists, not by the Wesleyans, or by Congregationalists.

Is not baptism regarded as an initiatory rite into Christianity?

No, into discipleship, with a view of their being taught that which is necessary to their becoming Christians. There are some clergymen who believe that baptism effects regeneration, and that that makes them Christians.

For heaven's sake don't let us get into baptismal regeneration, or prevenient grace. Are you acquainted with the prayer in the Church of England Prayer-book, 'Dearly beloved, for as much as men are conceived and born in sin; and that our Saviour Christ saith, none can enter into the Kingdom of God except he be regenerate and born anew of water and of the Holy Ghost?'

I am aware that there is such a dogma as that; it is believed by a portion of the Church of England as stated baldly there, but none of the Evangelicals believe it.

Mr Justice Denman: Are we not wandering unnecessarily into theology now?

Mr Day: It is in order to get at the meaning of the word 'Christian'.

Mr Justice Denman: It comes to this. These persons, rightly or wrongly, foolishly or wisely, choose to consider, or did consider honestly, one way or the other (that may be a question for the jury), that it was an insult to the child to say that it was not a Christian. The rubric says that unbaptized children shall not have the burial service performed over them in the churchyard. Most learned ecclesiastical lawyers, Sir John Nichol and others, say that a clergyman is not bound to bury a child with the service who has been unbaptized. But any sort of baptism will do; baptism by Dissenters will do, provided there is water used and the words of baptism are uttered – that has been held quite sufficient. Really, the question in the case very much depends upon whether this was picking a quarrel on one side unreasonably, and unreasonably accusing the clergyman of a want of charity in saying those words, or whether it was not; but I do not see how we are helped in that by going into a long theological discussion as to what the rest of the Prayer-book says.

Mr Day: I only want to show in what sense the word 'Christian' was used; and that this gentleman, being acquainted with the Prayer-book, knew what Mr Drury meant when he said – if he did say – that the child was not a Christian – that he did not mean it as an expression of reproach, but that he simply meant that the child was not baptized.

Mr Justice Denman: There are many learned ecclesiastical lawyers who use the very same language.

Serjeant Parry: It is not merely that he said the child was not a Christian (of which one would complain very strongly), but when he came from the churchyard, according to his own account, the first thing he did was to explain to the father that his child was not a Christian while the corpse was in the field.

Mr Day: He explained to the father that he was unable to read the burial service, because the child was not baptized.

Mr Justice Denman: It really seems, except as regards the animus of the matter (of which the jury will have to judge), that it does not much matter whether a man said, 'The child is unbaptized, and therefore is not a Christian', if he said it bona fide, believing it to be true: it all depends upon the bona fides.

Mr Day: I wanted to make clear the sense in which the term was used by Mr Drury.

Re-examined by Mr Serjeant Parry.

How long had you been reading before Mr Drury interfered?

Three or four minutes; and then after he interfered I read another three or four minutes.

Then did you threaten Mr Drury by word or by gesture till he pointed to the corpse of the child, and said, 'It is not a Christian'?

There was not the smallest approach to anything of the sort. I solemnly swear that I had not a feeling of the kind, much less an act, until that moment. After Mr Drury locked the gate and left, I read a few verses; there were only two or three verses remaining; then I offered an extempore prayer.

You were not able to perform any service in the churchyard?

Oh dear, no! we never attempted it. After the child was buried, we returned to the meadow and completed the service. That was before we went to Mr Smith's. The service was the same as I always read elsewhere. When we were driving to the meadow I heard Mr Gooding say something about the antecedents of Mr Drury.

Serjeant Parry: Your lordship is aware that there is certain language used about the nunnery which my learned friend, Mr Day, has not cross-examined upon. I did not know whether in examination in chief I should be permitted to ask whether the witness had any intention to attribute immorality in that sentence.

Mr Justice Denman: I did not know that there was any suggestion of it. From my reading I should not have thought that there was any suggestion of immorality.

Mr Day: I did not attribute to Mr Tozer that he intended any suggestion of immorality when writing these words.

The witness: Certainly not.

Mr Day: What I pointed out was this, that the use of that language, together with other references in another part of the libel published by the defendant, brought Mr Drury as he stated into a great deal of contempt.

Mr Justice Denman *(to the witness)*: You had no intention to impute any immorality?

The witness: No. It was founded on reports I had heard about the rows at the nunnery.

Mr Day: All I intended to say was that it was unfortunate to introduce any matter of this sort. The nunnery was described as a very different place from heaven, but I did not impute to his gentleman that he intended to charge immorality.

The court then adjourned for lunch.

(v) *Minor Witnesses*

During the afternoon, ten minor witnesses were called, each substantiating some small part of Mr Tozer's account.

The Bishop of Norwich confirmed that Drury was under monition from him – a fact which Drury had denied – and the judicial document was produced, dated May 29th, 1878, ordering the removal of certain articles and ornaments from the church. He also testified that other proceedings had been taken against Drury in 1863 and 1864; that he recognized Mr Smith as churchwarden, whereas Drury did not; that he directed that Smith should have the keys of Akenham church whenever he needed them – something that Drury had refused; and that the condition of the interior of the church was 'not so good as it ought to be'. The Rev. George Stokes – the Rural Dean – was more explicit. He confirmed that he had witnessed the bishop's instructions to Drury, and that the church was in such a dirty and dilapidated condition that he 'would have been very sorry to have to sit down in any part of it'. Stokes said he had also witnessed the strange scene – described in his evidence by Joseph Alfred Smith (the 'Protestant Churchwarden') – when Smith, having been unable to get the church keys from Drury following the bishop's directions, had resigned three times within a quarter of an hour, and had been just as rapidly reappointed by Drury. And another witness – Charles Richard Steward, an Ipswich solicitor and registrar – confirmed the evidence of the bishop's monition by describing how he served it on Drury in a field between Claydon and Akenham:

On Thursday, May 13th, 1878, I met . . . the Rev. George Drury in a field in Claydon, and handed him a duplicate of the . . . monition. He refused to accept it, stating that he never received anything of the sort except through the post office. I told him it was my duty to deliver it to him in person, and on my attempting to place it within the girdle which he wore round his waist, he came at me with both his fists, and threatened to knock me down *totidem verbis. (Laughter.)* I beckoned him away with my hand, and requested him to act as one gentleman towards another. He replied that I was not a gentleman, but a rascal. *(Laughter.)* He passed on, and I told him I had served him personally, and he said I had not. I told him I should leave the document, together with the letter from the bishop, on the ground, which I accordingly did then and there.

Ebenezer Edward Gooding – farmer and employer of Edward Ramsey, gave a detailed account of the funeral which bore out Mr Tozer's description in every respect, but testified clearly on one point in particular, which he repeated under cross-examination. This was the fact that he had certainly informed Drury of the change of time from 5.00 p.m. to 5.30 p.m.

'It was fixed,' he said, 'at half-past five instead of five, because Mr Tozer could not get there as early as five, as he had some engagement. I told Ramsey what I had done with reference to Mr Tozer, and I sent a boy, named Fayres, to Mr Drury to inform him of the postponement of the hour.'

The boy messenger – William Fayres – was called before the court, and, with a piece of evidence short and sweet, completely corroborated Gooding's account:

I was to say, 'Please, Mr Drury, the funeral is to take place at half-past five in the afternoon'; but if they could not be there quite at the time he was to forgive them, for they had to go a long distance. I took the message to Mr Drury's house. I saw an old lady, and gave her the message. She said, 'Stop a minute, and then I will hear if there be any message back.' She was away about a minute. I heard someone speaking. Then she came back, and said, 'There is no message back.' I said, 'Thank you.' (Laughter.)

In very brief statements, Edward and Sarah Ramsey, the dead boy's parents, then upheld Mr Tozer's description. Ramsey made it plain that he had told Waterman, the sexton, when they had both gone to tell Drury that the child was unbaptized, that '. . . we should very likely hold a quiet service in Mr Smith's meadow,' and, in his account of Drury's disruption of the service, he upheld the words Tozer had included in his account.

He said the child was not baptized, and was therefore not a Christian, and three or four times he made use of language, 'That child is a heathen.' This was in the hearing of the child's mother and myself. Dr Drury then said he must go and teach his parishioners that these proceedings were wrong . . . Mr Drury said twice in my hearing that he must go and teach his parishioners that these proceedings were wrong.

Mrs Ramsey, too, had without any doubt been deeply upset by the attitude and language of the sexton:

Mrs Sayers went with me. We went to choose the spot for the grave. I told Waterman I should like the child to be buried close by Mr Rowland's tombstone, and he said he would dig it there if Mr Drury would let him. He said it was consecrated ground, and he was afraid Mr Drury would not let him. Waterman said, 'Now comes the pinch for not having it baptized, for there would be no service over it, and in a manner it would be buried like a dog.' I said, 'Yes, there would, there would be a quiet service held in Mr Smith's meadow before going into the churchyard.'

Mrs Sayers, a close friend of Sarah Ramsey, confirmed these words:

. . . he said that was where the parents were to blame for not having their children baptized, for there came the pinch. It would have to be buried like a dog, for there could not be a service held over it. Mrs Ramsey said they intended to hold a quiet service before taking it into the churchyard.

And finally, George Garnham – a labourer and friend of Ramsey – confirmed the account of the funeral. Having lived in Akenham for twelve years, he was also able to confirm the frequency – if that is the right word – of the services held there.

We used formerly to hear the bell every Sunday, but I should think previous to the occasion of this funeral, there have not been half a dozen services in the year at the outside. I have often seen Mr Drury go to the church on Sundays, sometimes he unlocks the gates, and sometimes he does not. He waits there five or ten minutes and then goes back again.

Serjeant Parry then said that this closed the defendant's case, and the case was adjourned to Tuesday morning.

5 *The Summing Up**

TUESDAY, MARCH 11TH, 1879

(i) *Preliminary Questions*

The trial of this case was resumed today at the Court of Common Pleas before Mr Justice Denman.

Mr Merewether said that the witness Waterman, the sexton, was now present if his Lordship desired to ask him any questions.

The witness was then recalled.

Mr Justice Denman: I have read the evidence you have given, but I do not know that I quite understand it. Are you the clerk only, or clerk and sexton also?

I am clerk and sexton.

Did you dig the grave?

Yes.

When did you do that?

On the Thursday.

Did you choose the spot?

No. The Rev. Mr Drury told me to dig the grave on the north side.

But the exact place where the grave was dug did he choose, or did you?

I did; there was only me there.

When did you first hear what time on Friday the funeral was to be?

On Tuesday evening.

I thought it was then arranged to be on the Thursday?

So it was.

I asked about Friday.

It was to be at five o'clock on Friday afternoon.

Who said it was to be at five o'clock?

The mother.

When did the mother tell you that?

On the Wednesday.

When did you first hear that it was to be at half-past five?

I never heard anything about half-past five.

* From *East Anglian Daily Times*, March 12th, 1879.

Did Mr Drury tell you that it was to be half-past five?
No.
Mr Justice Denman: I have no other questions to ask the witness,
but I will allow any cross-examination if it is desired.
The witness was not cross-examined.

(ii) *For the Defence*

Serjeant Parry then summed up the case on behalf of the defendant.
He said:
May it please your lordship, gentlemen of the jury, you are aware
that the plaintiff complains here of the publication of a libel injurious
to him and to his character, and the defendant in his statement of the
defence says that the matters which are stated in that libel are true in
substance and in fact, and that the language and phraseology are
nothing but a fair criticism of a matter of great public interest. I propose to show you that in every respect that defence is made out by the
evidence which you now have before you upon both sides, upon the
part of the plaintiff and of the defendant. My learned friend, in opening
this case to you, told you that the object of the defendant in publishing
this defamatory matter was to get up some public agitation relating to
the Burials Bill, and that in point of fact the whole conduct of the
parties was nothing more than the carrying out of a premeditated intention of aiding the political agitation which is now going on in respect
to burials within the churchyards of the Establishment. Now, gentlemen, I propose to show you, and I believe that I shall do so to perfect
demonstration, that there is not a word of truth in that suggestion, and
that the only person who is really responsible for all that occurred in
that churchyard, and for the subsequent publication of the account of
what occurred, was the plaintiff and him alone – that if it had not been
for him that burial would have passed off with perfect propriety and
tranquillity; that it was his desire to take advantage, if possible, of the
proposed burial of a Dissenter within the churchyard, to publish his
views about baptism and about the burial service, and that it was his
deliberate intention in going to that churchyard that evening for the
alleged purpose of receiving the corpse to insult the living and really
defame the dead, and that if it had not been for him this case of action
could never have arisen, and that he is the last person in England who
ought to complain of the remarks that have been made about his conduct. He has brought it entirely upon himself by his own equivocation
and intolerance. I do not intend to shrink from my duty in this case,
or to take any intermediate course. I intend, on the part of the

defendant, to submit to you that there is no language too strong that could be used to designate and denounce the conduct of Mr Drury, the plaintiff.

Now, gentlemen, let me, if I may, contrast the conduct of those who were related to this child and to his parents with the conduct of Mr Drury . . . What was the conduct of the father and the mother of this child? What was the conduct of the gentleman who employed the father of this child – an agricultural labourer?

The poor child died upon the 19th of August . . . It is impossible to reproach the father and the mother for the loss of their child, and it is impossible to reproach Mr Gooding with having done all he could to assuage and mitigate the sorrow which the parents naturally felt. The father is a Dissenter. According to Mr Drury it is a crime to be a Dissenter. The father knows, or I dare say has heard before, that as regards the child of a Dissenter, there are some difficulties in the way of its burial – difficulties that may be started, and are started, by intolerant men, but difficulties that are never started by men who really have within them a spirit of Christianity, and desire to carry out its laws and its purposes. The poor man goes to Mr Drury, tells him of the death of the child, and asks if he can bury it on Thursday. Mr Drury says, substantially, 'Yes, but go to my clerk.' Can any one doubt that that clerk is Mr Drury's agent in these matters . . . and that when children of the poor, and especially the children of the dissenting poor, come to speak of a burial, and to learn how it can take place, that he must possess himself of the fact, above all others, whether the children have been baptized. Mr Drury denied that Mr Waterman, his clerk, ever had to ask questions of that kind. Waterman, the clerk, said, on the contrary, that it was his duty to ask them because in all probability Mr Drury would not ask them himself . . . Accordingly, when at the instance of Mr Drury, Ramsey, the father of the child, went to Waterman, one of the first questions almost that Waterman asked was whether the child was baptized . . . Waterman hearing that the child was unbaptized, went back that evening to Mr Drury and gave him that information. Ramsey went with him, but not inside the house; he stood outside a glass door and heard the conversation, and overheard Mr Drury say, 'Then I can read no service over it, it must be buried behind the church.' When I put that question to Mr Drury, he denied that he ever heard that the child was unbaptized on the Tuesday evening; he said he did not hear of it till Thursday morning, and to show his equivocation, which I lay great stress upon, he said that was one of the reasons why he went to bury the child, because he wished to explain

to the father that he could not have any service read over it in the
churchyard because it was unbaptized. That was one of the reasons
that he gave. He made out that he only heard of it on the Thursday.
Why? Because the funeral had been appointed for Thursday afternoon.
Therefore, if he had wished to do as he says and always desired to do,
if he had wished to tell the parents that it was better to have a funeral
service in the cottage, why did not he do it? It is untrue to say that he
advised that course. He said it here to put himself right with you,
because he knows full well that his conduct has been equivocal, and
requires explanation. He says it is his practice to advise baptists to
have the service read in their own residences before the funeral takes
place. Then why, in the name of truth, and I venture also in the name
of kindly feeling, did not he go to this poor man on the Thursday
morning and say, 'Ramsey, I think it would be better, to avoid all
scandal and annoyance, that some service should be read over the
child before its corpse is taken to the grave.' He did not do it. I ask you
why; I think you will have no difficulty in giving an answer.

He heard the next day – we cannot have a doubt of it – on the
Wednesday, that it was the intention of the parties to hold a burial
service in the meadow adjoining the church, because we find that
Mrs Ramsey on that day went to Waterman . . . She had been to the
churchyard and had selected a place near the grave of a Mr Rowland –
somebody whose memory she respected. What was Waterman's
reply? 'Oh, that is consecrated ground; your child is not baptized,
it cannot be buried in consecrated ground.' Gentlemen, who used
the term 'consecrated ground'? Can you have a doubt that amongst
the people in Akenham, as in the thousand villages in this country, the
difference between the ground where unbaptized and baptized children
are buried is unconsecrated and consecrated ground . . . and does not
Waterman, the clerk, bear that out? Does not he say, 'What a pity
your child was not baptized.' Now, here comes the pinch of the case –
'because it is not baptized it will be buried like a dog.' Whose language
is that? It is the language, no doubt, of the alleged libel. It is the
language of the publication which is complained of, but it is also the
language of Mr Drury's own clerk . . . 'Your child, because it is unbaptized, will be buried like a dog.' She replied, 'There will be some
little service over it; we have arranged that there shall be; in the
adjoining field' . . . Do not you believe that Mr Drury well knew on
that Wednesday that there was to be this little service, and if he did not
seek for, and mean and intend that there should be, a scene, that his
views should be promulgated, that he should teach his parishioners a

great lesson? If he did not mean that, why, when he heard on the Wednesday, as he must have heard . . . did not he then go and carry out what he says is his benevolent wish, and say, 'You had better not have the service in the open field, it may create some excitement and some little sensation . . .' That was not Mr Drury's conduct. He lay by, and he then, as I submit to you, had made up his mind to have a scene at Akenham church, and to promulgate the wretched views he entertained upon the subject of baptism. My lord said that if a man declares that in his opinion an upbaptized child is not a Christian that he may do it. Gentlemen, he may. There are a number of theological dogmas which men may entertain, and entertain sincerely, and no human being has a right to interfere or to complain. But if a man entertains a theological dogma, the practice of which is grossly insulting to the feelings of others, and he puts that dogma into practice in order to insult the feelings of others, has he a right to complain of anything which may be said against him? I submit that he is not . . . You may remember another incident, and one by no means unimportant. I asked Mr Drury, 'Were you not aware that the service on Friday was to be at half-past five instead of five?' I asked him whether he did not receive a message on the Friday morning respectfully requesting him to let the service be half-past five instead of five, and he said, 'No, he did not.' Gentlemen, that is untrue, as far as I can judge . . . How does that bear upon Mr Drury's conduct; how does it become important to see whether Mr Drury did or did not receive that message? Mr Drury made as his complaint that the funeral was to take place at five. 'I have been here for half an hour; pray bury the child, get rid of it and then say what service you like.' Is that excuse true? I submit that it is not true, and when Mr Drury made that excuse, he knew it was not true, because he had already been asked to postpone the funeral . . . Is there any proof that this was got up for the purpose of irritating Mr Drury and making political capital out of it? Will my friend when he comes to address you have the boldness to again assert that all this was done, not out of consideration for the feelings of the parents, but for the purpose of irritating Mr Drury? I think if he does so after this evidence, you will not listen to him with assent. It appears to me that no other inference can be drawn from the conduct of Mr Drury, but that he himself was the intended discordant element in this transaction, and that he cannot complain of anything said of him; he cannot ask you for damages for any language however vehement, and, if you will, passionate, which may have been used in one or two articles that have been published about him.

My friend's theory was that Mr Tozer was selected as a person capable of coping with Mr Drury, and of turning to account the plot that had been entered into. Is there a word of truth in that? You have heard Mr Tozer examined . . . Mr Tozer said that he had not the slightest idea beforehand that he should even encounter Mr Drury, he had no reason to believe that Mr Drury would be present. Mr Drury has said that it was his duty to be present.

I very much doubt that. He says it is his duty to receive the corpse at the gate of the churchyard. Is that so, that it is his duty to receive the corpse of an unbaptized person? The rubric says, 'The priest and clerks meeting the corpse at the entrance of the churchyard, and going before it, either into the church or towards the grave, shall say or sing.' That is the baptized corpse that it is their duty to bury, not the un-baptized corpse which Mr Drury told you he was in the habit of meeting. I do not know whether he thought that he was right in meeting it or not, but I say it is not the rubric that orders him to meet it. Then there was the sixty-eighth canon paraded before us by Mr Drury, and he said, if he did not meet the corpse upon that occasion, that he was liable to be suspended for three months. That canon says, 'No minister shall refuse or delay to bury any corpse that is brought to the church or churchyard, convenient warning being given him thereof before, in such manner and form as is prescribed in the Book of Common Prayer.' Now, there is no manner or form prescribed in the Book of Common Prayer for an unbaptized corpse; this relates only to an ordinary burial, and when Mr Drury said that he should have been liable to suspension, depend upon it if articles had been taken out or issued against Mr Drury for not being at the gate of that church to receive this unbaptized corpse, he would have pleaded, and with perfect success, that it was unbaptized, and that he, as a clergyman of the Church of England, had no duty whatever to perform. I read this canon to show that Mr Drury in telling you all this about his duty in meeting the corpse at the gate is deceiving you . . . I say if he conscientiously believed it was his duty to be there and to receive this corpse on this occasion, his conduct is not in the slightest degree mitigated; that is, the conduct of which he was guilty when he was there and when the burial service was going on in the field. All these matters, I say, were within the knowledge of Mr Drury. The child was unbaptized. He knew it on Tuesday; on Friday morning he had been asked to postpone the service till half-past five. Well, the service took place. Is there anything at all in what Mr Ramsey did or what Mr Gooding did, or what Mr Tozer did before arriving at the meadow, that anyone could censure? Was not everything done that could be done? There was the cart. The farmer had lent his cart and horse to carry the child from the cottage, some three-quarters of a mile to the place where it was to be buried. Mr Smith, church-warden of the parish, a Dissenter, had allowed his meadow to be used. The child arrives there; the coffin is placed upon the ground . . . Now, gentlemen, up to this time Mr Drury cannot complain. Then we have to see what he did, and for that purpose we must refer to the account in the alleged report.

You will remember that the publication was made after a very careful examination by Mr Tozer, Mr Gooding, and Mr Smith. They did not do it rashly. Something had occurred which, no doubt, had wounded their feelings considerably, and they thought it right that what had occurred should be made public. I say, gentlemen, that the sooner there is an end to the possibility of such a scene as that which has been described, the better for all classes of the community, and the better for infidels, if there are any in this country. I shall fearlessly ask you whether you do not think it was a proper matter to make public. That man Waterman has had the effrontery to state that he heard Mr Tozer say to Mr Smith, 'I will give Mr Drury such a dressing,' or, 'I will make this matter public.' Now, Mr Tozer swears that that was not true, Mr Smith swears that it was not true, and Mr Gooding swears that it was not true. I ask you whom do you believe? . . . Waterman told you that he never said that the child would be buried like a dog. Poor Mrs Ramsey tells you that he did say so, and her friend, Mrs Sayers, tells you that he did say so. Whom do you believe? You have seen Waterman with his curious demeanour in the witness box, while my friend was so ably cross-examining him; do you believe him or do you believe those ladies, for I call them ladies although they are in a humble station? . . .

Now I go to what occurred in the meadow. Mr Drury had been waiting at the church door, he says, for half an hour. He says he had heard nothing about the change from five to half-past five. I say he did, but my observations and arguments do not depend upon that. Suppose he had waited. Was he irritated; and had he determined, during that half-hour, to do what he did to bring about this great scandal? For a scandal it was, and is so called in the newspaper. The service would probably not have taken ten minutes; but what does Mr Drury do? If he had waited ten minutes, or, I believe, even five minutes, he would never have been annoyed by this inquiry, and the public would never have been disgusted with the details of it. Why did Mr Drury not stay there if he had not a bad and wicked mind and in-

tention? If it had been the case of one of your children, or a child of a
superior class of society, he would not have dared to feel annoyed,
with all his high notions of the priesthood. . . . I say if he had waited
five minutes longer nothing on earth would have occurred that any
human being would have complained of. He says that when the corpse
was laid in the meadow he went away from his gate three or four yards,
and that he began to explain to the father that his child could not have
any service read over it – not the burial service of the Church of
England, but any service – because it was unbaptized. You will see
that all along Mr Drury intended that no service, if he could possibly
prevent it, should be said over that child until after it was in the grave.
He says that the first thing that happened was that Mr Tozer came to
him and clenched his fist. Now, gentlemen, is that true? Witnesses
have been brought before you – witnesses besides Mr Smith, Mr
Gooding, and Mr Tozer – Garnham, Ramsey, and Mrs Ramsey; they
have all been called and they state most positively that Mr Tozer was
reading for three or four minutes; that they were all standing in a semi-
circle, some with their hats off; and that after Mr Drury entered the
meadow and spoke to the father, Mr Tozer did not forbear reading,
and that it was only after his voice became so loud that Mr Tozer went
and spoke to him. Now, Mr Drury, in stating that Mr Tozer came up to
him and put his fist in his face as soon as he came into the field, is stating
what is untrue. It may not be untrue to his knowledge, but it is untrue
as a matter of fact, and it shows that his statement of what passed is
not to be relied upon, because there are five or six witnesses who tell
you most distinctly that Mr Tozer never approached him or stopped
reading for three or four minutes. Now, let us look at the statement of
what really did take place. I shall ask you to say that it is true, and I
hope you will do so . . . This is the statement: –

'Incumbent: 'The time for this funeral was five o'clock, it is now
more than half-past five, and I request you to convey the remains to
the grave at once.' The minister continued reading, and no one paid
the least attention to Mr Drury's request. With a face as rigid as steel,
his lips firmly fixed at one end of the mouth, and slightly curved in an
upward direction at the other, expressive of disgust, the incumbent,
said: 'I have been waiting over half an hour, and it is not reasonable
that you should keep me here until you are pleased to finish these
proceedings. No one attempting to reply he continued: 'Why cannot
you take the coffin to the grave, and then come here and hold what
service you please??'

– Mr Tozer says that that is a correct description, and can any of you doubt but that Mr Drury was in a vile temper, and animated by anything but a Christian and proper spirit? As to this description of his features, if it is true, it is not libellous. Mr Tozer says distinctly that the statement was correct, and others have said that Mr Drury's manner was indignant, and that he subsequently treated the corpse with indignity.

'The reason for the interruption will be easily apparent to our readers. It was not so much Mr Drury's hurry as the repugnance to a religious service of any kind being held over an unbaptized child.'

– Well, there is nothing in that observation. 'Mr Tozer still took no notice of the obstruction, but continued quietly reading portions of Scripture. Incumbent: "I must again request you to defer this service until after the remains have been interred." Mr Gooding: "Pray, sir, do be quiet; the service will not last many minutes." ' If that was true, why did this man Mr Drury reiterate this request? Had he a good motive or had he a bad one? Did he intend to do anything that was worthy of him as a minister, or did he intend, if he possibly could, to prevent that service being performed, and, taking advantage of his position as rector or vicar of the parish, to force these people to resist? His conduct is unexplainable upon any other ground than that he went to interfere – that he was the discordant element, and that it was he who inflamed the temper of the people about it. He must have felt that he did so. When Mr Gooding quietly said to him, 'Pray, sir, do be quiet; the service will not last many minutes,' why did he not hold his tongue? . . . There is but one answer to the question: he was resolved to be insolent, he was resolved to be vindictive, and to have his own way. Whether that was because he had waited for half an hour, or because he regarded the service with contempt, I do not know, but in any way he was wrong, and I ask you to say so.

'Incumbent: Do not tell me to be quiet; I have a duty to perform, and I shall do it.'

– What duty? Will my friend explain what duty the Incumbent had to perform? With all his ingenuity he cannot do it.

'I must teach my parishioners that these proceedings are wrong.'

– They are not wrong, they are not immoral, they are not unlawful, they are not irreligious. And why should he dare to say that? You will see that his anger is mounting up, and that every word he utters shows you the temper he was in, and the determination to have his own way, to stop the service and force the people to put the child into its grave before any service could be read over the body.

'Mr Tozer moved slightly towards Mr Drury.' You cannot, I think, doubt that this is right. No doubt his passion or his temper was up in consequence of what Mr Drury had done.

'Mr Tozer: "I respect you as a gentleman, and I would not willingly offend your religious convictions, or your conscientious scruples, but do let me beg you to be quiet for a few minutes, we shall not be long.' Was not that true?

'Incumbent: "What has that got to do with it?"'

– There is a naggling temper! Cannot you in that phrase hear the man? Just imagine a question of that kind put by a minister of the Christian religion at a time like this.

'What has that got to do with it'? Then Mr Tozer uses language which undoubtedly is strong, but I hope you will say it is justified –

'Mr Tozer: Oh, I supposed you were a gentleman, a Christian, and a minister of Christ.

'Incumbent: I don't see what religious convictions or scruples have to do with it.

'Mr Tozer: Well, I have no wish to hold a discussion with you, but I appeal to your manhood, and beg you not to torture the feelings of these poor people at a time like this.

'Incumbent: That is all nonsense; manhood and feeling have nothing whatever to do with it; your proceedings are altogether wrong, and I must teach my parishioners that I cannot sanction them.'

– Mr Drury has sworn that he never said that. He has not fenced with that question as he has with so many, but he swears he never said it. It is proved by half a dozen witnesses, certainly four or five, that he did say it, and that, according to one witness, he repeated it twice. He had no right to say it; he feels that he had no right to say it, and, therefore, he denies it. . .

Mr Tozer: Well, sir, I thought if you were not a gentleman, or a Christian, you might possibly be a man; I am sorry to have been mistaken.

'Incumbent: I suppose you call that Christian?

'Mr Tozer: Very, and for that reason I fear you are incapable of appreciating it. You have a very priestly garb, and I suppose you take that as equivalent to being one; but you are destitute of the spirit of your Master, and you have not even a spark of humanity in you, or you could not be capable of this conduct.'

– That is strong language if you will, but I say it is language that is not unjustified by what had happened. It is the language that a man of strong feeling would use.

'Incumbent: I do not see what humanity has to do with it.' (There is no doubt that when he said that he was speaking the truth.) 'That child (pointing to the coffin on the ground with his umbrella) has not been baptized, and it is, therefore, not a Christian, and I object to its being buried as such.'

– I do not know whether the exact words 'as such' were used or not; my friend was almost jocular about them; but that is the substance of what was said, beyond all doubt.

'The secret of Mr Drury's interference was now disclosed, and it produced an instantaneous effect upon Mr Tozer. As quick as thought he drew himself up to his full height (close upon six feet) and brought his right arm dangerously near to Mr Drury's head, and, with his eyes flashing fire and his voice trembling with emotion, he said, "If it were not for harrowing the feelings of these poor people, I would very soon silence your brutal speech." '

– Was it a brutal speech? I do not fear what your answer will be. I shall call attention more minutely to what Mr Drury meant when he said that the child was not a Christian.

'Though decked in the garb of a priest, and holding the office of a minister, you are a disgrace to humanity. Incumbent: Don't shake your fist in my face. Mr Tozer: I was not shaking my fist in your face, but you justly deserve to be made to feel it. Incumbent: And you call that Christian? Mr Tozer: Perfectly.'

– Of course Mr Tozer was excited, and he depicts his own excitement. Mr Drury would have had no action for libel at all if Mr Tozer had not written this himself. If a shorthand writer had been present he would, of course, have reported exactly what passed. If Mr Tozer is to blame he has himself pictured his own conduct.

'Incumbent: You are a Baptist, and yet you can come here and perform a service over a child that has not been baptized, and is not, therefore, a Christian.'

– Why should he say that? What right had he to complain of a Baptist performing the ceremony over an unbaptized child? He himself need not do it, but why should he complain of a Baptist minister performing such a service and telling him with insolence that he had no right to do it?

'Mr Tozer: I have no desire to hold a controversy with a man so destitute of the commonest feelings of humanity as you are, and if this were not a funeral I would very soon bundle you out of the meadow.'

– No doubt he said what he meant, and what he would have tried to do, but that is not defamatory to Mr Drury, because it is called for by Mr Drury's own conduct.

'Incumbent: This is a public path, and I have as good a right to be here as you have. Mr Tozer: Just so much and no more. We have carefully avoided everything that could reasonably wound your religious scruples, and we came here because it is a public footway, and you have no right to interfere with us. Incumbent: I have the right to teach my parishioners that it is wrong to perform funeral rites of a Christian form over the remains of an unbaptized child.'

– If you believe that he said that, can you doubt that he intended to prevent this humble service being performed? He had made up his mind not to perform it himself, and I do not blame him for that; but he has no right to go further, and say that nobody else shall perform such a service . . . Of course, nobody could complain of his teaching his parishioners, but here he is interfering with a service that was being performed in the field by other parties. . . . Then the father of the child, a very respectable man, says, 'Come, Mr Drury, I shall have something to say to you if you do not allow the gentleman to go on with the service.' Do you believe that? If you do there is an end to Mr Drury. Just imagine a labouring man, who would lift his hat to Mr Drury as he walked along with his cassock and his three-cornered hat, being hurt by what Mr Drury was doing, as to say to him, 'Come, Mr Drury, I shall have something to say to you if you do not allow the gentleman to go on with the service.' How gross must have been Mr Drury's misconduct! Then the wife says to her husband, 'Never mind the parson; let Mr Tozer go on with the service.' She saw that her husband was getting angry, and, like a true woman, she tried to check it.

'Incumbent: I have been waiting here more than half an hour, and it is unreasonable for you to expect me to remain while you conduct this unwarrantable ceremony.

'Mr Gooding: Allow me to remind you, sir, that you refused to perform any service yourself. After that you were not asked to be present, and no one wishes you to remain.

'Incumbent: How could I perform a service over a child that was not a Christian.

'Mr Tozer: Don't repeat that, sir, if you do you may have cause to regret it. The sooner you take yourself off this public highway the better.'

– Again he repeats the insult: –

'Incumbent: If you do not at once take the remains to the grave I shall lock the gate and go.

'Mr Tozer: No one asked you to come, and no one wishes you to stay.

'Incumbent: I shall certainly lock the gate and leave.

'Mr Tozer: Go to heaven, if you like; it would be a happy deliverance for the world if you and all your priestly tribe were there; though I fear you will stand a poor chance of getting there. Take yourself away from us, and I don't care where you go.'

– The language there may be warm language, such as, perhaps, in his cooler moments he would not use, but it is not in any way defamatory of Mr Drury. It is only in answer to an insult of Mr Drury. Mr Tozer says – 'I had myself lost five or six children, and I felt most acutely the observation that he made about the child not being a Christian.' If you believe that you will understand Mr Tozer's feelings, and, to a certain extent, sympathize with them.

'The incumbent locked the gate and went – not to heaven, but to Claydon, which, so far as the rectory and the adjoining nunnery are concerned, is a very different place.'

– In a subsequent part, in the article from the *Christian World*, something is said about Claydon being close to a nunnery. I must say, when I heard the interpretation put upon that, I never was more surprised in my life . . . I had plenty of evidence, but Mr Drury himself admitted that there had been a great disturbance at this nunnery, that the whole country knew of it. I am not going into the inquiry, but, rightly or wrongly, it was asserted that he had kept a young lady at the nunnery against the will of her parents. In that he must have been entirely wrong. You have heard from Mr Steward, who acted for the father, that he endeavoured to procure her release. He applied for a *habeas corpus*, but did not succeed. Then violence ensued, and Mr Drury took part in that violence. Can you doubt what his character and temper are, and that that is what was alluded to when the church was spoken of as being close to a nunnery?

Then it is stated in the alleged libel that Mr Tozer completed the service, and so on. That is really not denied. The service was concluded, and there is no doubt that Mr Drury went away, finding that he could not carry out his illegal and intolerant purpose. Now I shall ask you whether you do not believe that statement to be true, and if the facts contained in it are true, is not the publication amply justified, and ought Mr Drury to complain of that which he himself has brought about? Now, before I dwell upon any of the other alleged libellous matter, let me refer to the articles inserted from other papers. First, there is the article in the *Daily Chronicle*. 'If the Christian religion depended for its vitality upon such ministers as Mr Drury, it would become a byeword, to be scorned by every section of the community.' Now, is that so? I ask you to say that it is.

. . .

'The Editor of the *Christian World* favours us with an advance proof of an article to appear in this week's edition in relation to the Akenham case. It is headed "A Pestilent Priest", and is as follows: The demon of discord is still haunting the tomb. The vampire of superstition flaps its repulsive wings over the graves of the unchristened. The dead babes of Baptists are consigned to the devil by the priests. The ecclesiastical jugglers failed to handle them, and their souls perished! No drops of consecrated water fell upon their innocent foreheads, and endless fire is their only portion! These pestilent priests dare to tell us that He who loved all the little ones on earth will spurn them from Paradise unless they go in by the Pharisees' door. The "burial scandals" of the Ritualists are becoming a national disgrace.'

– I hope you will notice the terms of this article. If Mr Drury is included in it, he is included with a number of others. This is an attack made upon the proceedings of certain priests in the Church of England in a newspaper which undoubtedly had a right to discuss them, and the attack is made, no doubt, in consequence of the Burial Scandal and the scene in the meadow near Akenham churchyard . . .

. . .

Then it goes on: 'Bad as all these burial scandals are, there has, perhaps, rarely been one so bad as this; for when Mr Drury refused to inter the child no one complained. The grave was dug, and the sexton paid for his work; and the Independent minister of Ipswich – who curiously enough has written strongly in defence of an Established Church, as against the extreme Liberationists – would have endeavoured to sooth the bereaved parents and call forth devout thoughts and holy resolves in the minds and hearts of the sympathizing neighbours, and no unpleasantness would have occurred. But he chose to sacrifice the gentleman, and even the man, and became a mere heartless priest, than whom there is no viler creature on the face of the earth. "What has humanity to do with it?" asked he, when rebuked by the friends of the sorrowing parents for his cruel words; and truly humanity was far enough from having aught to do with his conduct in the case. The very lowest type of ordinary humanity would be dismayed, or become angry, at the scene witnessed in that Akenham meadow, whither came this pretended minister of Christ, for the single and gratuitous purpose of irritating the living and insulting the dead. One can almost fancy that only toadstools will henceforth spring up where stood this priest uttering his maledictions over that tiny coffin, laid down there on the bare earth for want of the parish bier, which the charity of the parish church, in the person of its ruler, had refused. It had nothing to bestow in that hour of pain but curses.'

– Now, gentlemen, your answer to the question that will be submitted to you will be very important indeed. You are performing an important public duty, a public duty which will not be ephemeral, because, although the verdicts of juries, perhaps, have not the same influence upon the administration of justice as the decision of judges, there is no doubt that they have an immense influence upon public opinion; and in arriving at a conclusion upon this case, you, gentlemen, are exercising a great public duty; and I ask you to say that although the language of this article in the *Christian World* is vehement, passionate, if you will, although it contains very strong expressions, directed not only against priests who think with Mr Drury, but against Mr Drury himself, yet that the conduct of Mr Drury justified the remarks that had been made, and that he has no right to complain of them in a court of justice.

You remember my cross-examination of Mr Drury as to what he meant when he said, 'This child is not a Christian' – repeating it two or three times to Mr Ramsey, the father, who is very likely to be right. Now, I thought it right to ask Mr Drury this question, whether he had not preached and taught this doctrine; and one of his answers was, 'I cannot remember that I ever did,' and afterwards he no doubt denied it more positively, 'that such children cannot enter into the kingdom of heaven; that they can only be placed in hell where they shall never have the sight of the living God.' I read from a book in my hand when I put that question. I ask you, Do you not believe that when this man went into the churchyard and pointed with indignity to the child and said, 'It is not a Christian, it is a heathen,' he meant to tell the parents that the child would never enter the kingdom of heaven? If so, is there any language that can be used towards such a man that he or any human being can complain of? If he believed it he ought to have kept his belief to himself. He says it with a deadly purpose, intimating that the child is lost for ever because it has not undergone sprinkling by water by a priest. I should be ashamed of a man who, criticizing Mr Drury's conduct, did not criticize it in vehement and strong terms, using the strongest epithets he could possibly use. 'The dead babes of Baptists are consigned to the devil by the priests. The ecclesiastical jugglers failed to handle them and their souls perished! No drops of consecrated water fell upon their innocent foreheads, and endless fire is their only portion.' I asked Mr Drury whether he had not taught that, and his answer was, 'This is an open question,' – almost a worse answer than if he had told us that he had taught such an atrocious doctrine. I do not wish to interfere with any theological belief, for I know how varied it is . . . but when a priest like Mr Drury, holding this doctrine, enters a field where there is the corpse of a child, and in the presence of the parents insults them and insults the whole community; the case is very different. I care not if Mr Drury be a conscientious man. Conscience has often been pleaded for some of the worst crimes of humanity – for the martyrdoms of the Middle Ages, for the massacre of St Bartholomew. I say that when this paper tells us that Mr Drury uttered his maledictions over the corpse of that child, it is fully justified.

. . .

I submit to you that there is nothing in all this that Mr. Drury can complain of. There are some personal observations that might or might not have been spared, but there is nothing to justify an action for libel. There is another little passage about Akenham church, and it has been proved that it is true. You have heard that the church is in a dilapidated and filthy condition. The bishop would naturally be reluctant to say too much, but you have heard from others what the condition of the church is. Mr Drury will not even obey his bishop in the matter, and he would rather have his church in a filthy state than have it cleaned by a churchwarden who is a Dissenter. Mr Drury knew well that Mr Smith had been elected as churchwarden by the parish, but you heard how he fenced with my question on that subject. Mr Drury derives an income of £260 a year from this church and £240 from Claydon; but he actually allows the church to remain in the condition which you have heard. Is there any harm in Mr Tozer alluding to that in this article? As to the monition, you have heard the evidence of Mr Steward. He is the solicitor who served the monition, and as Mr Drury would not receive it he thrust it into his girdle. Mr Drury then squares up to him and calls him a rascal and no gentleman. What does Mr Drury mean by asking for damages to reinstate and rehabilitate his character? Can any damages put Mr Drury in a different position from that which he now holds? My friend cross-examined Mr Wilson, the editor who was called before you. Mr Wilson does not feel ashamed that he inserted this article. He says, 'I was exercising what I believed to be my duty as a journalist and the publisher of news, and informing the world what had taken place, and I did not exercise my duty until I had inquired about the facts in every possible way.' Mr Wilson believed

7

the facts to be true, and it is for you to say whether he was not justified in that belief. My friend has intimated that the whole life of Mr Drury for many years has been raked up, that we have gone up into his character more than we should have done. Is that so? Before you give a verdict either for or against Mr Drury, surely you should know Mr Drury, who he is, what he is, and what he has done. Mr Drury has gone out of his own neighbourhood, where he is well known, to bring this action. Did he expect if he brought his action in London that no inquiry would be made about him as to his antecedents? If he did it was surely a great piece of infatuation. He could not expect because he came here in a different dress from that which he ordinarily wears that some inquiry would not be made about him. It has been stated that he was associated with Brother Ignatius. I do not know that there is any great crime in that, but, gentlemen, Mr Drury is a minister of the Church of England, and is bound by its laws, therefore it was right that you should know who and what he was. He has received three monitions from his bishop. He denied the last monition, and in denying it, I will not say that he was stating that which was false, but he was equivocating. He has been in the habit of performing ceremonies of the most extraordinary description in his parish. He has associated with his ministry a thing unknown to the Church of England – a nunnery or a convent; he has been performing what he calls mass, a thing unknown to the Church of England. He says, 'I complain of being damaged in my character as a member of the Church of England.' Is he damaged? Can he be damaged? Ought he to be in the Church of England? Pray reflect upon these matters. What about that scene in the convent? I will dwell no more upon it now. Then what are the articles that he has been ordered to remove? A crucifix, a second communion table, and a sanctus bell. I do not suppose he will obey the monition unless he is compelled to do so. One of the proceedings against him was for preaching in an unlicensed place, the monastery at Norwich. Then you have heard of the chasuble, dalmatics, albs, stoles, maniples, caps, thuribles, processional cross and banner. Remember, this gentleman is a minister of the Church of England; can he be more injured than he has been by his own conduct? Listen to the words he uses of the Church Association, of which the Bishop of Norwich is a member – 'a body of assassins'. He is capable of the foulest language, and yet he is here before you complaining of a libel. You remember about the case of assault, when he denied that he used a red-hot poker and said it was a piece of wire eighteen inches long, and half an inch thick, and then (when there was a laugh) he reduced the thickness to a quarter of an inch. What right has this man to complain? How does this man brand the faith of the great majority of the Church of England? He speaks of Protestantism as poison, I have no doubt he has said deadly poison. I entreat you, unless you are coerced by some powerful motive which I cannot for a moment understand, do not give this man a verdict so that the world may imagine that he is a person who under any circumstances whatever has a right to complain of what has been written and published of him.

(iii) *For the Plaintiff*

Mr Day then addressed the jury on behalf of the plaintiff.

He said:

Gentlemen of the Jury, after the powerful address which has been made by one of our great masters, it would have been almost as well if we had been allowed a little time wherein to gather ourselves together and reflect that we are in a court of justice, and consider what are the issues we have to try. Gentlemen, the plaintiff in this case has been held up to public execration, and I am sure you will listen to the observations which I, as his advocate, have to offer on his behalf. He has been attacked by denunciations more severe even than those inserted in the newspaper. He is denounced as a man who is not only unworthy of the Christian ministry, but as without the slightest particle of humanity in his breast. This case has been introduced as a case of humble parents anxious to derive some consolation from a ceremony performed over the body of their child. Of course I appreciate such motives; but I venture to suggest to you that that is not the origin of the case. I say that this was regarded by certain persons as too good an opportunity to be lost; and the service was not intended for the comfort of the parents, but to aggravate and annoy the Incumbent. You have heard of the sixty-eighth canon, gentlemen; but let me tell you that by that canon, and by the statute law, the minister is responsible for the burial of a body; and that is the reason why Mr Drury was at the churchyard. My friend says that his object was to insult the living and defame the dead. If you think so, give your verdict against him. But did he go for that purpose? You have heard the account that has been given of what passed. After the funeral had taken place, they all adjourned to Mr Smith's, and there the account was concocted, and there various suggestions are made, and amongst others, suggestions as to the state of Akenham church. We will say no more about the state of the church except this. The bishop went there and was there for a quarter of an hour, when the repairs and other matters were being discussed. Now, I think, we must consider that this passage in the newspaper report, referring to the state of the church, is as highly coloured as the rest of it. The dead birds, as we know, are relegated to the south aisle, and that is the reason why the bishop was not supposed to see this deceased bird, but one cannot help feeling that in this part of the report, as well as the rest, many flowers of rhetoric were used, which were culled by the Rev. Mr Tozer from his garden at Ipswich, when he was about to compound the report, and I do not suppose that you will take it to be literally true ... So much for the Akenham church; now we come to the facts as alleged connected with the libel.

My friend, Serjeant Parry, calmly assumed that this report is a perfectly correct report, and he has argued upon that basis. Now, gentlemen, as I told you before, I am not going to take away the characters of other people. My client is here to clear his own character, not to assail other men's characters. He is not going to say, nor am I on his behalf, that Mr Tozer has said one word here that he does not consider a reasonably fair representation of what took place. But as I said before, is it likely that a man labouring under the excitement that Mr Tozer so graphically depicts here should do, word for word, question and answer, what is set out here? Is it in human nature to do so, and is he more likely to do so because he is assisted by the varying recollections of Mr Gooding and Mr Smith? I do not say that Mr Wilson would willingly insert what he knew to be untrue. It was sufficient for him that it was sent by Mr Tozer; that it was a very graphically written thing; that it occupied a couple of columns of his paper; that it was a sort of thing that would create a vast interest in the Christian world, that is to say, in the world of charitable people; therefore he said, 'It is a capital thing, an admirable thing, highly coloured; just the thing for our paper,' and he takes care that advance copies are sent, out of charity, to all papers that are likely to re-produce it and comment upon it, and most of them called 'Christian' – Christian this, Christian that, and Christian the other, including that most Christian of all Christian papers, the *Christian World*. Now, let us look at the report. Mr Tozer, having consulted with Mr Gooding and Mr Smith, and having made some notes in other company, probably referring to the state of the parish church and the history of Claydon, and so on, begins his report with: 'A few days since, a working man, in the employ of Mr E. E. Gooding, of Akenham Hall, lost a child, who was about two years old, both parents being Baptists. The child was never baptized.' Then he goes on to say that Mr Drury 'positively and peremptorily refused its burial in the consecrated ground, but gave permission for it to be buried behind the church in unconsecrated ground.' My friend says that is a mere figure of speech. He speaks about its being consecrated in the popular sense. I do not know what consecrated in the popular sense is. In one sense this court is consecrated to the law, and some people consecrate a garden to orchids; 'set aside' is the popular meaning, but that is not the meaning of the sense of it here. It is consecrated with a capital C here, and it is distinguished from the unconsecrated ground which has not a capital letter. To ascertain the meaning of the word consecrated here, I will fall back upon that Christian paper, the *Christian World*, where they say, 'No drops of consecrated water fall upon their innocent foreheads.' They mean there to distinguish between the ground that has been consecrated by religious ceremony and unconsecrated ground, and no man knew that better than Mr Tozer, who tells us in his earlier days he was a member of the Church of England, that he is familiar with its Prayer-book, and knows its history and laws. When he says unconsecrated ground, he is holding up Mr Drury, or intends to hold up Mr Drury, to execration because he would not allow the child to lie in consecrated ground in an ecclesiastical sense. The report says that Mr Drury very sternly refused to bury the child, but he was never asked to. He said that he would be there and walk before the body to the grave, and would assist at the burial and see that its remains were deposited with reverence in the grave; but he would not read the burial service of the Church of England, which the law prohibits him from using under the circumstances. My friend Serjeant Parry looks upon Mr Drury as an outlaw, a *caput mortuum*, against whom every man's hand ought to be raised, and he asked him, 'Would not you have thrown earth upon it.' Yes, gentlemen, he would have cast earth upon it as you may cast earth upon the coffin of your nearest and dearest relative when you accompany it to the grave . . .

'They paced up and down their respective paths, one inside and the other outside the church boundaries, with a defiant air that reminded us of two game birds pluming themselves for a brush.' What does that indicate? If Mr Drury had written it what would my friend Serjeant Parry have said? He would have said, 'Here is a clergyman describing himself; he is come down to insult the living and defame the dead; he feels himself already a game bird pluming himself for a brush.' I ask you, gentlemen, what state of mind does this betray in Mr Tozer. What has he come down here for? Has he come down here to draw the parson – to have a scene with the parson – to badger the parson? He it is who describes himself as the game bird pluming himself for a brush.

It is sufficient for my purpose that it was in his mind – that he looked upon himself as what he calls a champion of the faith – whatever that may be. . . He was coming down to do great battle . . . and going to write his own despatches, and highly coloured despatches they are, but he does not sign them.

. . . Mr Tozer told us that there may have been about thirty persons present. How did thirty persons come to be present out of a population of seventy or eighty, scattered over a large agricultural parish in Suffolk? What brought thirty persons there in the busiest time in the year, the harvest time? Gentlemen, if you are acquainted with the hours of labour of agricultural labourers, you know well that they do not leave their work at five o'clock or half-past five in the thick of the harvest. But who expected a scene? Those expected a scene, and those only, who had prepared a scene. No one had prepared a scene here except those persons who from some motive or other had determined to do that which they thought would irritate Mr Drury, and give them an opportunity of making some political capital out of the matter. Do you believe that a 'quiet burial' would have caused thirty inhabitants of Akenham to be gathered together at that spot at that time? Nothing caused them to be there except the expectations of a scene, which they knew had been prepared for them by those persons who were endeavouring to betray Mr Drury into some indiscretion or impropriety or, at any rate, to supply material for newspaper comment. . .

'No bier could be procured, and the coffin was placed in front of the churchyard gate.' As I pointed out in opening, biers are not used at the funerals of infants. Nobody asked for a bier; nobody asked the sexton to provide one. If they had wanted a bier they could have had one, but it is made a grievance that none was used although the use of one was not anticipated. My client complained of the funeral being late, but they never say that they had sent him a message that it would be late. Even a clergyman of the Church of England is entitled to some little courtesy, and they might have said. 'We are very sorry, we shall only be a few minutes longer' . . . According to his own account, Mr Drury went up to the parents of the child and said, 'You might as well have the child buried, and you can have the service afterwards.' Then he explains why he could not read the service. Surely that was no unkind thing. Surely it commends itself to one's notion of what was right. Mr Drury was desirous of creating no ill-will. He had no desire to live in enmity with his parishioners, and he simply explains that he cannot read the Burial Service because the child was unbaptized. Then reference is made to his garb, but what harm in the world does a man do by wearing a cassock? Perhaps some of you gentlemen indulge in the luxury of dressing-gowns, and they would be very inconvenient garments if you had not a cord to put round them. Every ulster has a belt to it, and we are told in some books of authority to gird up our loins. I do not know or care whether a clergyman wears it for convenience or symbolically. Gentlemen, whatever may be said about Mr Drury, he seems to have evidenced so much of the 'Spirit of his Master' that he displayed a meekness which is much to be commended. . .

The learned counsel commented at great length upon the other portions of the alleged libel, and in conclusion, he asked the jury to award such an amount of damages to his client as would express their sense of the moral wrong to which he had been subject, and would enable him to leave the court feeling that his character, as a gentleman and a man, had been established to the satisfaction of a jury of his fellow countrymen.

(iv) *Judgment*

Mr Justice Denman: Gentlemen of the Jury.

. . .

At the outset I have to say that I shall endeavour to be as concise as possible, because great public inconvenience would result if I were not able to conclude this case today. In the observations I shall make I shall endeavour to clear the way as much as possible at starting, so that your minds may be directed to the true considerations which ought to actuate a jury in a case of this kind, and not to any spurious, false, or unjust considerations, such as the law would entirely abhor and repudiate. You ought fully to understand, and it is necessary in such a case as this that you must be greatly on your guard against thinking that you are sitting there as champions of any particular creed, that you are there as bound to take any particular view of the right or the wrong of any theological doctrine. You are not sitting as a court of theology or of divinity; you are sitting there to come to a verdict in an action of libel, and the nature of that I will presently explain to you. Still less are you there to allow yourselves in any way to be led to come to a verdict with the view of amending or altering any law that you may think wrong. You are there, sworn to give your verdict according to the evidence in the case, and you are solemnly bound to take the law, not to make yourselves responsible for any proposition of law, but to hold the judge to his responsibility in that matter, and to take any law that he may lay down to you, which is liable to be construed, if it be right or wrong, as the law of the land with reference to the case; then, taking that as the law, decide the case according to your true belief and your consciences as regards the evidence which has been before you tending the one way or the other.

Now, this is an action of libel, and the law of libel is very shortly stated indeed. It has been commented upon by the counsel on both sides, and by neither in the least degree inaccurately, as far as I know; but it is better that you should have it in the fewest possible words, laid down to you so that you may be under no mistake about it. The definition of libel, given as shortly and as well as I can find it anywhere, is found in the simplest and most ordinary book which we lawyers use. It is as follows: 'In the case of words published by writing, it is only necessary, in order to make them a libel, that they should be calculated to degrade or disparage the plaintiff, and hold him up to hatred, ridicule, or contempt, to make them actionable.' People are very apt, in talking of libel in private life or in ordinary parlance, to confound two things, and that is, to talk of a thing as libellous only with reference to whether it be true or not. Sometimes you have heard a common answer to that, which is not very easily understood by laymen, but is intelligible to lawyers – the old saying, that the greater the truth the greater the libel. In one sense it is true, and in this sense, that before the jury can say that the defendant in any case is guilty of a libel, they have to look at the libel itself with reference to its truth, without reference to justification or anything of the kind – to look at it as a writing, to put themselves in the place of the person of whom it speaks, and then ask themselves, 'Is that a writing which, without any supposition as to its truth one way or the other, leaving that for after consideration, is that a writing which holds me or anyone up to hatred, ridicule, or contempt?' – That is the consideration tending to disparage or degrade, or lower a man in the estimation of his fellows, or to hold him up to hatred, ridicule, or contempt; and that is the question wholly for a jury. There was at one time of our history a great battle over that, whether the judge had any function in the matter or not, and whether it is wholly for the jury. It is wholly for the jury in the first instance to say whether it is a writing that holds up the person of whom it speaks to hatred, ridicule, or contempt, or whether it disparages or degrades him or tends to lower him, or such like things. That, therefore, is the first consideration in this case. Is this a libel? When I come to call attention to it, I shall have a word to say about considerations which usually do actuate juries one way or the other in such cases, but not very much – it is undoubtedly your function. Then supposing you come to the conclusion that it is a libel, then arises another question, and that is however libellous it may be the defendant alleges it is true in substance and in fact. That does not mean undoubtedly that every syllable is true, but that it is a substantially true and accurate statement of facts relating to the person complaining. Is it substantially true, is the question. If all those statements which you think libellous are proved to be true, then the defendant will be entitled to a verdict. But suppose that there are any left not proved to be true, libellous and disparaging statements unwarranted by the facts, and to any appreciable extent left not proved to be true, then arises the question of damages, and the question of damages will always depend more or less, of course, as to how much is proved or how much is not proved, and what course of conduct has been pursued by both sides, all of which are questions purely and entirely for a jury, and with regard to which counsel address juries forcibly on the one side and on the other in most cases, and with which the judge has very little to do indeed, though even then he may sometimes give useful assistance by pointing out some considerations that ought to bear one way or the other. That is the end of this case, and the first question being, is this a libel or is it not? It is necessary to glance at the thing itself; its history, its contents, and the general assertions which it makes one way or the other; and as to some in this case it is necessary that there should be some explanation, because it turns upon a question which is to some extent a question of law.

Now, as this alleged libel appears in the *East Anglian Daily Times*, it is a very long document, and it appears in the paper rather in the shape of a second leading article of a country paper than in any other capacity, one would say. Here is the *East Anglian Daily Times*, then comes a London letter, then comes this article, headed in very large letters, 'Burial scandal at Akenham; passage of arms between the Rev. George Drury and the Rev. Wickham Tozer.' Now, the history of this we have pretty fully developed by the evidence. It is not an article which emanates from the staff of the paper so to speak, but it is a letter written by an Independent minister, who seems to have the faculty of using his pen and using it pretty strongly, as I think you will be of opinion. It comes to the paper which takes an interest in affairs connected with burials apparently, and the editor of the paper, who is also proprietor and publisher to a considerable extent, scans it and considers it, because he tells us he makes alterations in it here and there, touches it up, and corrects the proof sheet, and eventually it is published deliberately in his newspaper as an article sanctioned by him, perhaps more fully so than is usually the case where the proprietor or publisher of a paper in that sense causes an article to be published. The heading

of the article is somewhat altered from that which was originally proposed by the writer of the article. It was originally headed, 'A passage
of arms between two ambassadors of peace.' That is altered here –
'Burial scandal at Akenham: a passage of arms between Rev. George
Drury and Rev. Wickham Tozer.' This article is written originally by
one of the principal actors in the scene which it describes. I cannot help
rather agreeing with Mr Day that if he was so very anxious really to
bring forward publicly that which he believed to be a great scandal in
the conduct of or in the prevention of a burial service, it would have
been far better if he had sent it to the newspaper in the shape of a letter,
purporting to be by someone who had seen the thing, and not in the
shape of a leading article as it would appear to be, because one could
not help feeling it was possible that the very fact that a man wrote
under disguise as it were, purporting to be not that which he really was,
might cause him to exercise a freedom, and to indulge in flowers of
rhetoric. One of the questions, of course, in the case will be whether it
has induced him to state under the shelter of an apparent article in the
newspaper things which are reckless, and which he would not have
stated if he had written in the avowed capacity of an actor in the scene.

The learned judge then proceeded to comment upon the statements
in the alleged libel . . . With reference to the use of the service over the
body of an unbaptized person, it was really a matter of law upon which
there was no doubt whatever. The rubric of the church expressly
stated that the service should not be used in the case of unbaptized
persons, and, indeed, in some of the later part of the alleged libel it was
admitted that so far as that was concerned, Mr Drury would be within
the law in refusing to perform the service of the Church of England
over an unbaptized child. They might say it was wrong, and they
might have their opinion about it, but that was really the law, and they
were bound to look upon that as an established fact in the case. The
learned judge went on to say that one could not help feeling that this
was a sensational article, and if writers in newspapers, in order to ridicule people, spiced the articles with things immaterial to the question
they were writing about, showing thereby an animus, which looked as
if it were intended to injure or vilify the people of whom it was written,
that was for the consideration of the jury, in coming to a conclusion as
to whether the article was libellous or not. Mr Drury considered it
part of his duty to meet the corpse at the gate of the churchyard; that
was a point upon which he (the learned judge) felt there was considerable doubt; and he could not say that Mr Drury's view was
absolutely wrong. There was no doubt that Mr Tozer used very insult-

ing language in saying that the plaintiff was doing something unworthy of a gentleman and a Christian, and the jury would hardly say that that was language which, when used by a clergyman of any denomination, would not be very disparaging and very degrading. In the absence of any justification, it must be held libellous. He could not see why pointing to the child with an umbrella should be exactly indicative of any intention to insult the child or the parents. Then, with regard to the statement that the child was not a Christian, and he objected to its burial as such, he was bound to call attention to the law of the Church upon that subject, because Mr Drury ought not to be made a victim for anything which was prescribed by the law of the land, however unreasonable dissenters or the jury might think it. In a celebrated case, decided by John Nichol in 1809, this question was raised, and the judge stated that as the law in the rubric, which formed part of the statute law of the land, forbade the burial service to be used for persons who died unbaptized, it was not a matter of expediency or of benevolence whether a clergyman should administer or refuse that service, because he was expressly enjoined not to perform the office. He finally came to the conclusion, that if the child died unbaptized, it was the duty of the minister, and he was enjoined by law, not to perform the service. It was for the jury to say whether the language used by Mr Drury indicated any intentional or reckless departure from the sort of language a charitable and fair man might use, or whether it was such language as was intended to insult. It was said on the one side that he was intending to irritate the living and to insult the dead, and on the other side it was put that they were endeavouring to pick a quarrel and to annoy him, and do a thing as unpalatable as they could, and that the whole thing was got up for the very purpose of annoying him.

The learned judge then dealt with other passages of the libel . . .

The case had been so put on both sides, that it was not necessary that they should remember all the points in controversy, because the defence had put it, and Serjeant Parry had repeated it, that he imputed to Mr Drury that he went to the funeral with the intention of 'irritating the living and insulting the dead', whereas he denied anything of the sort, and said that he simply acted in the discharge of his duty, and that the defendant and his party went there with the intention of having a burial conducted offensively close to the churchyard, and to keep him there looking on while they performed a ceremony which was simply for the purpose of annoying him, and that it was done with a sinister motive, and for the purpose of gaining political capital – for the purpose of getting up a Burial Bill or something of the sort. Now, he was bound to tell them that if that was so, and if the article was written for the purpose of insulting and irritating the plaintiff, that would be no justification for their publishing such an article. He was bound to go further, and say that if they published the libel utterly regardless of his character or regardless of accuracy, and stated things that were not true, then the mere fact that they were actuated by a desire to make capital of it, and to get up a scandal for the purpose of promoting a particular Bill in Parliament, it would be what the law called malice. This would not be a right or legitimate mode of treating other people, and it would not be treating the plaintiff with the respect that one human being owed to another. No one had a right to carry out any by-ends by putting into print or publishing of another person that which degraded and disparaged him, and the only justification of it would be the truth of it, and if it was substantially true that would be a justification. But if it was not substantially true, and some by-motive was the object, such as to disestablish the Church of England or bring in a Burial Bill or anything of that sort, that would be just the very thing the law would not sanction.

After pointing out the law of libel more particularly to the jury, his Lordship continued: – Now, this is a lamentable case. I most cordially and heartily sympathize with the observations of my brother judge when this case was in its earlier stage. I most heartily wish the parties had seen fit to assent to his view. Nothing can be more damaging to Christianity itself than to see fights such as these in courts of justice. That is my opinion. It enables enemies of the Lord to blaspheme, and to point with scorn, and say, 'See how these Christians love one another,' in a very different sense in which the Christians of old were spoken of. You have had a better opportunity than I have had to judge whose fault it is that any suggestion of this sort was not accepted at a previous stage of the case. His lordship concluded by saying that he had felt very much hampered in the matter by not having the opportunity of seeing how Mr Drury gave his evidence. This made him very diffident as to any observations he might make on that head, so that he felt it was entirely and wholly with the jury, and that he had better not comment on the demeanour or bearing of the witnesses on the other side, for fear he should do any injustice to either side. It was emphatically a case for the jury to decide, and he would now leave it in their hands.

(v) *Verdict*

The jury, in fact, took no more than ten minutes to decide. They returned a clear verdict for the plaintiff (Drury), but awarded damages of only forty shillings.

This small amount of damages, bearing in mind the very special significance attached to this point by both advocates in their summing up, raised a question about costs. Counsel for the defendant (Wilson) evidently thought that one implication of the low figure was that Drury might still be obliged to meet his own costs; but the judge thought not.

Mr Digby: I do not know what your Lordship under the circumstances will do about costs – whether you will deprive the plaintiff of costs considering the way Mr Day put it.

Mr Justice Denman: We had better leave it where it is, I think.

Counsel for the plaintiff (Drury) then tried for larger damages. But again, since the forty shillings was enough to give the plaintiff costs, the judge let the matter rest.

Mr Merewether: I think your Lordship might do more for us. If I may be permitted to parody what my friend said – after the way it has been put by Serjeant Parry.

Mr Justice Denman: That gives you the costs, does it not?

Mr Merewether: Yes.

Mr Justice Denman: I think the language is rather too strong . . .

Not only the guilt, but also the heavy burden of costs fell, therefore, upon Frederick Wilson, even when the moral stature of Drury's action in the whole affair had been deliberately rated so low. A very definite verdict and judgment – it could hardly have been better calculated to leave grievances and differences unresolved.

6   *The Law's Comment on the Law*

This was the end of the matter in court. The Akenham Burial Case was settled. But what a settlement!

On legal technicalities, by the law of the land, the editor of the *East Anglian Daily Times* had, by the findings of a jury, committed an act of libel. The Rev. Drury was upheld. But in its action, the same jury had also pronounced another verdict. Mr Day, closing his speech for the Rev. Drury, had plainly asked the jury:

> . . . to award such an amount of damages to his client as would *express their sense of the moral wrong to which he had been subject,* and would enable him to leave the court feeling that his character, as a gentleman and a man, had been established to *the satisfaction of a jury of his fellow countrymen.* (My italics.)

These were direct words, making a direct request. The jury gave an equally direct answer: *forty shillings!* The judge, too, was in no doubt. 'We had better leave it where it is, I think.'

And so – the court left it.

Brought by violent public disputation into the places of the law, however, the Akenham Burial Case did not end there. Out of the court it went back again; back into the troubled arena of social facts, social problems, social sentiments, social interests, and the struggle for social justice, out of which it arose. The law had made its comment – explicitly and implicitly – but, in itself, it could not alter the deeper, unavoidable roots of social malaise.

OUTCOME

1 *Immediate Press Comment*

Immediately, the wider comment of the press began. The very day after the verdict was published, the *East Anglian Daily Times* (March 13th, 1879) collected the first reports.

THE AKENHAM BURIAL CASE

DRURY V. WILSON

Nearly all the London and the principal provincial dailies comment at length on the above case, and we give below some extracts, impartially selected, from the articles published yesterday.

Daily Telegraph

'Although he has obtained a verdict, with forty shillings damages, we cannot say that the Reverend George Drury, of Claydon, was well advised when he insisted on giving to a local libel the wide publicity secured for it by making it the subject of a suit in the High Court of Justice. There are many cirumstances of his position and career which do not look well in the "fierce light" thus thrown upon them; and to understand the final brawl beside the grave of a little child we must revert to some other facts in this clergyman's biography. Mr Drury has been rector of Claydon for thirty-three years. Service is held in the church "about twice a month"; if there is no congregation there is no service; and that this sometimes happens seems only natural, for, as the parish clerk states, "There are no people in the parish except Dissenters." The church is "dilapidated and dirty"; the clerk admits that he has never cleaned it; and Mr Drury refuses to give the key to the churchwarden. This gross neglect carries us back to the worst years of the last century, when priests and laity were alike indifferent to spiritual life or decent ceremonial. But Mr Drury is not a mere drowsy parish priest, for he seems to have a talent for keeping himself in hot water. He has been "admonished" by his bishop for the use of illegal ornaments in the church – namely, "a crucifix, second altar, sanctus bell, chasuble, dalmatics, copes, thurible, processional cross and banner" – a kind of finery oddly associated with the dirt and disorder of a ruinous and rarely-used edifice . . . There is a convent also at Claydon, and at one time a riot arose owing to his detention there of a girl named

Rolfe. When the people broke in, Mr Drury helped her to escape, and threw a basin of water at one of her pursuers. She was carried off against her will, was afterwards confined by her father in a lunatic asylum, but finally got back to the nunnery. On one occasion Mr Drury was fined five pounds for assaulting a man with a red-hot poker. He has publicly denounced the Church Association as worse than the "Ancient Body of Assassins"; and he had stigmatized Protestantism as "poison". In fact, he appears to have been at feud with his parishioners for, as he himself admits, twenty years; though he calls it "persecution". His Christian forgiveness of his enemies, however, is on a par with the gentleness of the Irish wife who, on being told by a clergymen that she should win back the love of her bad husband and "heap coals of fire on his head", interrupted the advice by the words, "I have tried boiling water, sir." '
After reverting to the circumstances of the burial our contemporary continues: – 'It was clear that what is called "brawling" when the offence is perpetrated in a church was committed on this occasion by Mr Drury himself. His right to refuse to read any service at the grave gave him no authority whatever to interfere with a service performed in a piece of ground that formed no part of the churchyard. Nevertheless, he apparently wished to emphasize his refusal and to magnify his office by ostentatiously displaying the privation suffered by Dissenters when they were denied full funeral rites. Nobody can blame any clergyman for obeying the rubric which forbids the reading of the Church Service over the bodies of those who are unbaptized; but every right-minded minister feels that such refusal is a very painful part of his duty. No person of even ordinary good feeling would like to proclaim his prohibition, to shout it into the ears of a father and mother standing by their child's grave, and deriving some consolation from passages of Scripture or prayers read or spoken at a time when they were bowed down by sorrow. It would almost seem as if a long course of narrow clericalism hardened the heart, as if a minute attention to forms and ceremonies and ornaments drove out the spirit of the Founder of Christianity, who, when He gathered little children to Himself, certainly made no distinction in favour of those who had been baptized. An argument not without its force in favour of an Established Church is that, taken at its lowest, it secures the residence of at least one gentleman in each parish. At Claydon, where the spiritual advantages of the Church seem utterly non-existent, in the face of congregations who will not attend, the public must decide whether this residual gain is accomplished. An incident like this will do more to force on a solution of the burial question than all the arguments of Mr Osborne Morgan or all

the wisdom of the House of Lords. Were every parish priest in England endowed with charity and common sense, the whole dispute would have died down long ago; for individual arrangements or local compromise would have evaded opportunities of strife. But, while it is only a small minority of clergymen who are capable of acting in a narrow and intolerant spirit, we must remember that even exceptional scandals do enormous mischief to the Church. There is a class of ecclesiastics whose conduct tends, if unchecked, to degrade Christianity among us and re-encrust it with silly superstitions. The distinctions which men of this school so emphatically proclaim between "consecrated" and "unconsecrated" ground, between service and no service, are survivals of old beliefs too gross to be incorporated in our Articles or Rubrics. Churchyards were "consecrated" at first, not because anybody ever believed that the condition in the future world of the dead person whose body was buried therein could be affected by the ceremony, but because the mediaeval Christians firmly put their faith in an almost forgotten superstition. They thought that devils roamed about the earth seeking for human bodies into which they might enter, and that the bishop's blessing and the sign of the cross and the holy water used would guard the graves thus surrounded from those legions of imps. The same belief accounts for that "watching" of the corpse which in Ireland and other countries has degenerated into the convivial "wake". No intelligent clergyman of the Church of England would give credence to the superstition, but the Ritualists, in reverting to the rites of the Middle Ages, have a great tendency to revive also much of their childish credulity. For instance, Mr Drury told the Independent minister that the service he was reading could be of no use to the child; though doubtless this quarrelsome parson believed that, if he himself had read it, a certain efficacy might have attended the ministrations. On that point he, too, goes beyond the faith of our Church. The Burial Service is read not because of any magical influence supposed to be wrought in favour of the dead, but for the solace of the mourners, and the edification of others who attend. Even Roman Catholics, who attach great importance to the ministrations of their priests, look upon the matter from the same rational point of view. It is only a few hot-headed and ill-informed Ritualists who seem to regard consecrated ground and Church services as adjuncts of a kind of sacerdotal conjuration producing a mysterious effect.'

Standard
    'The unhappy differences, religious and political, which together

constitute what is commonly known as the Burial Question, have never led to a scandal more painful and revolting than the case of *"Drury* v. *Wilson"* . . . the Jury, in returning a verdict for the Plaintiff with forty shillings damages, must be taken as having given a very significant expression of opinion on the question.

• • •

'The alleged libels which appeared in the defendant's paper, though perhaps more objectionable and scurrilous in their terms, were comparatively unimportant, as being the natural and inevitable results of the first publication. The question of justification the jury answered without hesitation in the negative. It must be taken as established that the literary effort of Mr Tozer was an unfair and exaggerated distortion, written in a partisan spirit, of what really took place; and that the editor of the *East Anglian Daily Times* was extremely indiscreet to insert it in his publication. In saying this, we by no means intend to imply that the conduct of the plaintiff throughout the whole transaction was unexceptionable. Quite the contrary. It is fair to presume, from the very moderate amount of the damages awarded, that the jury, while carefully abstaining from indicating by "contemptuous" damages an opinion that the action ought not to have been brought, nevertheless thought that the plaintiff was not entitled to the full sympathy which a man who brings an action for libel occasionally receives. It is notorious that many clergymen of the Established Church abstain from asking inconvenient questions as to whether infants brought for burial have been baptized or not. The conscientious convictions of Mr Drury may not have allowed him to take that course, but he should clearly have abstained either from provoking an altercation on the subject, or from yielding to such provocation in the presence of the mourners and of the dead. . . . We all know – and if there were doubt, the disclosures in the present action would be sufficient proof – that but too many Dissenters are eagerly watching to find the joints in her armour, and are not ashamed to draw the bow which is to pierce them, even in the most sacred moments, and on the most holy ground.

'The editor of the *East Anglian Daily Times*, from his own point of view, was probably not unwise. More than one of the journals which followed his lead made capital out of the sensational scandal which Mr Tozer had promulgated, as an illustration of the expediency of some such measure as Mr Osborne Morgan's Bill, and even as an argument in favour of the Disestablishment of the Church. Ill-suited as politics and religion are to each other, religious politicians are notoriously the keenest of partisans, and the most enthusiastic of supporters. To gibbet a parish clergyman as a "pestilent priest, uttering his maledictions over a tiny coffin", is an outrage upon decency and religion, viewed in connection with the real facts upon which the accusation was based; but it was, doubtless, an acceptable service to certain political parties and to certain religious sects. No one suggests that the editor of the *East Anglian Times* would willingly insert, for political purposes, anything which he did not believe to be true; but the verdict of the jury must be taken as establishing that the editor did insert this particular report on wholly insufficient and exclusively partisan evidence. It is not with such weapons that the contest on the burial question is to be concluded, or that the Established Church can be successfully attacked.'

Daily News

'The case of "*Drury* v. *Wilson*", though nominally an action against the proprietor of a provincial newspaper, was really a dispute between two persons whom we will not call rival ministers of religion, but who are certainly professors of antagonistic creeds . . .

. . .

'A more unpleasant story has rarely come before the public. That a funeral is not the best opportunity for a party fight is a stale and, we fear, an unprofitable maxim. The Conservative Party has set the example of selecting the churchyard as the arena of political conflict. But in the case of Mr Drury there was no pretence of legal title, no shadow of ecclesiastical claim, to justify intrusion upon the rites of an alien sect, or the enforcement of Anglican doctrine (if Anglican doctrine it be) upon a Nonconformist congregation. A man who, by his own admission, informs the company of relatives round an open grave that the body they are interring is not that of a Christian, may or may not be justified by theological technicality, but he certainly deserves the thanks of his political opponents for the help which he has unconsciously rendered to their cause.'

Daily Chronicle

'The action for libel brought by the Rev. George Drury, rector of Akenham, in Suffolk, against Mr Wilson, editor, publisher, and proprietor of the *East Anglian Daily Times*, was last night concluded. After a patient and protracted hearing of three full days the special jury found their verdict for the reverend plaintiff, with forty shillings damages. This is much the same as the traditional farthing so often given, and the only reason we can imagine why the larger amount was awarded is because it carries the plaintiff's costs, which upon a farthing verdict would have been doubtful, as the jury, from reading law reports, were probably well aware . . . The Rev. George Drury, who acts as pastor without parishioners, is a most ritualistic rector. He would doubtless prefer the title of "priest", but the vulgar villagers will only call him "parson". With the intense intolerance of a medieval monk, he lays down dogmas and doctrines worthy of the darkest ages, speaks of Protestantism as "poison", and courteously calls the Church Association an "ancient order of assassins". With a ruined church and no congregation, he passes his time saying Mass in a monastery, superintending a convent, and walking about in a cassock and biretta. He has been proceeded against by his bishop for ritualistic practices in the way of vestments, banners and processions, but has always treated the monition with some contempt. Such we find, from the evidence publicly proved in a court, is the church, and such the rector, a stranger to his flock, an opposer of his bishop, and now the successful party in this action for libel upon his personal and priestly character, with an award of forty shillings by way of damages.'

Similar reports were received from the *Globe*, **the** *Echo*, **the** *Manchester Examiner* **and the** *Leeds Mercury*. **All debated the justice of the award of damages and costs:**

'A most unsatisfactory termination' is the verdict of the *Echo* upon the result of the case . . . 'This clergyman, who calls his fellow-churchmen "assassins", who had been fined for assaulting a man with a red-hot poker, who has a clerical income of over £500 a year with residence, and yet who has driven his congregation away and allows his church to be in a most dirty and deplorable condition, comes into court demanding heavy damages for libel because a little strong language was used in regard to conduct calculated to rouse the blood of the meekest and most long-suffering of men . . . The verdict will be received with general surprise. If the account given by the newspaper really was a libel, Mr Drury ought to have had substantial damages; if he did not deserve substantial damages, the *East Anglian Daily Times* does not deserve to be mulcted in the ruinous costs [not much less than £1,000] of a three days' trial.'

And all shared the conclusion of the *Examiner*:

'. . . There can be little doubt that technically the report of the scene at Akenham contained a libel. It is, indeed, a difficult thing for a man to write an account of a row in which he has been engaged without making mistakes and libelling his opponent. The verdict might be set aside on a new trial, but we question whether it would be worth while carrying the matter further. Though the result is against them on the trial, Mr Tozer and the Akenham Nonconformists must feel that substantially they have gained their case. They have shown that the existing law of burial authorizes an intolerable outrage, and they have been the means of exposing a deplorable scandal in the church, and one which appears to defy treatment so long as the Establishment is protected by its present constitution.'

Legally, Mr Wilson and Mr Tozer had lost the case; morally, they had won it.

These were now by no means small provincial papers fighting in the cock-pit of their own locality or region, but widely influential newspapers making national comment. Their agreement on the implications of the verdict was a massive manifestation of public opinion. During the next ten days press statements of the same kind appeared throughout the country, and flooded into the office of the *East Anglian Daily Times*. One or two quotations will be enough to indicate their nature.

South Wales Daily News (March 14th, 1879)

What better argument for the disestablishment of the Church of England than that such a man as this Suffolk rector should be allowed to take the pay of the Church while doing the works of Rome, and apparently glorying in it? The Church of England has indeed come to a serious pass when . . . a mock monk ('Father' Ignatius) finds access to pulpits which it is illegal for Noncomformist clergymen to enter; when a Suffolk rector can double his fist in the face of his bishop's representative, and not blush to call Protestantism – which he is paid to teach – poison! Yet the men who are systematically dishonouring the Church as by law established, clamour for liberty of conscience. Who denies them liberty to think and to worship as their conscience directs? Nobody. But is there an organized Church in the world which allows its tenets to be morally trodden under foot, and its principles made the subject of derision, without bidding the recreant teacher take himself off to more congenial associations?

Woodbridge Reporter

Mr Drury sued the publisher of the *East Anglian* for £2,000, and the jury, after his lordship's ruling, gave him the first figure of the sum sought to be obtained, cutting off all the os. Mr Drury is to have £2 for the injury he alleges he has suffered through the severe strictures that have been made upon him. Looking at his past history – seeing how often he has been in unpleasant circumstances – we think £2 will more than cover any injury that can by any possibility have fallen upon him by recent comments in the public press . . . Forty shillings is almost an insult to offer any man, who has been publicly branded 'a monster', 'a disgrace to humanity', and 'a pestilent priest' . . . Our contemporary contended in this matter bravely. Believing it was publishing absolute truth, and thinking this was needful to be known, in the interests of freedom and religion, it has refused all compromise, but has fought the battle to the bitter end.

Among many other criticisms, the *Liverpool Mercury* (March 15th) commented:

On a review of the whole case, we must say that this burning and shining light of Suffolk strikes us as a very strange person to term the child of a God-fearing Baptist farm labourer 'not a Christian, but a heathen'. He cannot fill his pews, and he objects even to fill his graves. He has been rector of Akenham and Claydon since before 1863, and, judging from what was brought out at the trial, the result of some twenty years' ministry seems to be 'a filthy church' and 'no congregation'. . . How long is this to last . . .

The *Whitehall Review* pointed out that Mr Day, Drury's counsel, was himself a Papist. The *Christian World* strongly upheld the stand Mr Wilson had taken, making it clear that Rev. Drury had insisted upon legal action despite the fact that the pages of the *East Anglian Daily Times* had been deliberately made available to him for any 'explanation or disclaimers', and pointing, too, to the deep public interest aroused and the fact that the court was crowded throughout the three full days of the trial. It also issued a 'special extra edition', containing the whole of the proceedings, so that readers could judge for themselves beyond any 'selectivity' of press reporting.

Like the *Christian World*, the *Harwich Free Press*, the *Ipswich Free Press*, the *Bolton Weekly Journal*, the *Essex Telegraph*, and others, also voiced the desire for a general subscription to cover the *East Anglian*'s costs. It is interesting to see that this expressed desire arose from newspapers throughout the country. It was no selfishly or locally engendered thing. It was evidence of the solidarity of the press, a communal expression of the importance of the action of the press, and, especially, a communal concern for its freedom. The most forthright statement of all came from Scotland – the *Greenock Telegraph*.

. . . The case has just been tried in the Court of Common Pleas, and has resulted in a verdict favourable to the priestly pursuer, who has received forty shillings damages. This will take most people by surprise; and we venture to say that the feeling of astonishment will be considerably increased on a perusal of the evidence that was produced at Westminster. That evidence conclusively demonstrated that the report in the Ipswich paper was substantially accurate . . . Yet the jury guided by some inscrutable motive, actually concluded that the Akenham priest was entitled to receive forty shillings of damages . . . That the *East Anglian Daily Times* should have been put to serious expense for daring to report a public incident that imperatively demanded still greater publicity, is only another illustration of the unsatisfactory character of the law of libel and the occasional fatuity of English juries. But . . . the public will no doubt make good the pecuniary loss in which it has been involved; and we shall be glad to hear that the Scottish friends of religious equality have sent some practical expressions of their sympathy to the Ipswich editor.

On the verdict in general, the *Edinburgh Daily Review* believed that comment

. . . is, we think, unnecessary. The facts are plain enough to carry with them their own moral, and we rejoice to believe that nine out of every ten members of the Church of England will condemn as heartily as the most uncompromising Nonconformist the conduct in the affair of the churlish State official who was the occasion of such an outrage upon common decency.

The *Examiner* thought that:

If Mr Drury has acted like a Christian, then Christianity as practised is a farce, and a very dismal sort of farce too.

This particular spate of reports was ended by one from the *Croydon Advertiser*, which decided:

It must must have been a very 'special' jury which gave a verdict of forty shillings to the 'Reverend' George Drury, of Akenham. It seems impossible to reconcile such a verdict with the evidence, except on the supposition that the jury was 'specially' selected . . . This Akenham priest carried out his peculiar views with a vigour worthy only of a Zulu, and roused the whole countryside to the highest pitch of indignation by his intolerance. The editor of an Ipswich newspaper described the scene perhaps too literally, and made some comments perhaps too strong, for this special jury. But can any comments be too strong for a case like this? The venerable Serjeant Parry ably defended the editor, and unsparingly lashed the 'reverend' complainant; but the 'special' jury returned a verdict which has astonished all England, and probably no one more than Drury himself. For the sake of humanity, we hope . . . that this burial scandal may be prevented from being repeated by a readjustment of the Burial Laws . . . The record of the case reads more like a legend of the sixteenth, instead of a sober fact of the nineteenth century.

These quotations, however, are taken from only a selection of the reports that appeared. Among the many other papers drawn upon by the *East Anglian Daily Times* **were, for example, the** *Norfolk News, Leeds Mercury, Newcastle Chronicle, Sheffield Independent, Weekly Despatch, Cambridge Independent Press, Suffolk Chronicle, Saturday Review, Essex Standard* **and the** *Aberdeen Journal.* **On March 17th, the** *East Anglian Daily Times* **had drawn attention to a strange parallel:**

The editor of the *Ipswich Journal* is also a leader writer on a Conservative newspaper known as the *Exeter Gazette*. It is an interesting and instructive study to compare his utterances at Ipswich and Exeter, which, similar as they are in such phrases as 'parson baiting', differ so widely in their estimate of Mr Drury's conduct. Which of the articles presents him in the truer light we leave our readers to determine: –

Ipswich Journal.	*Exeter Gazette.*
The scene which took place last August at the gate of the secluded churchyard of Akenham was a parson-baiting, and nothing more or less.	This minister of the Gospel (Mr Tozer) seems, as far as can be gathered, to have been selected to fill the situation of parson-baiter.
The jury to whom the Rev. George Drury appealed have affirmed this view, which indeed was taken in these columns from the first. We are not, therefore, surprised at the result; any other	What is called the Akenham Burial Scandal Case was brought this week to a conclusion, alike unsatisfactory to the plaintiff, the defendant, and the public. The Rev. G. Drury has obtained a

ending to the case would have been a gross injustice.

A scandal has been created, but a British jury has shown that the average Englishman's view of the affair is that they who sought to create political capital on the lid of a poor child's coffin are the only scandalous parties.

There was much ingenuity displayed in the whole arrangements for the infliction of pain on the Rev. George Drury. He was there to perform a duty, and his tormentors knew that he would be.

verdict for forty shillings and costs against the Editor of the journal that maligned him, but this cannot be held to represent any great solatium.

All persons, to whatever religious denomination they may belong, will regret that this case should have been brought into court at all, as the undoubted tendency of its details is to bring religion itself into contempt. In some respects we are almost tempted to say that the Church of England clergyman and the dissenting minister who figure in this case are 'Arcades ambo'.

Nevertheless, though Mr Drury's action in the matter does not come out well from close examination, that of Mr Tozer, the dissenting divine, appears in a very invidious light indeed. Mr Drury behaved not only indiscreetly, but with undue harshness, and in these respects his actions need not be endorsed by the approval of Churchmen.

Stung by the charge implicit in this piece, the *Ipswich Journal* – in true Vicar of Bray manner – reared itself up and lumbered into action, presenting some further press reports in its train. Its opening blast came on March 18th:

The editor of the *East Anglian Daily Times* has just received a lesson from a British jury, which we had hoped would have cured him of the habit of making what we will call reckless statements. Bought wit is proverbially best wear, and the only reservation of the ancient proverb to that effect is not to pay too high a price for the article. But even the high price has not in this case secured our friend a good article. We have to complain of a very impertinent piece of recklessness – we are using a longer word than is necessary – perpetrated in yesterday's paper. We find there, set out in double columns, a portion of our article on the Drury *v.* Wilson case, from Saturday's paper, and opposite it is another article from the *Exeter Gazette*. Prefixed to these is a statement that the Editor of the *Ipswich Journal* is also leader-writer to the *Exeter Gazette*. This statement is utterly false – we use a shorter word this time, but a shorter yet would only correctly characterize as wanton a piece of impertinence as could be expected to emanate from any one above the ranks of stable boys and street sweepers. The editor of the *Ipswich Journal* is not leader-writer to the *Exeter Gazette*; which paper is in no need of assistance from any but its own able and accomplished editor and its own staff. We leave to our readers to judge whether assistance be needed nearer home. What can these friends of the defeated party in Drury *v.* Wilson – who are about to vindicate his character as a journalist and salve the wound inflicted by a jury, by subscribing to pay his costs – think when they find him so soon again convicted of publishing reckless misstatements?

By way of staunch support, it carried, on the same day, a 'Press Opinion' from the *Church Times*:

We have . . . to point out the scandalous manner in which the case was sought to be prejudiced by the introduction of irrelevant matter of a kind which was thought likely to throw the mind of the British juror off its balance. In the first place, a great point was made of the dirty and neglected state of Akenham church, with a view to show that Mr Drury was negligent of his sacred duties. But it was not stated that Akenham was within a mile of Claydon, with which the benefice is consolidated, that its gross population was only eighty-four; that the few farmers of the parish were all Dissenters, and would not come to church; and that it was the business of the churchwardens, and not of the rector, to keep the edifice clean. Nor was anything said about the frequent and well-ordered services at Claydon. Next an attempt was made to get Mr Drury to avow a belief in what is really a Calvinistic, and not a Catholic tenet, namely, that, as one of their writers has put it, 'there are children not a span long crawling about on the floor of hell'. Of course, Mr Drury believed nothing of the sort, but he has been reviled in the grossest way on the assumption that he had preached this doctrine to the parents in the hope of causing them pain. Next Mr Drury's connection with Brother Ignatius, who had once a house at Claydon, was brought in, and he was charged with having helped to detain a young lady against the wish of her father, Dr Rolfe. But it turned out that this young lady was of full age when admitted into the

convent, and that Dr Rolfe had allowed her to go there; that afterwards an attack was made on the house by a score of men, who searched
in a most indecent manner the room of the Mother Superior, who was
ill in bed; and that having carried off Miss Rolfe by force, her father
shut her up in asylum for a year, and then dying, left her penniless. In
the end all these attempts at prejudice, though enforced by Serjeant
Parry in his best Old Bailey style, broke down and the jury found for
Mr Drury. What is more, the Dissenting organs, though furious at the
result, are one and all constrained to confess that Mr Tozer's conduct
in supplying the report, as if from a third person, was altogether improper. In a word, the getters-up of the attack on Mr Drury have fared
very much like the zealous magistrate in one of Sir Walter Scott's
novels, who snatched up his 'Protestant flail' in a panic, and broke his
own head with it. We are not certain whether the failure of Serjeant
Parry's impassioned invective does not mark the reaction which has
set in against anti-ritualism, more distinctly than almost anything that
has yet occurred.

Like the *East Anglian*, the *Ipswich Journal* had its following, and
produced some – but far fewer – supporting comments from
other newspapers. Some of these – like the *Norwich Argus* –
gloated more than a little over the *East Anglian*'s burden of costs.
Even the *Saturday Review*, after a fairly moderate piece entitled
'A Churchyard Squabble', ended with this emphasis:

It will probably be hardly necessary to advise the editor of the *East
Anglian Times*, the next time he applies to Mr Tozer for a contribution,
to make sure that Mr Tozer is describing the deeds of others rather
than his own. Any little lesson of this sort is usually mastered with
surprising rapidity when it is impressed on the memory by a bill of
costs.

The *Ipswich Journal*'s last offering of press reports appeared in a
'Supplement' on March 22nd. A balanced piece came from
the *Guardian*:

This case in itself must be so utterly painful to all serious men, that we
should not care to dwell upon it, except for certain points of public
interest which it suggests in relation to the present position of the
burial question.
    . . . It is certainly not a little suspicious that Mr Tozer, who is
wholly unconnected with the Baptists, and who, on the point of the
general necessity of baptism, ought to be substantially at one with the

Church of England, should have been put forward to officiate on this occasion, in preference to the Baptist minister, who appears to have been consulted . . . But, even supposing that the arrangement which secured Mr Tozer's valuable services was accidental, and that his violent conduct on the occasion was to be excused by mistake and excitement, what is to be said of the article which he drew up for the *East Anglian Times*, carefully speaking of himself in the third person, as if it proceeded from an admiring but impartial reporter, introducing statements which appear questionable in point of fact, and dragging in irrelevant matters, simply to excite odium against Mr Drury and against the Church to which he belongs? It is too obvious to be denied that its main object was to make capital for the cause of political Dissent, and especially on the burials question . . .

Nor can any one venture to extenuate the grossness of the libels against Mr Drury. . . In spite of the abusive eloquence of Mr Serjeant Parry, and the obvious local prejudice against Mr Drury, the jury could not help recording a verdict in his favour, though they affixed nominal damages; and the judge most justly allowed the payment of the costs to fall on the defendant. There is a limit to endurance to gross personalities, even from a provincial newspaper. It is well that those who direct the power of the press should be taught that an unpopular man, exposed to all the bitterness of the *odium theologicum*, has some protection against anonymous invective and slander. . .

The *Exeter Gazette* voiced its own protest at an earlier accusation – feeling as much maligned, though not so hotly concerned, as the editor of the *Ipswich Journal*. For once provincial papers were involved in nation-wide controversy and debate.

The *East Anglian Daily Times* does the *Exeter and Plymouth Gazette* the honour of asserting that a leading article in last week's issue on the Akenham Burial Scandal must have been penned by the editor of the *Ipswich Journal*. Our radical contemporary is even able positively to state, out of profundity of knowledge, that the leading articles in the *Gazette* are written by the editor in question. Our contemporary is welcome to the assumption that all wisdom, all common sense, and all disgust at dirty actions reside in East Anglia; but here in the West we have a certain reputation for originality to maintain, and we must disclaim the soft impeachment that our leaders come from Ipswich.

And the *Graphic*, ranged with these few others behind the Vicar

of Bray, managed to get in its sting not so much about Disestablishment as about the true nature of the Dissenters – revealed
in this case in all its nastiness and vulgarity.

Nonconformists also have something to learn from the miserable story.
None of them, we presume, would be prepared to defend the conduct
of Mr Tozer. He displayed an extraordinary want of judgment, tact
and self-control. Yet he merely presented the ordinary temper of many
Dissenters in an extreme form. Nonconformists, as a rule, are not content to protest against the Established Church; they watch it with
jealousy, and nourish feelings regarding it which ill accord with their
general principles as to the conduct of life. The result is that fiery persons like Mr Tozer, placed in exceptional circumstances, blaze out in
wrath and fury, and bring discredit upon themselves and the ecclesiastical system to which they belong.

Besides these professional journalists, the writers of 'letters to
the editor' had been exercising their zeal. Pens up and down the
country had been stabbed at paper just as swords into the sides
of their enemies. A London correspondent to the *Rochdale
Observer* had been an eye-witness of some of 'Father Drury's'
earlier doings:

I happen to know a good deal about the villages of Claydon and Akenham, and the Popish Anglican rector there, the Rev. George Drury,
who was the plaintiff in this action against the *East Anglian Times*. For
more than twenty years that man's conduct has been a cause of mis-
chievous petty local war and of bitterness of feeling in the district in
which he unfortunately holds a living, and the conditions of the existence of our Established Church are such that for such conduct as that
which this clergyman was guilty there is no redress except such as
that which comes of its exposure by the press. A poor man and woman
go out to bury their little dead child, two years of age, and while a
Christian service is being read over the coffin the clergyman goes up to
the coffin and points to it, and stops the burial service by declaring that
the child is not a Christian, because it has not been baptized. In the
local newspaper appeared a description of the occurrence, to all intents
and purposes correct, and after hearing the evidence the jury declares
this description to be a libel, and gives the clergyman forty shillings
damages with costs. I have heard only one opinion expressed of this
verdict, and that is an opinion strongly condemning the decision of the

jury. More than fifteen years ago I saw an extraordinary ritualistic procession pass from Claydon church to Akenham church, with this Mr Drury and the well-known Father Ignatius at its head. In the procession were carried banners representing bleeding hearts, and other such emblems as one may see in a village in Belgium, and when these banners were set down in the church the faithful made obeisance to them as they passed by them. At that time such forms of medieval idolatry as these were constantly practised at Claydon church. They were, in some extent, I believe, modified some time after in obedience to an order of the Court of Arches.

The Bishop of Norwich, having had little success in pressing home his admonitions of Rev. Drury, was content simply to dissociate himself publicly from the 'Order of Assassins'.

THE BISHOP OF NORWICH AND THE CHURCH ASSOCIATION

Sir, – In your report of Serjeant Parry's speech, in the case of *Drury v. Wilson*, he is stated to have said, 'Listen to the words he uses of the Church Association, of which the Bishop of Norwich is a member.' The Bishop of Norwich is not, and never has been, a member of the Church Association.

I shall be much obliged if you will insert this correction of Serjeant Parry's mistake.

Yours faithfully,

Monk Soham Rectory, March 12*th,* 1879   ROBERT W. GROOME

It is quite clear that Anthony Trollope had no need to go far in search of material for his clerical novels!

But some correspondents were more concerned about an issue altogether different from the theatre of the absurd in the Church: the freedom of the press. Here is the most sturdy and unconquerable letter of all. An anonymous letter; a letter out of the people.

Sir, – I am not a Dissenter, but I am greatly mistaken if the people of England will allow the decision of the Court of Common Pleas to be final in the case of Drury *v.* Wilson.

If this decision is to be final, then the freedom of the British press may be considered as a matter of past history in England.

I, personally, care not a straw for the *East Anglian Times*, or any other paper, but if civil and religious liberty are to be crushed out of England and the English people, it shall not be done without the protest of one

WORM

Throughout the noisy week following the trial, however, the spate of press reports and correspondence was interspersed by a few more dignified leading articles from the editors concerned. These, too, took different sides. On March 15th, the editor of the *Suffolk Chronicle* summarized matters in this way:

The Akenham Burial Scandal has at last got through the court, and the Reverend George Drury has by this time learnt how small an estimate is placed by a disinterested jury upon his grievances . . . It cannot be denied that some amount of interest gathered round the case of *Drury v. Wilson*. Dramatic incidents were not wanting to add their piquancy to what would otherwise have been a prosy affair enough . . .

As for the political motive, we discard that at once. There is no doubt that Mr Tozer, when he wrote his narrative of the burial scene, was righteously indignant at the conduct of Mr Drury . . . It would have been better, had Mr Tozer not possessed himself of a dual character. He should have confined himself to his ministerial office, that being the office he sustained in his conflict with Mr Drury, and not taken upon himself the functions of a reporter. He was a leading actor in the scene, was labouring under considerable excitement, and could not bring that coolness and impartiality to bear upon his narrative which would have been the case had a professional reporter been present. And it was just here that Mr Wilson, as we conceive, erred. A spirited dialogue written by one of the disputants, aided by the memory of other disputants, was certain to have a bias . . . Then the defendant, in copying into his paper strongly-worded articles from other journals, did not smooth matters . . . to copy them looked much like a determination to throw whatever wordy brickbats came in the way at the head of the rector of Claydon and Akenham . . .

As to Mr Drury's part in the scene, it was lamentable. Why could he not have stopped at home instead of mixing himself up with those pestilential Dissenters. He must have known that it was a Dissenters' gathering, since his church-clerk says he is the only Churchman in the parish, and Mr Drury knew very well he was not about to attend the funeral of that pillar of the Church. Why, too, go through the farce of protesting against a service over an unbaptized child, when he cannot

8

say that the child was worse off for not having been baptized? The reverend gentleman needed not to have troubled himself about the matter. Do we do him injustice if we say he was in no amiable mood when he trudged across to Akenham church – the home of spiders, where birds cease from chirruping, and where it can scarcely be said the remains of unbaptized children are at rest? Undoubtedly the reverend gentleman is a man of strong convictions. He may have a holy horror of Protestants, especially of Baptists. But one's convictions must be held in subordination if they run counter to the popular idea of Christian forbearance and neighbourly obligation. The action which has just been disposed of will not bring peace to Mr Drury; it will not strengthen the Holy Catholic Church, as represented by him; it will not bring Akenham closer to his heart. Theology will not be benefited by his confessions as to the destiny of unbaptized children – and brotherly kindness, which is a trifle better than theology, will not be promoted. The only parties benefited are members of the legal fraternity . . .

For ourselves we fervently hope that burial scenes, of whatever sort, will soon cease. It is really too bad that churchmen should connive at a system which they would not dare to originate, nor, so far as they are individually concerned, venture to put into operation against their neighbours.

On the same date, the editor of the *Ipswich Journal* was as immovable in his own conviction that the entire Akenham incident could be most fittingly described as 'THE AKENHAM PARSON-BAITING' (the title of his article). The half-hour delay in the timing of the service and the arrangement to hold it as close as possible to the gate of the churchyard were – he insisted – deliberately calculated to inflame and torment Drury. And the Dissenters, in doing this, had had no more feelings for the parents than 'the nails which held the parts of the coffin in their places'.

Ipswich and its neighbourhood are to a great extent lowered in the public estimation, by the fact that men exist hereabouts who can meanly, and with a vile craftiness which is inexpressibly shocking, scheme and carry out a plot of the nature revealed in the trial of Drury *v.* Wilson; but if the event has the effect of attracting public attention to the hollowness of that melancholy sham called the Burials agitation, there will after all be some compensation for having been the scene of even this contemptible squabble.

Two days later (March 17th) the editor of the *East Anglian Daily Times* made his own pronouncement: flatly ridiculing and re-jecting, again, any idea that the incident had been a 'plot'. The press, he showed, had known nothing whatever about the burial until after the event. Wickham Tozer had officiated by accident – being the only Nonconformist minister Gooding had been able to find. And the relationship between Gooding and Ramsey had been not only one of employer and labourer, but of lifelong personal acquaintance. Gooding's concern for Ramsey, in this situation, was therefore thoroughly understandable. To inter-pret the wish to hold a service over the child in the meadow as a piece of theatre deliberately contrived to 'bait' the rector – simply because the rector was known, in fact, to be a man prone to such 'baiting' – was an absurdity no sensible person could entertain.

Nevertheless, the day afterwards, the *Ipswich Journal* de-scribed Claydon's reception of Drury, after the trial, as nothing less than the homecoming of a public hero. The rector was: '. . . met with a most warm and enthusiastic reception, and was greeted with loud cheers, many congratulations, and much hand-shaking.' Indeed, the report went on: 'Had there been time to make the necessary preparations, it was, we believe, the intention of the parishioners to have erected a triumphant arch . . .' The most interesting thing about this article, however, was that it contained, also, an account of what might be called Drury's 'Victory Sermon'. This, in fact, is the only record of the reasoning on which Drury himself rested his action in refusing to read the Burial Service over the unbaptized. Preached on the following Sunday, from the text: 'Go ye, therefore, and teach all nations, baptizing them in the name of the Father and of the Son and of the Holy Ghost,' the gist of it was this:

'Before considering the subject of baptism . . . it is necessary first to explain the meaning of . . . the word "teach", which does not, in this place, mean . . . to convey knowledge as schoolmasters and mistresses do to their pupils, but rather to admit pupils to their schools; and many persons, instead of translating the words, "go and *teach*", translate them, "go and *make disciples* of all nations, *baptizing* them . . ." so that if a person asks how anyone is made a disciple of Jesus Christ, the answer is, "by baptism" . . . Persons are made Christians or disciples of Christ by baptism according to the plain teaching of the Holy

Scriptures, and there is no other way. If persons are baptized they are Christians; if they are not baptized, they are not Christians. Nothing can be plainer than this . . .

'Why is the burial service "not to be used for any that die unbaptized, excommunicate, or have laid violent hands on themselves"? Because neither one or the other of them are members of the Christian family, neither of them are recognized as being brethren of the same society: neither of them are pupils or disciples in the school of Christ, or, as we generally say, Christians. You perceive that they are all outwardly in the same position regarding the society which is called the Church: the unbaptized have never been admitted into it; the excommunicated have been expelled from it; and those who have laid violent hands on themselves have cut themselves off from it. They are neither of them recognized members of the Christian family. You see the same in all societies, benefit clubs, and unions . . . The members are admitted after being elected, by perhaps only inscribing their names in a book and paying a small fee. This, though only a small ceremony, makes them members . . . It is the same with the Church – the outward visible Church – and its members. Persons are admitted to membership by baptism. If they are not baptized, they are not members; if, after being baptized, they are expelled by excommunication, they cease to be members; and if they lay violent hands on themselves, they separate themselves from the society by their own act, and cease to be regarded as members of it; and not being members, the service which is appointed to be read at burials of those who are, is not to be read at their burial.

'Moreover, the reading of the service does not depend upon the spiritual condition or moral character of the person buried. A person who has lived a bad life, who has been a vagabond, who has been a notorious sinner, who has oppressed the poor, who has committed robbery or murder, is to be buried with the same service, the same rites and ceremonies as those who have lived good, holy, and irreproachable lives. It is not a question of moral character. The priest who buries has not to inquire what kind of life the deceased had lived, and judge and condemn, or forbid or allow, the burial to take place in such and such a manner and with or without the service. If he had to do this he would have to act as a judge, and he is not a judge but a minister . . .

'Let us be glad at least that the reading of the service at the burial of the deceased which has been set forth as a thing of vast importance to the unbaptized dead, and the refusal to do which has been proclaimed to be a crime of such magnitude that the English language can hardly

supply words sufficiently severe to denounce, does not depend upon
the moral character of the deceased, but only on the fact of his being
outwardly recognized a member of the Christian family; neither does
the reading of the service at the burial of the dead depend upon his
spiritual condition. He who dies in mortal sin . . . is buried in the same
manner and with the same service as he who has received the last
sacraments with every outward token of devotion . . . and why not?
The grace of God may have overcome the enmity, intolerance and
ignorance . . . and have effected his conversion and acceptance with
God at the last moment . . . while, on the other hand, he whom we
regarded as a saint, may, by a proud thought, have excluded himself
from heaven . . . have become less acceptable to God than the publican.
We cannot judge – it is not our province, neither have we the ability –
we leave judgment and justice to God, hoping the best for those who
are of the household and family of the faith, commending their souls to
God and committing their bodies to the earth as members of the same
head, and fellow-heirs of the same promise.'

Whatever may be thought of the *Ipswich Journal*'s account, and
of the sermon itself, it is a matter of fact that some members of
Firm Father Drury's parish and congregation subscribed for a
Bible – beautifully and ornately designed – which they presented to him in grateful recognition of the efforts he had undertaken in defending truth against error on their, and the
Church's, behalf. It still lies, though now unnoticed and forgotten, in a cupboard drawer in Claydon Church. It was signed,
however, by only one churchwarden.
   Was this presentation something akin to the forty shillings'
damages received? It is hard to tell.

This might have been thought to be the last of the story: two to
three weeks of press upheaval in 1879, as in 1878. But just a few
further comments were to come. On April 1st, the *East Anglian
Daily Times* carried a 'History of the Akenham Libel Case'. This
was not a summary of the entire story, as the title suggests,
but, in fact, the substance of the 'proof' prepared by Wilson for
his counsel, which had not been used at the trial because of lack
of time. It proved Wilson's fair treatment of earlier press reports on festivals at Claydon church, including one on a lecture
by 'Sir George Drury' on 'Protestantism and Popery' for which
Sister Mary – the Superior of the Claydon Nunnery – had

thanked '. . . the editor of the *East Anglian Daily Times* for his kindness on this and other occasions.' It gave evidence of Drury's own anger in past press correspondence – as, for example, when: '. . . he held up to ridicule a gentleman who had been his churchwarden at Claydon for ten or thirteen years, calling him an Anabaptist butcher.' But it concentrated chiefly on Wilson's own handling of the initial Akenham article. What is especially interesting is that, after Wilson's offer to print a final letter from both Drury and Wickham Tozer after the first week's intense exchanges, Wickham Tozer had, in fact, written such a letter. Drury, however, had not, and would not. This had not come to light before. As Wilson explained:

In August I was staying by the seaside at Felixstowe, and on Saturday afternoon, the 24th, went to a picnic on the river Orwell, which obliged me to stay that night at my house at Ipswich. The following day, I was walking to the train for Felixstowe, when I was overtaken by my manager, Mr Elkington, who was going down to Felixstowe to see me. He then showed me the manuscript of the report of the Akenham Burial written by Mr Tozer . . . I saw at once that the report would arouse a stormy controversy, and having a great dread of the *odium theologicum*, I did not relish the prospect before me, but felt that the burials question being one of great public importance it would be a dereliction of duty as a public journalist if I failed to insert the account of what had taken place at Akenham . . . The report appeared, and hot correspondence followed. I published letters, for and against Mr Drury, and though I consigned several to the waste-paper basket which attacked him, I published every one that came in his favour. I find that I published seven letters for Mr Drury and thirteen against him . . . At the end of a week, considering that the matter had been exhausted, so far as any public good to be derived was concerned, I stopped the correspondence with the following notice: –

THE AKENHAM BURIAL CASE

We have received further letters on this subject, but it has now been thoroughly discussed; and, as far as we are concerned, the correspondence must end, unless the principal actors – the Rev. G. Drury and the Rev. Wickham Tozer – desire to address the public through our columns. We observe in a letter to the *Ipswich Journal* that a writer, who appears thoroughly to know Mr Drury's mind, expresses his apprehension that any reply to an attack made in the *Daily Times* might not obtain 'free and unaltered admission'. Mr Drury has many times been allowed to address the public at length through our columns when, as his friends stated, no other Suffolk newspaper was open to him. He is at perfect liberty to avail himself again of the privilege, and, having been vehemently attacked, we promise him that any letter shall appear unabridged and unaltered.

Mr Tozer had sent me a letter to insert, but I declined to publish it, unless Mr Drury wrote first and his letter involved, in justice, a reply.

Wilson was sufficiently fair to delay printing Wickham Tozer's letter for six weeks, until he had heard more. Then, Drury's solicitor wrote to him saying that Drury would not enter into a newspaper correspondence, but demanded an apology under the threat of bringing an action. Wilson then went to Akenham himself, inquired into the circumstances of the burial, found that all the people he saw testified to the truth of Wickham Tozer's account, and therefore decided to stand by the report in his paper. Drury's obduracy, again, seems clear. And certainly there seems no evidence whatever of personal malice on Wilson's side. It was a matter of free and truthful reporting of an issue he thought publicly important.

One other comment – noted in the *Liberator* (April 3rd) – was worth while in showing very clearly the disgust felt by many *within* the Church of England as well as by many outside it. Coupling Drury's proceedings with those of another High Churchman, the *Record* (a Low Church journal) had said:

It might be supposed that to such men the welfare of the Church would be their highest possible consideration: yet in both these cases *they have made it to stink in the nostrils of the people committed to their charge*, and have alienated alike their respect and affection for it. There are, indeed, conceivable circumstances in which it may be a positive duty to run counter to popular convictions, and, under the requirements of conscience and in defence of the sacred claims of truth, to maintain a resolute protest against them. But in the cases to which we refer the odium has been incurred by violating the law of the Church, disdaining the authority of its rulers, and contradicting its most clearly pronounced decisions.

And the *Liberator* itself not only upheld the principles underlying such condemnations, but also the necessity and rightness of vigorously expressing them – despite any risk of libel. Morality should not be hamstrung by the law.

We think such condemnation is much more worthy of respect than the cool criticism of those who are shocked that Mr Tozer and the editors of certain journals should have expressed themselves so strongly about Mr Drury's conduct. They did well to be angry; although their anger may have been too vehemently expressed. This parochial clergyman distinctly sought to interfere with the liberty of the subject, in trying to prevent the completion of a burial service which was in no way illegal – which did not infringe on his own legal rights, and which was the least consolation to be had by the bereaved parents, under specially afflicting circumstances; and we hope the day will never come when similar arrogance and intolerance will not be resented with English resoluteness.

A final letter summed up the widespread distaste that had come to be felt about the whole matter.

Sir, – How much longer are our burial laws to continue to permit, if not invite, such scenes as have been recently described? In England long custom has led mourners to look for a religious service at a burial. To be by law forbidden to hold such service in the customary place – viz., at the grave, is felt to be a hardship and a wrong . . . When parents are weeping by an open grave they need nothing to aggravate their sorrow. Whether they are church people or dissenters, words of religious comfort are then looked for and valued. Who would be injured by free permission for such to be spoken I really cannot see. Another generation will hear with wonder and with indignation of the law which now, in rural England especially, insults dissenters and all the unbaptized dead.

With still greater surprise and shame will the clergy of that generation remember that it was the wearers of their cloth who clung to an inhuman and unchristian law when all other classes were anxious to remove it. How long will those who ought to be the readiest to all acts of kindness, have to be dragged reluctantly or by force to the removing of all stumbling blocks out of their brethren's way? . . .

A.Z.

2 Costs and Committees of Support

In the trial itself, and in all the following press discussion, much had been made of the question of costs. 'Drury-supporters' tended to gloat over the large bill that Wilson had to meet. 'Wilson-supporters' expressed a wish to play their part in meeting it. Unsolicited contributions were, immediately after the end of the trial, coming into the office of the *East Anglian Daily Times*. Among the many letters mentioning costs, one – appearing in the *Suffolk Chronicle* on March 15th – was official.

Sir, – Mr Wilson has gallantly defended himself, the press, and the public . . . and in the opinion of many his services are worthy of general recognition. Unsolicited subscriptions towards the heavy costs incurred in defending the action have been sent to me by entire strangers, as well as from neighbours, who are desirous of expressing their approval of the disinterested manner in which Mr Wilson has acted throughout. These sums have been forwarded to Messrs Alexander's and Co's Bank, where the subscriptions of those who likewise wish to share in the defence of this suit may be placed previous to the formation of a committee. – I am, sir, &c.,
Akenham, Ipswich, March 14th, 1879   J. A. SMITH

This was from our old acquaintance – the 'Protestant Churchwarden'. From that time on 'Committees of Support' sprang up quickly. First a 'Local Committee' was formed; a 'London Committee' and an 'Eastern Counties Committee' rapidly followed. The *Christian World* also had its own list of subscribers. Advertisements of these committees and statements about the progress of their funds appeared in many papers. The lists of contributors showed from what various sources and in what various sums the money flowed in, and were evidence in themselves of the breadth of support and the depth of feeling that lay behind the whole matter.

Contributions came from individuals all over the country: London, Tunbridge Wells, Leeds, Ashton-under-Lyme, Bristol, Nottingham, Liverpool, Bradford, Frome, Reading, Dublin,

Plymouth, Wisbech . . . hardly a place was unrepresented. And the contributions came from all levels of society: from the proprietor of the *Christian World* and a Member of Parliament, each with sums of £105, to 'A Baptist, Weybridge' with a sum of sixpence. And the contributors' descriptions were themselves of interest. There was 'Half-Inch Wire, 1*s*.', 'Father, Mother, and Five Little Heathens, 5*s*. 0*d*.', and 'Anti-Pestilence, 5*s*. 0*d*'. There was 'Forty Shillings' and 'Damages', each with, appropriately, £2. There was 'Fiat Justitia', and 'Twenty-one Protestants, Claydon', making it clear that not all Rev. Drury's Claydon parishioners had contributed to his presentation Bible or welcomed him on his homeward journey from the trial. And even the birds of the Akenham and Claydon churches – dead or alive – were remembered by 'An Akenham Sparrow'. Some even waxed poetical:

> I tell thee, churlish priest,
> A ministering angel shall my sister be,
> When thou liest howling.

The first London list reported £304 7*s*. 6*d*.; the *Christian World* list, £185 19*s*. 0*d*.; the Eastern Counties list, £140 3*s*. 0*d*.; a joint Eastern Counties and London list, £201 19*s*. 0*d*.; and a later Eastern Counties list, £243 4*s*. 6*d*.

There was no doubt whatever that Mr Wilson's costs would readily be met.

3 *Success and Celebration*

Earlier, the *Ipswich Journal* had felt able, with some elation, to record the homecoming from his trial of the Reverend George Drury. So now (on June 7th), the *East Anglian Daily Times* – backed by the enthusiasm of a much warmer and much wider support – could, with evident delight, print this account of its own celebration:

PRESENTATION TO MR. F. W. WILSON

On Friday afternoon, at the Golden Lion Hotel, Ipswich, the sum of £900, raised by national subscription, for the purpose of defraying the costs in the trial of *Drury v. Wilson*, was publicly presented to Mr. Fred. Wm. Wilson, proprietor and editor of the *East Anglian Daily Times*. The main facts of the case are, of course, in the recollection of almost every newspaper reader in the country, but it may be as well to state that the proceedings arose out of circumstances which occurred at the village of Akenham in August last, when the Rev. Geo. Drury, rector of Claydon and Akenham, interrupted a burial service which was about to be performed in a field outside the churchyard of the latter place by the Rev. Wickham Tozer, Congregational Minister, of Ipswich. Mr Tozer wrote a report of the proceedings, which was inserted in the *East Anglian Daily Times*, and on this and articles from other papers quoted by the *East Anglian Daily Times*, was founded an action for libel, Mr Drury claiming £2,000 for damage done to his character. The action was tried in the Common Pleas Division of the High Court of Justice in March last, and resulted in a verdict for the plaintiff, with forty shillings' damages, which, however, carried costs. Both local and general subscription lists were opened, and about £950 was promptly raised, the subscribers including Peers, Members of Parliament, Magistrates, Liberal and Conservative Churchmen, Nonconformist ministers and laymen, and the proprietors of both London and provincial newspapers. The sum of £900 was devoted to the payment of the costs, and with the balance the committee purchased two magnificent bronzes of armed crusaders, each standing about thirty-three inches high, and a marble dining-room clock, on which was the following inscription: – 'Presented by 600 subscribers in grateful recognition of his services to the cause of religious freedom, equality, and humanity,

235

to Frederick William Wilson, proprietor and editor of the *East Anglian Daily Times*, together with the sum of £900, the amount of costs incurred in defence of the action *Drury* v. *Wilson*, in the High Court of Justice, Westminster. Ipswich, June 6th, 1879.' Lord John Hervey was expected to preside at the presentation ceremony, but was unexpectedly prevented. In his Lordship's absence the chair was occupied by Dr W. A. Elliston, who was supported on his right by Mr Wilson, Mr Carvell Williams, the Rev. J. F. A. Hervey (rector of Shotley), Mr Benjamin Birkett (solicitor to the defendant), and on his left by Mrs Wilson, Mr James Clarke (proprietor and editor of the *Christian World*), Mr J. T. Miller (Claydon Hall), Mr Joseph Smith (churchwarden of Akenham), in all about fifty ladies and gentlemen being present.

The company having partaken of an excellent luncheon, the Chairman, in opening the proceedings, read two letters which had been received from Lord Waveney and Lord John Hervey. Lord Waveney said, 'I regret that I shall not, I fear, be able to attend from my drill work. But I will ask you kindly to express my complete sympathy with the object, and you may remind the hearers that if it depended on the Lords, right would have been done already.' [Applause.] Jord John Hervey wrote as follows: –

Woodlands, Ipswich, June 3rd, 1879.

Dear Sir, – I have made an unfortunate mistake about the day of making the presentation to Mr Wilson, and find I am engaged to be at a place near Grantham on Thursday next, and following days.

I am sincerely sorry for the mistake, which is entirely my own. I am afraid I must give up being at the luncheon. Will you kindly tell Mr Wilson that I fully intended to be present. I do think it was of great importance that attention should be called to the state of things in the parishes of Claydon and Akenham, and I do feel that more still requires to be done.

The civil and ecclesiastical disabilities to which Akenham is now subjected are a scandal to church and country. It is a shame that things should continue as they are, and some public protest ought to be made.

Yours truly,

JOHN W. N. HERVEY

The Chairman again rose to propose the toast 'The Queen', but, before doing so, expressed his extreme regret, which, he said, was doubtless shared by all present, at the absence of Lord John Hervey.

He was quite sure that but for Lord John's many engagements he would have been glad to be present. He gave the health of the Queen, and in so doing he expressed the hope that, in addition to the many beneficent Acts which had been passed in her Majesty's reign, she might live to see the burial laws of the country in such a state that such scenes as that which occurred at Akenham might not possibly take place in the future. *(Applause.)*

The toast having been duly honoured, the Chairman called upon:

Mr Clarke, who read two letters which he had received, the one from the Secretary (Mr A. J. Shepheard), and the other from the Treasurer (Mr Henry Richard, M.P.), of the London Defence Committee. Mr Shepheard said: 'I only got back to town late yesterday afternoon, and find several appointments which quite put it out of my power to go down to Ipswich today. I am very sorry for this, as I should much liked to have been present, and to have joined in the congratulations of the day.' Mr Richard wrote as follows: –

Boscarn, Looe, Cornwall.

My dear Sir, – I am sorry that engagements formed in this part of the country before I was aware of the time fixed for your meeting at Ipswich will deprive me of the pleasure of being with you on Friday. Otherwise, I should have been very glad to have accompanied you and Mr Williams on so interesting an occasion, which will, I hope, subserve a twofold purpose – that of vindicating the right of free discussion, and of administering a rebuke to ecclesiastical intolerance. I am quite sure that there are many members and many clergymen of the Church of England who deplore and deprecate as much as we can do such incidents as that which took place at Akenham, and would gladly see their Church relieved from the danger of the repetition of so great a scandal.

I am, my dear sir, yours very truly,

HENRY RICHARD

Mr Clarke went on to speak of the suddenness with which he had been called upon to make the presentation of the amount of the London subscription, a task which was by no means uncongenial to his feelings. He referred to the circumstances of the Akenham case, and, with reference to the conduct of Mr Tozer, said, whatever the troubles that may have followed upon the visit of this good Samaritan to the house of mourning, he could not fail to have had the approbation of his own conscience and of all men and women who can appreciate a generous and Christian deed. *(Applause.)* A service of Scripture reading and prayer, in a meadow adjoining the dismal spot supposed to be more holy than the surrounding ground, was perfectly lawful and right, and if priestly claims had not interfered with the service no scandal would have occurred; but the solemn and peaceful group of mourners was rudely interrupted and censured by one dedicated to the service of a Master who wept by the side of the grave, and blessed little children as heirs of His kingdom, though they had not been baptized. *(Hear, hear.)* Feelings of indignation, of necessity, had vent, and it was incumbent upon those who had witnessed the outrage to let the world know what social wrongs could be perpetrated in the rural districts of England by ministers of our National Church, in order that public opinion might be aroused to put an end to them; such scenes being not only a disgrace to our professedly Christian character, but to our common humanity. It was no private matter which concerned only the few inhabitants of Akenham; as the many debates on the injustice of our burial laws in the House of Commons, and the condemnation of them in the House of Lords had long before been sufficiently testified. The editor of the *East Anglian Daily Times* did his simple duty in printing the report that was supplied to him by those whom he could trust, and his justification, on public grounds, was shown in the use made of the report by contemporary journals in all parts of the kingdom. *(Cheers.)* It was still possible, however, to make men offenders for a word, and the hero of the story appealed to 'Father Antic, the Law', for protection against certain of the statements and criticisms which his conduct had provoked, and for punishment to be inflicted upon those who had dared to expose what had been done to the public gaze and reprobation. They were well acquainted with the trial that followed, and how after three weary days a jury at Westminster decided that some few of the words printed were too strong, and awarded to Mr George Drury, not the £2,000 that he asked for, but two golden images of her Majesty the Queen as adequate compensation for the injury that had been done to his clerical reputation. *(Laughter and cheers.)* Unfortunately this was a land of costly law, and it not unfrequently happened that the man who gained his cause suffered almost as much as he who lost it. Probably Mr Drury himself did not find the damages he obtained sufficient to meet his disallowed costs. *(Hear, hear and laughter.)* It was because of Mr Wilson's unflinching conduct in a matter of great and growing public interest appertaining to not less than half the nation, that the hundreds of people up and down the land who had subscribed this fund desired to do honour to him by holding him harmless against the costs incurred in the suit – which, it should be remembered, he need not have defended if he had been willing to play the part of a craven journalist and make an abject apology for the report he had permitted to appear. *(Cheers.)* He might thus have had 'peace', but certainly without 'honour' – *(laughter)* – and because he sacrificed ease to duty, he *(Mr Clarke)* had, in the name of the metropolitan and other subscribers to this fund, apart from those in the Eastern Counties, to ask Mr Wilson's acceptance of a cheque for £680. *(Loud cheers.)*

The Chairman next called upon the Rev. J. F. A. Hervey to present to Mr Wilson another cheque, which would make, with the one just presented by Mr Clarke, a handsome sum, by which to express their feelings on this question. Before doing so, however, he would ask them to drink the health of Mr Wilson, and to sympathize with him in all he had had to undergo in the past, and give him their well-wishes for anything that he might have to do in the future that was right and just. *(Cheers.)* Thanks to the spirited course which had been taken by Mr Wilson, and the influence of the press, the story of the Akenham case was circulated throughout the length and breadth of the land, and people who had not thought carefully on this subject began to think whether similar things might not happen to themselves. *(Hear, hear.)* It was a matter that affected everybody, for if anyone was born they must die, and must, as a matter of course, be buried, at least according to the present law, which so far as that went was perfectly just, burial having many advantages over any other system of disposal. But burials must be effected without such scenes as that which took place at Akenham. *(Cheers.)* Speaking of religious intolerance, the chairman said there was still an immense amount of intolerance in the world, and all those who had any leanings towards it could not do better than read a lecture given a few years ago by Professor Max Müller on 'The religious census of the world'. They would be surprised to find what a small number of Protestants – or, in fact, of the whole Christian community – there was in the world, compared even with the Buddhists. He thought it would do us good to reflect on such facts as these. *(Hear, hear.)* If the reformed Protestant Church treated with contumely or indifference those who differed from them, they could not expect to do that good which they ought to do. *(Hear, hear.)*

The toast having been drunk with enthusiasm, the Rev. J. F. A. Hervey rose to present the sum of £220, which, he said, had been raised by Mr Wilson's friends and neighbours in the Eastern Counties, in addition to that which had just been handed over by Mr Clarke, and in doing so he should like to say a word upon the burials question. He did not know how many clergy of the Church of England he could speak for, but he knew that two or three years ago four hundred clergymen signed a memorial in favour of the question being settled consistently with feelings of charity, humanity and religious freedom. *(Cheers.)* The clergy, with whom he thought, regarded the present state of the burial laws, and such occurrences as that which took place at Akenham, with no less feelings of sorrow, of regret, and of shame than could be experienced by any Nonconformists. *(Applause.)* They had no wish to maintain, in connection with the burial of the dead, any exclusive privileges whatever; they only wished that all should stand on an equal footing, and if the present state of things was done away with, they would feel that one more injustice had been swept away, that one of those barriers which tend to separate man from man had been removed. *(Cheers.)* Referring to the inscription which had been placed on the clock, Mr Hervey said he considered Mr Wilson had done a public service, not only in aiding the removal of the unjust burial laws, but in drawing attention to the present scandalous state of the parish of Akenham. He would not refer to any individual, but he did say that the condition of the parish constituted a public scandal. *(Hear, hear.)* He trusted that, though the trial was over, they had not heard the last of Akenham, and that some steps would ere long be taken to remove the scandal and the injury that was caused to true religion by the present state of affairs. The Bishop of Norwich would shortly be visiting this town, and he suggested that a memorial should be presented to him by the inhabitants of the parish, requesting him to institute an inquiry into the condition of the church and the state of the parish. In conclusion the rev. gentleman presented to Mr Wilson the cheque for £220, and the pair of bronzes and clock, as a mark of the confidence and esteem of the subscribers; expressing a wish that he might long live to support the cause of religious freedom, equality, and humanity. *(Loud cheers.)* At a subsequent stage of the proceedings, Mr Hervey read a rough draft of the memorial which he proposed should be presented to the Bishop, and which would be something to the following effect:

We, the undersigned inhabitants of the parish of Akenham, and others, desire most respectfully to call your Lordship's attention to the state of things now and for some years past existing with reference to the condition of the parish church of Akenham and the conduct therein of Divine service. We desire to represent to your Lordship that the interior of the church is in a most neglected and filthy condition, and that the churchwarden is unable to obtain access to the building for the purpose of keeping it in due order and repair; that the fabric itself is falling into ruin and decay, and that Divine service is only performed in it at rare and irregular intervals of time. We, therefore, pray that your lordship will be pleased to direct an inquiry to be held for the purpose of ascertaining by whose default this most unhappy and discreditable state of things has arisen, and in order that the grave public scandal arising from its continuance may as speedily as possible be removed, the church henceforth kept in proper order, and the services duly performed.

Mr Wilson, whose rising was the signal for loud cheering, said they had put into his hands on that day the most difficult task he had ever been called upon to perform, and that was to thank them adequately for the splendid gift with which they had presented him. He did return to them his sincere thanks, and not only to those present, but to the many absent friends who had subscribed. There were times when we could not see the end of things that we undertook, and he certainly had no idea when he inserted the now famous report that such great results would follow. He confessed that at times he had had a little anxiety as to how it would all end, but if he could have foreseen this happy result all anxiety would have vanished. *(Cheers.)* Having been a newspaper proprietor and editor for fifteen years, he knew, when the statement was put into his hands one quiet evening last summer, the pits and quicksands into which its publication might bring him, and worldly wisdom would have dictated the suppression of the report. He felt, however, that, as a journalist, he should fail in his public duty if he withheld the report, for, whichever side might be wrong, it equally proved the necessity for the amendment of our inhuman burial laws. *(Cheers.)* He felt that it was a contest of civilization against barbarism, and Christianity against antiquated superstition. Mr Drury had received forty shillings' damages, which had cost him £120 in money, and much more, he trusted, in regret. Through their liberality he (Mr Wilson) had nothing to pay, and their applause had shown him he had nothing to regret. *(Cheers.)*

Mr Clarke asked leave at this stage of the proceedings to say something about the part Mr Tozer was forced by circumstances to take in this affair. No intimate friendship had prompted him to desire that the service he rendered should not be passed over without some sort of recognition. It seemed evident that if the editor of the *East Anglian Daily Times* was to be commended for inserting in his paper the report of an occurrence of which the public were entitled to be informed, as one of national interest, they were guilty of a manifest absurdity if they said that the writer of the report was not also deserving of commendation and thanks. Had Mr Tozer, Mr Joseph Smith and Mr Edmund Gooding been thinking only of themselves, they would, doubtless, have permitted the indignity offered in their presence to pass without rebuke, but they happened to be English gentlemen, to whom it is not given to submit tamely to oppression, especially at the hands of those persons who, even in the days of Cowper, went about our parishes

> Girt with a bell-rope
> That the Pope had blessed.

Mr Clarke went on to point out that there are times when a selfish prudence was deserving only of our scorn, none of our great reforms having been wrought by prudent people, and Mr Tozer was to be commended, even if he were not too prudent on this occasion. It was not improbable that this miserable superstition and social iniquity would continue until some Nonconformist minister of note should determine to enter a churchyard and conduct a funeral service over the remains of a departed friend. He would, of course, be haled to prison, but the Burial Bill of Mr Osborne Morgan would be passed in both Houses the very next session of Parliament. Looking at the matter in this way, he felt that they owed to Mr Tozer a debt of gratitude, and as a recognition of that debt, combined with a slight attempt at its discharge, and for future encouragement, he asked his acceptance of a cheque for fifty pounds.

The Rev. Wickham Tozer, speaking of a remark of the *Daily Telegraph*, that Mr Drury had a talent for keeping himself in hot water, remarked that this reverend father had another talent, which was equally obvious to all who knew him, and that was, of getting other people into hot water. *(Laughter.)* He certainly managed to get him (Mr Tozer) and several others into very hot water, and kept them there for a good many months. When he sat down to write the simple report of the occurrence at Akenham he little thought he was writing what would be read with avidity and interest in most of the towns of England, in many of the colonies, and in America and other countries. He heartily rejoiced at the success that had attended their efforts to indemnify Mr Wilson for his losses. It was, in his judgment, a duty which the Christian public owed to themselves. He took it that they declared by the presentation that Mr Wilson was perfectly justified in publishing the report, and that they regarded him as representing now the liberty of the press. *(Hear, hear.)* He (Mr Tozer) had been accused of writing too strongly, but it seemed to him that it was not a question of style, nor of strength, but of truth. *(Applause.)* If the strong words were used – and he was sorry to say they were – how could he do otherwise than report them? He carefully considered the step he was taking before he wrote the report, and the question occurred to him whether he ought not to tone down his own words, as it would be very difficult to make people understand the extraordinary provocation he received, but he resolved to be truthful, let the consequences be what they might. *(Cheers.)* He was in the peculiar position of having to report himself as if he were not himself, but a witness of his own acts; otherwise, he should certainly have left out all personal allusions that were not essential to accuracy. He might be permitted to regard the presentation which had been so liberally made to him as an expression of opinion that he had not altogether disgraced himself as a man, or the denomination to which he belonged. *(Hear, hear.)* It had been said by some that he ought to have done more, whilst others said that he ought to have done less. It was all very well for people to sit comfortably in their arm chairs, and say what he ought or ought not to have done, but they should put themselves in his place. *(Laughter and cheers.)* He could not have done more without disgracing himself, and he certainly could not have done less. He went to Akenham to perform an act of brotherly kindness, and he should for ever have been ashamed of himself if he had allowed Mr Drury or anyone else to have prevented him doing it. *(Cheers.)* That simple act of humanity had cost him many anxious days and sleepless nights, but their kinds words and kinder deeds would go very far towards redeeming the episode from the pain and regret with which hitherto he had only been able to regard it. In conclusion, Mr Tozer said if he had done anything which would contribute to the passing of the Burials Bill, it would be the honour, of all others, that he should desire. *(Cheers.)*

Mr Carvell Williams, who was received with cheers, said it was desirable that it should be known that he was down here simply as a member of the committee formed in London for the purpose of raising the money to pay Mr Wilson's costs. He was also drawn here by the fact that circumstances had caused him to take, perhaps, a greater interest in this burials question than any other man in England. He was very much amused whilst listening to the speech of Mr Drury at the opening of the trial, that this affair was planned to aid in the Burials Bill agitation. If the opponents of the burials laws had got the affair

up, surely they would have taken care not to give Mr Drury an opportunity to bring this trial, and to deprive him of the very small triumph
which he had thereby gained. He thought that the people connected
with this transaction were suddenly called upon to perform a very
difficult, and, as far as Mr Tozer was concerned, a very painful task,
and one from which many men would have shrunk. *(Hear, hear.)*
They might fairly have thought

> It not meet at such a time as this
> That every slight event should have its comment.

But Mr Tozer was called upon to face a piece of more than common
intolerance; for Mr Drury's offence lay not in the fact that he refused
to bury the child, but that he stopped and interrupted the service outside the church gates. That was a distinct interference with the liberty
of the subject – *(hear, hear)* – and if after the proceedings had been
published Mr Wilson had abjectly withdrawn his report, a distinct
injury would have been done to the cause of public journalism throughout the country, and clerical bigots would have had their hands
strengthened. He thought it was Daniel Defoe who had said, 'Publicity
is the soul of justice,' and in this case, as in many others, publicity by
means of the press was the only method of inflicting punishment on
offenders against the public. There was nothing which village tyrants
dreaded so much as the publicity which was given to their acts by the
press. He knew that many of the clergy were too wise, too humane, too
Christian, to use the weapon of the burial laws against Nonconformists,
but there were others who,

> Dressed in a little brief authority,
> Play such fantastic tricks before high heaven
> As make the angels weep.

(Laughter and cheers.) Mr Williams went on to speak of the determination of Nonconformists to secure perfect equality in connection
with the burial of the dead, and pointed out that in scarcely any other
country were such obnoxious restrictions placed upon interments.
When he explained the matter to some Americans they were so
astonished that they spoke of sending some missionaries over to England to teach Christianity. The Rev. Mr Hervey had referred to the
petition of four hundred of the clergy for a just settlement of the
burials question, but he asked, with all due respect, what was that
among so many? They must not forget that no less than 14,000 clergy
of the Church of England had signed a memorial in which they ob-

jected to any Nonconformist service whatever being allowed in the churchyards. And this it was which prevented the Government, otherwise so powerful, from dealing in a just manner with this question. It would have to be decided by the electoral body at the approaching general election, and he had no doubt of what the result would be. *(Cheers.)* It had been said that this agitation was got up for the purpose of promoting the disestablishment movement, but he contended that the best thing those who wanted the Church disestablished could desire would be the continuance of the burial laws. Strong as the Church of England was, she was not strong enough to stand many of these Akenham burial scandals – *(applause)* – and there were many who said that the longer these laws were maintained the more likely the Church was to be disestablished. But there were many things which they desired more than disestablishment, and one of these was to have peace in our midst, especially at such solemn times. *(Cheers.)* They did not wish to fight the battle of disestablishment over the tombstones. There, if anywhere, we should meet as fellow men, forgetting our differences while we blend our sympathies, suffering, perhaps, from some common calamity. *(Hear, hear.)*

The Rev. W. Dorling next addressed the meeting, speaking with regret and indignation of the state of things which prevails in the parish of Akenham, and protesting against the horrible, outrageous, and disgraceful condition of our burial laws. He concluded by moving a vote of thanks to the chairman.

Mr R. L. Everett, in seconding the motion, expressed his great surprise at the result of the trial. He thought the burial service was a public ceremony, and consequently liable to be recorded in the public press, and he could not conceive how twelve English jurymen could bring themselves to convict the *East Anglian Daily Times* for libel for publishing the report of the Akenham scene. He was heartily glad that their fellow-townsman would not suffer pecuniarily from the responsible position in which he put himself in performing a public duty – *(cheers)* – and he believed the affair would go a long way towards bringing about an alteration of the law. We had made wonderful progress towards religious freedom, but we were still suffering from one great injustice, which he hoped would soon be removed. *(Applause.)*

The Chairman having returned thanks for the compliment, the Rev. Wickham Tozer said he should like, before the meeting closed, to draw attention to the pecuniary sacrifices which Mr Clarke had made in connection with the affair; for not only had he given £100 to the fund, but he had spent something like £150 more in circulating the facts of the case, not only over the country, but all over the world. *(Cheers.)*

Mr Clarke acknowledged Mr Tozer's remarks, and said the *Christian World* existed for the purpose of doing good, and he was always glad to render any assistance in his power in the cause of right and justice.

Mr Wilson said he might mention what might be called the closing scene of the Akenham case. On the previous evening he assisted at the erection of a tombstone to the little infant who was the cause of their meeting that day. The inscription on it was – 'In memory of Joseph, son of Edward and Sarah Ramsey, who died on his second birthday, August 19, 1878', and underneath was the text, which he trusted they would consider appropriate, 'Suffer little children, and forbid them not, to come unto Me, for of such is the Kingdom of Heaven.' He hoped that this tombstone might long remain at the back of the Akenham churchyard, to 'teach' Mr Drury and the parishioners, though the parishioners were not nearly so much in need of it as the rector of the parish. *(Laughter and cheers.)*

The meeting then broke up.

The story of the Akenham Burial Case was almost ended.

AN ENDING

1 *The Death of Rev. George Drury*

Mr Thurston was not unduly diligent in following up the stories in his Black Book. Why should he be? He was a spectator: fascinated by what went on about him. He conducted his business meticulously, and – that aside – let his eyes rove avidly, restlessly, acutely over the events that took his fancy; the tangled affairs of those areas of social life that interested and concerned him. His set of cuttings on the Akenham Burial Case needed a good deal of supplementation, but, even so, it was enough to indicate the outline of the whole story and its implications. The celebration held on June 7th would have seemed to be the end of the whole affair; and, indeed, from that date onwards the concern and the uproar of the press ceased. No more ink was spilled on it – by way of either pens or printing presses.

But Joseph Thurston had a large human perspective, a long memory and an artist's touch. His keeping of cuttings was a noting down of short stories, a compounding of well-designed novels. One day in the winter of 1895 – on December 7th to be exact – *sixteen years* after the Akenham upheaval, whilst reading the *Suffolk Chronicle* in his room in the Butter Market, his eye caught one more relevant notice. He cut it out, and – finding room for it in his book immediately after the notice of the *East Anglian Daily Times'* celebration – he carefully pasted it in.

THE DEATH OF THE REV. GEORGE DRURY

The Rev. George Drury, who had been rector of Claydon-with-Akenham close upon fifty years, closed his eyes in death on Monday night, after a somewhat chequered experience as a clergyman of the State Church. He was seventy-six years of age, and was partly educated at the Ipswich Grammar School, then in Foundation Street, Ipswich, which street was in former times a strong Roman Catholic centre. Of that school Mr Drury's great-grandfather was headmaster, as well as rector of Claydon. The 'living' came down from great-grandfather and grandfather to the deceased gentleman. Mr Drury's father broke the ecclesiastical succession by entering the army; his mother was a French lady. Mrs Drury died twelve or fourteen years ago. Mr Drury leaves a family of two sons and six daughters; three of the latter are married. The elder son is seeking for his fortune beneath the Southern Cross; the younger, Mr Drew Drury, follows a pastoral life at Barham.

Mr Drury was a gentleman of eclectic tastes, but was better known for his advanced religious dogmas and ritualistic ceremonial. We rather fancy he occasioned some worry to the late Bishop of Norwich, whilst he fairly puzzled some of his parishioners and edified others, some at Ipswich, by his highly developed ritualistic practices in Claydon. The columns of the *Suffolk Chronicle* at the time bore ample proof of the excitement occasioned. Some of the farmers and Mr Drury did not get on well together. Perhaps a disinclination to make sufficient allowance for mutual misappreciation was as evident on one side as on the other. The dissentients had, however, the best of the argument, for the State Church is generally supposed to be a Protestant institution, whilst Mr Drury's ceremonial and teaching showed that as time went on he was a 'day's march nearer home', this last word representing Rome.

We well remember attending one of the midnight Christmas services at Claydon Church many years ago. It was a dreary night. We were bound in the first instance for the hospitable shelter of Claydon Hall, the then inmates of which were greatly annoyed by Mr Drury's ecclesiastical performances. The narrow Church Lane was unfamiliar, but we eventually found ourselves at our destination. After service, however, when rain and snow fell, on our return journey, we missed the road, taking the wrong turning. Where the horse took us to we know not, and are no wiser today. Of that night we have a vivid recollection – not only of the service, which was sufficiently advanced to please the most uncompromising member of the Church Union, but of the weary, wet and perplexing journey to Ipswich. Those intimate with the doings of Providence might perhaps consider such an experience a 'judgment' upon us for visiting the church with hostile intent – anyhow the experience was the reverse of pleasant, and had the late reverend gentleman been aware of it possibly he might have found consolation, have looked upon it as a sly bit of nature's retribution in advance of the descriptive article which we felt it our duty to write upon the extraordinary service which took place, now so many years ago.

Mr Drury was undoubtedly sincere in the course he took. Only a sincere man would have stood the test which he did not shrink from. Some persons may have been disposed to think that sincerity shaded somewhat into obstinacy, but throughout his ritualistic development Mr Drury was consistent. The parish was divided of course. The sturdy Protestant was scandalized; the follower of the rector, if he understood little of the doctrines expounded and still less of the performances at the so-called 'altar', was resolute and uncompromising, and so it happened that dissensions pervaded the parish; and whilst some cried aloud for the intervention of the bishop and for 'the law' – ecclesiastical law being, as is well known, a study in which the wayfaring man, though a fool need not err – others stoutly defended the rector. It was for the time being a somewhat miserable state of things; for the rector it would not have been all pleasantness, for the bewildered people the 'decent church which topped the neighbouring hill' became an object of suspicion. Of course Mr Drury was bound to come into collision with somebody over the grave of the unbaptized. A burial scene occurred at Akenham, and culminated in an action for libel against our daily contemporary, and in this Mr Drury was more successful than he was in converting his parish.

The reverend gentleman went the full length of his ecclesiastical tether. His dogmas were not only as a foreign language to the Claydon rustics, but his attire was a distinct innovation upon conventional habit. Today there is a clerical outfit affected by the advanced school, but nobody went so far in this direction as the rector of Claydon. He not only wore vestments in the church, but by reasons of his biretta, his long skirt, and girdle he became a picturesque object in his parish. His introduction of a nunnery and of nuns emphasized his antagonism to what, perhaps, he may have considered the dry-rot of Protestantism. Father Ignatius, too, made his eccentric start in Claydon under the auspices of Mr Drury. The fervid utterances of that gentleman still live in one's memory, whilst the genuflexions which used to take place in the church suffer no disenchantment by the lapse of years. They are as vivid in outline and fresh in action as though they occurred yesterday. Sometimes it has happened that a daring ecclesiastical innovator like the late rector of Claydon fascinated objectors by the brilliance of his oratory and compelled admiration by the profundity of his thoughts. That was hardly the case with Mr Drury. Not that neatness of epigram was wanting; but there was not the fire of the crusader. There was nothing particularly robust in his pulpit utterances; the excitement of which he became the centre was in the main due to the ceremonial novelties which he introduced. We have a strong desire to guard ourselves against the imputation of dealing unjustly with the memory of the deceased gentleman, for we do not impugn, and never have impugned, his sincerity. What we have said was that being a State clergyman he was either in his wrong place or the ecclesiastical government of the State Church was at fault. He stood by his claim to be considered a parish 'priest' in the ultra sense, and his ecclesiastical

superiors in the diocese appeared to be helpless. The Church pulpit
is a castle from which it is amazingly difficult to dislodge a cleric who,
from it, assaults, in hot and hearty fashion, the Protestant army,
asleep, perhaps, beyond its ramparts. That army in this case was not
asleep, but so far as its action against Mr Drury was concerned it
might as well have been.

Now all is over: the hot contentions; the struggles on behalf of a
revival of faded ecclesiasticism; the wrestling with unsympathizing
spectators – the rector is dead, and one would like to learn something
of the permanent results of the movement of which Claydon was the
obscure scene; whether Nonconformity is anything the worse, or the
State Church the stronger, or the faith of the Claydon people better
defined and more consolidated – whether life is brighter and individual
action more brother-like. There should be some compensatory results
for the turbulence which at one time existed. There may be. We are
setting up no censorship. After the storm comes the calm; what of the
calm?

The rectory of Claydon with Akenham is in the presentation of the
Drury family, and is worth £590 a year.

2   *A Second Funeral*

Five days later, on December 12th, Joseph Thurston took from the *Chronicle* what was to be his final piece.

The remains of the late Rev. George Drury, rector of Claydon and Akenham, were committed to the grave on Saturday afternoon. The procession started from the rectory at half-past two o'clock. The coffin, covered with lovely wreaths of flowers, was carried upon a bier, the bearers wearing blue cassocks and white surplices. A large number of the parishioners followed, all classes being represented, and there were many signs that the deceased rector was highly esteemed and deeply lamented. With the clergy were the choir, at whose head was a cross-bearer, and who wore scarlet cassocks and white surplices. The opening sentences of the Burial Service were sung, and, as the body was borne along the nave and deposited in the chancel, 'I know that my Redeemer liveth' was feelingly played by the organist and choirmaster. Candles had been placed upon the chancel screen, within the chancel, and in the space beyond the communion rails, and these lighted up the somewhat gloomy interior.

During the service the odour of incense could be distinguished. First the hymn 'There is a blessed home' was sung; then the psalm was chanted. The lesson was read by the Rev. R. H. Faulconer, after which the anthem, 'Thou knowest, Lord' (Purcell), was sung by the choir in a manner which reflected the highest credit upon them. The hymn, 'Now the labourer's task is o'er', ended the first portion of the service.

As the body, mourners and congregation left the church the grand 'Dead March' in *Saul* was played upon the organ. The family vault in the churchyard had been opened and in it the body was deposited. At the vault the Rev. E. St G. Cobbold officiated, and at the end of the service the hymn, 'On the resurrection morning', was sung. The inscription on the coffin-plate was –

GEORGE DRURY,

Born March 2nd, 1819.

Died December 2nd, 1895.

R.I.P.

The body was enclosed in an elm shell and a massive oak coffin, lined with lead, with brass fittings. The vault was opened and the masonry work done by Mr C. Watling, of Claydon.

APPENDICES

1 Ipswich Journal: *Provisional Report*

On March 8th, 1879, the *Ipswich Journal* lost its 'parcel' containing its report of the first day's court proceedings; the reason
being given at the end of this piece. Even without the report,
however, it managed to produce this 'provisional' effort – containing not only fact, but also interpretation.

ACTION FOR LIBEL AGAINST THE
EAST ANGLIAN DAILY TIMES

HIGH COURT OF JUSTICE. – COMMON PLEAS DIVISION
Yesterday (Friday), March 7
(Before Mr Justice Grove)
DRURY *v.* WILSON

This was an action for damages for a libel alleged to be contained in a
report in the *East Anglian Daily Times*.

Mr Day, Q.C., Mr Merewether, Q.C., and Mr Poyser were counsel for
the plaintiff, instructed by Messrs Aldridge, Thorn, and Morris;
Mr Serjeant Parry, Mr Bulwer, Q.C., and Mr K. Digby were counsel
for the defendant, instructed by Mr Field Roscoe, for Messrs Birkett
and Bantoft.

Mr Poyser stated that the plaintiff was the rector of Akenham and
Claydon, in Suffolk; and the defendant was the publisher of the *East
Anglian Daily Times*. The defendant admitted that he published the
newspaper, and he pleaded that the paragraph was true, and also he
said that they were matters of public interest, and that the statements
did not exceed the bounds of ordinary criticism. Upon these pleas
issue was joined.

Mr Day, Q.C., stated the case for the plaintiff, and remarked that the
defence to the action was simply for the purpose of fostering and
fomenting a religious and political agitation, which ought not to be
introduced to the consideration of a jury. This action was brought by
the Rev. George Drury, the rector of Akenham and Claydon, in Suffolk,
and he complained of gross imputations cast upon him by the defendant, who was the Editor of the *East Anglian Daily Times*, a daily
paper published at Ipswich, and circulated throughout the county,
in a report of the burial of a little child two years old, of some poor

9

people living at Akenham. He could not help thinking, and he thought the jury would also speedily arrive at the conclusion, that the funeral was not dealt with as funerals should be. It was a most solemn occasion when parents gathered on the side of the grave, and these circumstances were taken advantage of by persons other than these parents, for the purpose of making an ostentatious display, which might have the effect of worrying and disturbing the clergyman on the one hand, and on the other hand of fostering the agitation for throwing open the burial grounds of the Church of England to other than the Church ministers. For some years past an agitation to that effect had been going on, and no doubt the promoters of the scene at Akenham church-yard thought that a favourable occasion presented itself for making a demonstration. Now in this particular parish there were very few parishioners who were members of the Church of England. The farmers were nearly all members of the various Dissenting denominations, and, perhaps, as a natural consequence, very few of the labourers were members of the Church of England. They would see that the articles which formed the subject of this action reflected upon the character of his client, as if he were the cause of the comparatively neglected state in which the church was found. On the occasion of this funeral communication was made with Mr Drury. The father called upon him and requested him to make arrangements for the burial of the child, and such arrangements were made, and he was prepared to discharge his duty as directed by the ritual of the Church of England. This funeral was taken advantage of – he would not say by the parents of this child, because he thought they were made a stalking-horse by agitators who wanted to make capital out of it. Mr Drury was very well known to be a clergyman who was a strict adherent to the ritual of the Church of England, and one who would not allow anything to be done which the law and the Church prohibited. It was not a matter now for consideration whether the Church of England should be established or should not, or whether any other religion should be established in its place, or whether there should be no religion established at all. Certain regulations were laid down in the rubrics of the Church of England, and Mr Drury was bound to obey them. Mr Drury was perfectly willing to provide for this child's burial in accordance with the rules and regulations of the Church of England, and at the instance of the father he appointed a Thursday afternoon for the burial, and nothing was said as to the circumstances or character of the funeral. Mr Drury had no communication with the father from that day until the body of the child was brought to be interred. But it was brought to his knowledge during the week that the child was the child of a member of the Baptist persuasion, and that he had not been baptized. Mr Drury was well aware that the Prayer-book of the Church of England stated that the rubric for the burial of the dead was not to be used for any that died unbaptized. It might occur to the minds of many people that it ought not to be so used, but that had nothing to do with the present enquiry. It was part of the law of the land that this office should not be used with respect to persons unbaptized. The Church of England considered that the right of baptism was an initiatory right into that Church, and that persons who had not been admitted into the Church were held not entitled to the use of its services. The plaintiff communicated with the father of the child that as the child had not been baptized it could not be buried with the services of the Church of England. This opportunity was too good to be lost, and two large farmers – themselves Dissenters – took care that there should be a religious service, if not in the churchyard, yet at all events under such circumstances that it should have a good political effect. He did not suppose that they expected any moral good from the service. They secured the services of two Dissenting ministers from Ipswich. The parents of the child were Baptists, but from some reason or other the Baptist minister did not interfere, but the Rev. Mr Tozer, an Independent minister, gladly availed himself of the opportunity of thrusting himself forward into the agitation. The funeral was put off until Friday. In the libel it was stated that the child was 'buried like a dog in unconsecrated ground', but did the Rev. Mr Tozer believe that, or did the parents believe that any benefit could be derived by the child from being buried in ground which, to use a phrase in the libel, had been 'subjected to the legerdemain of priests'. It happened, however, that the fact was that the child had not been buried in unconsecrated ground at all, for the ground was consecrated some 1,100 or 1,200 years ago. The whole of the ground was consecrated at the same time, so far as was known. It was an old custom in the church of Claydon, derived from times when that church was not, that a part of the churchyard should be set apart for those who were not of its community. He believed that the south side of the burial ground was the fashionable side, and the north side had therefore been set apart for those who were unbaptized. A grave was dug for this child on the north side of the churchyard. This did not affect the child; it scarcely affected the Rev. Mr Tozer; and as to the editor of the *East Anglian Daily Times*, probably he hardly knew the difference between the various points of the compass, even in a churchyard. The learned gentleman then read at great length the first libel, which consisted of a long account of the funeral of the child, in the course of which there was a long contest between the plaintiff and the Rev. Mr Tozer, who performed a burial service outside the church-yard, the plaintiff asking that the child should be buried first and the service read afterwards, so that he might not be detained. The learned counsel also said that this account was written by the Rev. Mr Tozer, and, therefore, very fully showed the feelings which animated him.

[Our parcel by the Great Eastern Railway was miscarried, and we are compelled to defer our report till Tuesday's paper, when we shall give it in full.]

2 *Burial Laws Amendment Act*, 1880

The newspaper reports already cited give ample proof of the widespread public feeling that the Akenham Burial Case aroused. But there is another area of evidence I have not (because of space) even been able to touch. For twenty years, the burials question had been debated by both Commons and Lords before, finally, the Act of 1880 was passed. The pages of *Hansard* are filled with speeches* remarkable for unbelievable prejudice, for careful legal nicety and balance, for outright fear of the crumbling of the Established Church, for nauseous good humour (from the Conservative side – when their case was almost lost), and many other variable qualities. Here, it may be of interest just to indicate the scale and kinds of grievances felt throughout the country, and the way in which the English (Established) Church seemed so much more intransigent than others, both at home and abroad.

The scale of grievance was best illustrated from Wales. Mr Roberts, from Abergele, claimed that the difficulty was by no means:

> . . . a manufactured or fancied grievance, *but a real practical grievance*, with which they were brought into contact almost daily. The majority of the people of Wales were Noncomformists; the cemeteries in the Principality were few in number, and very unequally distributed. Such burial-grounds as were attached to chapels were generally very limited in area; so that, as a matter of fact, parish churchyards in most districts formed the only burial-grounds available, and it was unfair that the right to use these parish burial-grounds should be clogged with onerous conditions by imposing the use of a Service which, though beautiful and appropriate, was distasteful because it was enforced upon them, and by debarring Nonconformist ministers from saying a word of comfort or of exhortation to their own people at the grave-side of their departed friends.

He gave examples drawn from the most eminent and the most ordinary people alike.

* The examples quoted here are drawn, very selectively, from debates in the House of Commons and the House of Lords between 1878 and 1880.

Reference had been made, he believed, in the House before to the funeral of the Rev. Henry Rees, the father-in-law of the hon. Member for Anglesey. Nearly 1,000 people had travelled from Liverpool, a distance of eighty miles, to attend the funeral of their pastor, and yet they were not allowed to hear a word spoken in the churchyard by any of the well-known ministers who were present. Similar cases had occurred since that time . . .

At Abergele, last spring, arrangements were duly made for the interment of an old woman in humble circumstances; the hour was fixed, the bell was tolled, and, as was the custom in Wales, a considerable number assembled to pay their last token of respect to the deceased; but the curate – generally very attentive to his duties – had forgotten the engagement; the vicar not being at home, the interment had to take place without any service, though the minister of the Presbyterian church, to which the deceased belonged, was at the graveside. An old man, however – a layman – ventured to break the law, and to offer up a short prayer before the friends left the churchyard. Those, therefore, who knew the condition of Wales, and the feeling of the people there, could readily understand that the Welsh were very anxious to have this grievance removed.

John Bright later substantiated the scale of this Welsh grievance with evidence collected by his friend Mr Richard (Member for Merthyr).

'In Carnarvonshire the Calvinistic Methodists, Independents, and Baptists have 240 chapels – of these 35 have graveyards and 205 have none. In Anglesea, there are 147 chapels belonging to the same Bodies – 25 have graveyards, and 122 have none. In Flintshire, the Calvinistic Methodists and Independents have 113 chapels – 13 of these have graveyards and 100 none. In Merionethshire the three denominations have 173 chapels – of these 46 have graveyards and 127 have none. In Denbighshire the Calvinistic Methodists and Independents have 133 chapels – of these 27 have graveyards and 106 have none. In Montgomeryshire the same two denominations have 155 chapels – of these 27 have graveyards, and 128 have none. In Cardiganshire the Methodists and Independents have 150 chapels – of these 48 have graveyards and 102 have none. In Carmarthenshire the three denominations have 225 chapels – of these 149 have graveyards and 76 have none. In Glamorganshire the Calvinistic Methodists and Independents have 332 chapels – of these 162 have graveyards and 170 have none.'

The total result is that, out of 1,668 chapels, only 532 have grave-yards, and 1,136 have none. And my hon. Friend has since stated an additional fact – namely, 'The Wesleyan Methodists (as distinguished from Calvinistic Methodists) have in North Wales 210 Welsh chapels; of these three have graveyards and 207 have none. In South Wales they have 101; of these 18 have graveyards and 83 none.' Therefore, in 1,426 out of 1,979 cases no burial grounds are attached to Dissenting chapels in Wales. I need not tell the House that, exclusive of Scotland, there is no portion of this Southern part of the Island in which the Established Church has done so little for the people as in Wales.

But the grievance extended far beyond the situation in Wales. There were, for example, recurring Catholic/Protestant difficulties. One was cited by Major Nolan.

At Shoeburyness, where there is a large garrison, not long ago – in March last – a Catholic soldier died. There they were obliged to have him buried under Protestant rites. This fact, as I have said, is entirely within my own personal observation – indeed, the soldier belonged to my own battery, and I had to make most of the arrangements for the funeral. A Catholic clergyman was allowed to say prayers in the dead-house of the garrison – there was no objection to that; but when the funeral procession arrived at the churchyard the Protestant clergyman performed the rest of the ceremony, and the comrades of the man who had lived all his life a Catholic saw him at the last moment handed over to a Protestant clergyman. It was not the fault of the military authorities that this happened, for there was no cemetery within forty miles. I say that the existing state of the law inflicts a great grievance, and I hope that it may be amended somehow.

Another distasteful scene – in Oxfordshire – was mentioned by Mr Walter.

'I remember some years since attending the funeral of a much re-spected Roman Catholic at Dorchester, whose ancestors were in the churchyard for many generations. The Roman Catholic bishop attended at the grave, when, in order to show their distaste to a Protestant ser-vice, he and all the relatives turned round their backs to the officiating clergyman. I never have forgotten the scene; and in order to prevent such a repetition I gladly accept the measure which will allow their burial by their own pastors.'

The Lord Chancellor, introducing the first reading of the final Bill in the House of Lords, in May 1880, made it very plain that extreme degrees of grievance existed, mentioning, as one example:

A case of certain Primitive Methodists in Norfolk who had been prosecuted by a clergyman because, having said prayers up to the entrance to the churchyard, but not beyond it, and having committed their dead to the ground, at the close of the church service they sang over the grave a hymn which was, in itself, perfectly unobjectionable . . .

Your lordships may depend upon it that this is not a case in which you can put the question aside, or decline to accept the responsibility of dealing with it, on the ground either that it is no grievance at all, or that it is an unimportant and a diminishing grievance.

There was also, he stressed, another source of grievance which could not be overcome by the expedient of setting up *separate* cemeteries and churchyards. Quoting an earlier formulation of Mr Plunket's (1824):

'The allotment of separate burial-places . . . would go to outrage the very commonest and yet most sacred feelings of humanity. It would have the effect, in many cases, of separating families as to their places of burial. A husband could not be buried with his wife, a brother near his brother, a father by the side of his son.'

He went on to describe:

. . . the case of a son who was a Churchman, whose mother, being a Dissenter, was buried in a Dissenting burial-ground with, I think, two children and a second wife of the father. On the death of the father the son, as a Churchman, determined to bury him in the churchyard, and not enduring the notion of separating in death his father's and his mother's remains, he gained access to the Nonconformist burial-ground, disturbed the ground and the remains which were buried there, and unlawfully took away, after the lapse of several years, the corpse of the mother, in order that it might be placed in the churchyard with that of his father at the time of the father's burial. Although the action was justly condemned by law, and is not likely to find imitators, yet I think it is a good illustration of the strength and depth of those feelings which make us desire to lie in death near to those whom we have loved in life.

The same point was emphasized by many. Mr Osborne Morgan read out – as an absurdity in which the law resulted – a short cutting from *The Times*, signed: 'A Sufferer'.

My first wife, a member of the Church of England, died and was buried in the consecrated portion of our public cemetery. My second wife was a Roman Catholic, and, of course, I laid her remains in the Roman Catholic portion. I am neither a Churchman nor a Romanist; but I had hoped that one of those two graves at least might be made available for myself. Our local authorities, however, say 'No', unless I agree to the religious Service; and when I complain of the hardship of having to pay for a third grave in the cemetery in which I have already purchased two, they point out that, under the circumstances, my proper course would have been to have married two Nonconformists.

And Mr H. H. Fowler took issue with the sneering innuendo of one bishop at the idea that the families of the middle and working classes should have the same sentiments – or pretensions? – as those of the aristocracy.

He *(Mr Fowler)* could understand that some representative of one of our great houses, whose family history had run side by side with our national history, would regard it as an extreme dishonour to be excluded from the last resting-place of his illustrious forefathers; and he could understand that to such a one the ancestral association would be a reality which would not attach to any modern cemetery. But . . . to Nonconformists, the words 'father', 'mother', 'husband', 'wife', 'parent', 'child', were as dear as they were to the proudest Peer that ever sat at Westminster; and though Nonconformists might lack 'ancestral association', they cherished in its deepest intensity that feeling of kinship, friendship, and affection which today, as 3,000 years ago, found its truest expression in the passionate utterance of the Jewish widow – 'Thy people shall be my people, Where thou diest will I die, and there will I be buried.' Not as Nonconformists, not as professing any creed, but on the ground of our common humanity, they claimed and clung to the common right of which nothing but an intolerant or vindictive legislation could deprive them – that of unbroken union in the last home, the family grave.

Finally, examples were given of the much greater degree of tolerance, compassion, and common kindliness shown – over this matter of burials – by other churches elsewhere. The 'case for Scotland' was put by Sir Charles Forster.

. . . as reference has been made to the liberality of the Scotch Church as to burials, I wish to give an instance of it which will powerfully appeal to the feelings of those hon. Members who sat, as I did for many Sessions, with the late Lord Marjoribanks, better known as David Robertson, the genial and popular Member for Berwickshire. When I visited him some time back at his hospitable abode at Lady-kirk, I was shown the parish church, rich in ancestral monuments and memorials of Flodden Field. There, not in the churchyard, but in what before the change of religion was the altar chancel, the vault of the Robertson family was situated. There, Sir, some few years after-wards, the honoured remains of our lamented friend were gathered to his kindred dust, the service being conducted in the old Scotch kirk according to the Episcopalian rites, and the words of interment pro-nounced by his own Episcopalian minister. Why will not English Churchmen take an example from Scotch Presbyterians in this respect, by throwing open their burial-grounds to their Dissenting brethren? Talk of additional cemeteries, silent burials, or approved selected ser-vices as fitting solutions of the question! Surely the true solution is to be found in the combination of common sense with the slightest tinc-ture of Christian charity.

A similar case was described by Mr A. M'Arthur from Ireland.

A friend of his who lived in one of the large towns of Ireland, informed him that a respectable Nonconformist died there not long ago, and in accordance with the only formality that was required, notice had to be given to the clergyman that a Burial Service was to be held in the churchyard. The time fixed happened to be the same time at which a Service was to be held in the church. The clergyman, instead of object-ing to the funeral taking place, wrote a very kind note to the Noncon-formist minister in which, after regretting the event, he said that he did not think the funeral would at all interfere with the Service in the Church, and, therefore, begged that it might proceed. Now, if they had a little more of that kindly spirit in England, and a little more of that disposition to meet each other in a friendly way, he thought a great many of the fears that had been expressed would be found to be groundless.

And Mr James Howard mentioned another example of Roman

Catholic tolerance when a friend of his, who had lived for several years in France, and now lived in Paris, lost his wife.

He desired to bury the body of his wife in a village churchyard in a different part of France, and where some other members of his family had been buried many years before. The funeral party went up from Paris to this village churchyard, accompanied by a Protestant clergyman, who conducted the service. They were met at the gates by the Roman Catholic priest, who appeared most cordial throughout. It occurred to his mind, upon the occasion, why should not the English Church on this burial question be as tolerant as the intolerant Roman Catholic Church?

But perhaps the most striking example was that presented by Mr Osborne Morgan. Arguing that the laity of England was becoming ashamed of the opposition being offered to the Bill, he went on:

They were ashamed of being told, when they went to Austria or Russia, or even to Turkey, that England on this question was lagging behind the most bigoted countries in Europe. Why, Cyprus was miles ahead of us in this matter. The other day an English soldier was buried in one of the parish churchyards of the Greek Church in Cyprus. Now, if a Greek sailor had happened to die in a rural parish in England, everybody knew that he could only have been buried by an Anglican clergyman with the rites of the Anglican Church. But what took place in Cyprus? Why, the Burial Service of the English Church was conducted by an English chaplain. A Greek priest was present, but the only part he took in the service was to bless the grave! Well now, he really thought that poor Greek priest might have taught a lesson of Christian charity to many an Anglican bishop; and if the acquisition of that unfortunate island should lead us to assimilate our Burial Laws to those of other and more barbarous counties, he, for one, would feel almost disposed to condone the means by which it was acquired.

Osborne Morgan was certainly right in this; many of the clergy of the Church of England were themselves sickened by the position adopted by some of their leading spokesmen. All too often the arguments of the Established Church showed themselves to be rooted in one thing only – stated very plainly (and approvingly!) in the Commons by Mr Newdegate.

Let the House remember that the proof of continuous identity in doctrines and services is . . . shown to be essential to the validity of the title to all religious and denominational property. By the principle of this Bill, the introduction of the various and diverse Services of different denominations into the churchyards of the denomination to which I belong will fundamentally invalidate our title to that property, and, in this respect, place the Church of England, as a denomination, in a position of inferiority, as compared with every other denomination in this country.

Property! Property! Property! That was the cry of the Church of England. But – after twenty years of debate, after ten years of intense and persistent campaigning, and helped by the final explosion of the Akenham Burial Case – the opposition was defeated. The Act that resulted is as follows.

BURIAL LAWS AMENDMENT ACT, 1880

An Act to amend the Burial Laws.

[7th September 1880.]

WHEREAS it is expedient to amend the law of burial in England and the Channel Islands:

Be it therefore enacted by the Queen's most Excellent Majesty, by and with the advice and consent of the Lords Spiritual and Temporal, and Commons, in this present Parliament assembled, and by the authority of the same, as follows:

After passing of Act notice may be given that burial will take place in churchyard or graveyard without the rites of the Church of England.

1. After the passing of this Act any relative, friend, or legal representative having the charge of or being responsible for the burial of a deceased person may give forty-eight hours notice in writing, indorsed on the outside 'Notice of Burial,' to, or leave or cause the same to be left at the usual place of abode of the rector, vicar, or other incumbent, or in his absence the officiating minister in charge of any parish or ecclesiastical district or place, or any person appointed by him to receive such notice, that it is intended that such deceased person shall be buried within the churchyard or graveyard of such parish or ecclesiastical district or place without the performance, in the manner prescribed by law, of the service for the burial of the dead according to the rites of

the Church of England, and after receiving such notice no rector, vicar, incumbent, or officiating minister shall be liable to any censure or penalty, ecclesiastical or civil, for permitting any such burial as aforesaid. Such notice shall be in writing, plainly signed with the name and stating the address of the person giving it, and shall be in the form or to the effect of Schedule (A.) annexed to this Act.

The word 'graveyard' in this Act shall include any burial ground or cemetery vested in any burial board, or provided under any Act relating to the burial of the dead, in which the parishioners or inhabitants of any parish or ecclesiastical district have rights of burial; and in the case of any such burial ground or cemetery, if a chaplain is appointed to perform the burial service of the Church of England therein, notice under this Act shall be addressed to such chaplain, but the same shall be given to or left at the office of the clerk of the burial board, if any, in whom any such burial ground or cemetery may be vested: Provided also, that it shall be lawful for the proprietors or directors of any proprietary cemetery or burial ground to make such byelaws or regulations as may be necessary for enabling any burial to take place therein in accordance with the provisions of this Act, any enactment to the contrary notwithstanding.

Paupers.

2. Such notice, in the case of any poor person deceased, whom the guardians of any parish or union are required or authorised by law to bury, may be given to the rector, vicar, or other incumbent in manner aforesaid, and also to the master of any workhouse in which such poor person may have died, or otherwise to the said guardians, by the husband, wife, or next of kin of such poor person, who, for the purposes of this Act, shall be deemed to be the person having the charge of the burial of such deceased poor person; and in any such case it shall be the duty of the said guardians to permit the body of such deceased person to be buried in the manner provided by this Act.

Time of burial to be stated, subject to variation.

3. Such notice shall state the day and hour when such burial is proposed to take place, and in case the time so

stated be inconvenient on account of some other service
having been, previously to the receipt of such notice,
appointed to take place in such churchyard or graveyard, or the church or chapel connected therewith, or
on account of any byelaws or regulations lawfully in
force in any graveyard limiting the times at which burials
may take place in such graveyard, the person receiving
the notice shall, unless some other day or time shall be
mutually arranged within twenty-four hours from the
time of giving or leaving such notice, signify in writing,
to be delivered to or left at the address or usual place of
abode of the person from whom such notice has been
received, or at the house where the deceased person is
lying, at which hour of the day named in the notice, or
(in case of burial in a churchyard, if such day shall be a
Sunday, Good Friday, or Christmas Day) of the day
next following, such burial shall take place; and it shall
be lawful for the burial to take place, and it shall take
place, at the hour so appointed or mutually arranged,
and in other respects in accordance with the notice:
Provided that, unless it shall be otherwise mutually
arranged, the time of such burial shall be between the
hours of ten o'clock in the forenoon and six o'clock in the
afternoon if the burial be between the first day of April
and the first day of October, and between the hours of
ten o'clock in the forenoon and three o'clock in the afternoon if the burial be between the first day of October and
the first day of April: Provided also, that no such burial
shall take place in any churchyard on Sunday, or on
Good Friday or Christmas Day, if any such day being
proposed by the notice shall be objected to in writing
for a reason assigned by the person receiving such notice.

Burial to take place accordingly.

4. When no such intimation of change of hour is sent
to the person from whom the notice has been received,
or left at the house where the deceased person is lying,
the burial shall take place in accordance with and at the
time specified in such notice.

Regulations and fees.

5. All regulations as to the position and making of the
grave which would be in force in such churchyard or
graveyard in the case of persons interred therein with
the service of the Church of England shall be in force as

to burials under this Act; and any person who, if the burial had taken place with the service of the Church of England, would have been entitled by law to receive any fee, shall be entitled, in case of a burial under this Act, to receive the like fee in respect thereof.

6. At any burial under this Act all persons shall have free access to the churchyard or graveyard in which the same shall take place. The burial may take place, at the option of the person so having the charge of or being responsible for the same as aforesaid, either without any religious service, or with such Christian and orderly religious service at the grave, as such person shall think fit; and any person or persons who shall be thereunto invited, or be authorised by the person having the charge of or being responsible for such burial, may conduct such service or take part in any religious act thereat. The words 'Christian service' in this section shall include every religious service used by any church, denomination, or person professing to be Christian.

Burial may be with or without religious service.

7. All burials under this Act, whether with or without a religious service, shall be conducted in a decent and orderly manner; and every person guilty of any riotous, violent, or indecent behaviour at any burial under this Act, or wilfully obstructing such burial or any such service as aforesaid thereat, or who shall, in any such churchyard or graveyard as aforesaid, deliver any address, not being part of or incidental to a religious service permitted by this Act, and not otherwise permitted by any lawful authority, or who shall, under colour of any religious service or otherwise, in any such churchyard or graveyard, wilfully endeavour to bring into contempt or obloquy the Christian religion, or the belief or worship of any church or denomination of Christians, or the members or any minister of any such church or denomination, or any other person, shall be guilty of a misdemeanour.

Burials to be conducted in a decent and orderly manner and without obstruction.

8. All powers and authorities now existing by law for the preservation of order, and for the prevention and punishment of disorderly behaviour in any churchyard or graveyard, may be exercised in any case of burial under this Act in the same manner and by the same

Powers for prevention of disorder.

persons as if the same had been a burial according to the rites of the Church of England.

Act not to give right of burial where no previous right existed.

9. Nothing in this Act shall authorise the burial of any person in any place where such person would have had no right of interment if this Act had not passed, or without performance of any express condition on which, by the terms of any trust deed, any right of interment in any burial ground vested in trustees under such trust deed, not being the churchyard or graveyard, or part of the churchyard or graveyard, of the parish or ecclesiastical district in which the same is situate, may have been granted.

Burials under Act to be registered.

10. When any burial has taken place under this Act the person so having the charge of or being responsible for such burial as aforesaid shall, on the day thereof, or the next day thereafter, transmit a certificate of such burial, in the form or to the effect of Schedule (B.) annexed to this Act, to the rector, vicar, incumbent, or other officiating minister in charge of the parish or district in which the churchyard or graveyard is situate or to which it belongs, or in the case of any burial ground or cemetery vested in any burial board to the person required by law to keep the register of burials in such burial ground or cemetery, who shall thereupon enter such burial in the register of burials of such parish or district, or of such burial ground or cemetery, and such entry shall form part thereof. Such entry, instead of stating by whom the ceremony of burial was performed, shall state by whom the same has been certified under this Act. Any person who shall wilfully make any false statement in such certificate, and any rector, vicar, or minister, or other such person as aforesaid, receiving such certificate, who shall refuse or neglect duly to enter such burial in such register as aforesaid, shall be guilty of a misdemeanour.

Order of coroner or certificate of registrar to be delivered to relative, &c., instead of to person who buries.

11. Every order of a coroner or certificate of a registrar given under the provisions of section seventeen of the Births and Deaths Registration Act, 1874, shall, in the case of a burial under that Act, be delivered to the relative, friend, or legal representative of the deceased, having the charge of or being responsible for the burial,

instead of being delivered to the person who buries or performs any funeral or religious service for the burial of the body of the deceased; and any person to whom such order or certificate shall have been given by the coroner or registrar who fails so to deliver or cause to be delivered the same shall be liable to a penalty not exceeding forty shillings, and any such relative, friend, or legal representative so having charge of or being responsible for the burial of the body of any person buried under this Act as aforesaid, as to which no order or certificate under the same section of the said Act shall have been delivered to him, shall, within seven days after the burial, give notice thereof in writing to the registrar, and if he fail so to do shall be liable to a penalty not exceeding ten pounds.

12. No minister in holy orders of the Church of England shall be subject to any censure or penalty for officiating with the service prescribed by law for the burial of the dead according to the rites of the said church in any unconsecrated burial ground or cemetery or part of a burial ground or cemetery, or in any building thereon, in any case in which he might have lawfully used the same service, if such burial ground or cemetery or part of a burial ground or cemetery had been consecrated. The relative, friend, or legal representative having charge of or being responsible for the burial of any deceased person who had a right of interment in any such unconsecrated ground vested in any burial board, or provided under any Act relating to the burial of the dead, shall be entitled, if he think fit, to have such burial performed therein according to the rites of the Church of England by any minister of the said church who may be willing to perform the same. *Liberty to use burial service of Church of England in unconsecrated ground.*

13. From and after the passing of this Act, it shall be lawful for any minister in holy orders of the Church of England authorised to perform the burial service, in any case where the office for the burial of the dead according to the rites of the Church of England may not be used, and in any other case at the request of the relative, friend, or legal representative having the charge of or being responsible for the burial of the deceased, to use at the *Relief of clergy of Church of England from penalties in certain cases.*

burial such service, consisting of prayers taken from the
Book of Common Prayer and portions of Holy Scripture,
as may be prescribed or approved of by the Ordinary,
without being subject to any ecclesiastical or other
censure or penalty.

Saving as to ministers of Church of England. 14. Save as is in this Act expressly provided as to ministers of the Church of England, nothing herein contained shall authorise or enable any such minister who shall not have become a declared member of any other Church or denomination, or have executed a deed of relinquishment under the Clerical Disabilities Act, 1870, to do any act which he would not by law have been authorised or enabled to do if this Act had not passed, or to exempt him from any censure or penalty in respect thereof.

Application of Act. 15. This Act shall extend to the Channel Islands, but shall not apply to Scotland or to Ireland.

Short title of Act. 16. This Act may be cited as the Burial Laws Amendment Act, 1880.

SCHEDULES to which this Act refers

SCHEDULE (A)
Notice of Burial

I   , of   , being the relative
[*or* friend, *or* legal representative, *as the case may be, describing the relation, if a relative,*] having the charge of or being responsible for the burial of *A.B.*, of   , who died at
in the parish of   on the   day of   ,
do hereby give you notice that it is intended by me that the body of the said *A.B.* shall be buried within the [*here describe the churchyard or graveyard in which the body is to be buried,*] on the   day of   , at the hour of   , without the
performance in the manner prescribed by law of the service for the burial of the dead according to the rites of the Church of England, and I give this notice pursuant to the Burial Laws Amendment Act, 1880.

To the Rector [*or, as the case may be,*] of

Schedule (b)

I   , of   , the person having
the charge of (*or* being responsible for) the burial of the deceased, do
hereby certify that on the   day of   ,
A.B. of   , aged   , was buried in the
churchyard [*or* graveyard] of the parish [*or* district] of   .

To the Rector [*or, as the case may be,*] of   .

3 Rev. George Drury: Some Characteristics (by his grandson)

Rev. George Drury's rectory (now the 'Old Rectory') at Claydon, was bought by Sir Laurence Grafftey-Smith, now of Coddenham, Suffolk, when he moved to England from France in 1960. Shortly after moving to the rectory, he had tried to find out more about Drury. His inquiry – addressed to the surviving Drury in Australia – had been passed on to Mr J. F. Warrington-Rogers, then of Hertfordshire, who was Drury's grandson (son of a daughter of Drury). The following is the letter Sir Laurence received. It is with his permission that it is published here, and the notes incorporated with it are his own.

August 1st, 1961

Dear Sir Laurence,

My cousin G. R. Drury has written asking me to tell you what I know of Claydon Rectory, and sent me your letter to him.

My Mother was a Drury, so the Rev. G. Drury was my grandfather, and all the history of their family I know of was told to me by her and by her sisters, my aunts. My grandfather was rather a stern and certainly a clever man, and always taking up some special hobby: when he had mastered it, he started another. The two gazebos and kitchen-garden wall were built by him to resemble a ruin, and I remember Ecclesiastical Commissioners made the Drurys do it up, in spite of their violent protests. In the field in the Rectory grounds there was a brick-kiln he had made.

I was born in December 1881, and he died when I was about 10 years old, and he must have been in the 70s then.

He also had quite a bit added to the Rectory to make more room for the servants. The grotto was built for his sisters in his father's time, and they used to drive over to Aldeburgh and collect the shells which cover the interior.[1]

When my grandfather came to live at Claydon Rectory, he changed the services in the Church from low to very high Church, and the Claydon people were mad about it. He had the 9-foot wall built along the road passing the Rectory, as they were always throwing stones and shouting: 'NO POPERY!'

Brother, later Father, Ignatius[2] came as a sort of pupil to him, and one incident I remember was when the local butcher had a big bonfire, Brother Ignatius happened to be passing and the butcher seized him and was going to throw him on the fire when an old woman rushed out and hit the butcher on the head with a pair of tongs or a poker, and Brother Ignatius got safely away. I may say that when my grandfather died, the people petitioned my uncle Drue Drury[3] to get someone for the living who would carry on the services as grandfather had, i.e. High Church.

I must tell you of the Lady in Grey who is supposed to haunt the Rectory. I never knew who she really was, but when the new rooms were added, my grandfather moved from his bedroom to one of the new rooms at the other end of the corridor, and the Lady in Grey used to walk to the room, and several times the key of the old room was found on the bed of the new room, where the old bed had been moved to. My Father, who was then engaged to my Mother, was staying with them and went up to the old room, which had become the guest chamber. He had not heard about the Lady in Grey, who had not been seen for some years, and when he came back to them, he said: 'I did not know that you had any-one else staying here.' They all said: 'There is no one else staying here except Father, who is in his study. What do you mean?' He said: 'I passed a lady in the corridor just now.' They said: 'What did you do?' He said: 'I bowed to her and she bowed to me, and we passed on.' They asked how she was dressed, and he said: 'She had a grey dress on.' Great excitement.

Some years later, my Aunt Nell Drury, who was married to Admiral Theobald and had a son Geoffrey about six years old, put Geoff on their bed in the guest chamber, and later on went up-stairs to put him into the little dressing-room, adjoining. He said: 'Mummy, such a dear old lady came and looked at me.' She said: 'Was she dressed in grey?' He said: 'Yes.' 'Were you frightened?' He said: 'No. She smiled at me and I smiled at her, and she went away.'

I fear I have written you rather a rigmarole, but hope it will be of interest to you.

Yours sincerely,
J. F. WARRINGTON-ROGERS

Note 1 This would date the grotto at around the 1820s. There were at least five George Drury Rectors at the Rectory, the first in the early eighteenth century; and the Father of my correspondent's grandfather and of the girls for whom the grotto was built was the penultimate one. The family were Patrons of the living.

Note 2 Extract from the *Dictionary of National Biography*, 2nd Supplement, Volume 2:

LYNE, Joseph Leycester. 1837–1908. 'Father Ignatius'

. . . In 1862 Lyne, who henceforth called himself 'Father Ignatius' issued a pamphlet in favour of the revival of monasticism in the Church of England. This publication excited vehement controversy. Together with one or two kindred spirits, Lyne formed at Claydon, near Ipswich, a community which was frequently menaced by Protestant violence. The Bishop of Norwich refused him a licence to preach and subsequently inhibited him.

In 1863, Lyne acquired premises at Elm Hill, near Norwich, in face of local opposition. Special Masses celebrated for the community by the sympathetic Vicar of St. Laurence, Norwich, produced further conflict with the Bishop . . .

(The local population still believes that the mock-ruins referred to in this letter are ruins of some old monastery.)

Note 3 As Patron of the living.

In his letter of thanks to Mr Warrington-Rogers, Sir Laurence expressed sentimental regret that the mock-ruins should prove to be of such recent origin, saying that many people had suggested to him that they, and the grotto, might date from the first Rev. Drury's period. He also asked him to confirm his own assumption that the bedroom vacated by his grandfather (with the interesting sequel of the appearance of the Lady in Grey) was the so-called 'Oak Room' which he now used as a guest-room. The following is an extract from Mr Warrington-Rogers' reply.

August 6th, 1961

. . . I am sorry you are disappointed with my reminiscences which were told me by my Aunts and Mother, but I think they are pretty accurate. My other grandfather was the Rev. J. C. Warrington-Rogers, who was Rector (or Vicar) of Blakenham, so the two families knew each other pretty well. I was born at Bramfield, Suffolk, where my father was curate, and we soon came to Bower

Cottage in Claydon. My memory starts from there. He got the living of Aspall and shortly after the Vicar of Bramfield died. The people of Bramfield petitioned the Bishop for my Father to have the living, and I was there until I was 16, when he died.

My grandfather Drury took up stone-carving as another hobby, and he carved the pulpit in Claydon Church and the gargoyles on the top of the tower. This was probably when the Church was enlarged, and it is quite possible that surplus masonry was used to build the walls of the kitchen-garden and the towers.[1] As for the grotto, it could easily have been built in the seventeen hundreds.

Grandfather Drury loved law cases. He was also Vicar of Aken-ham, and when the Chapel Minister insisted on burying one of his people in the Churchyard, he went there and stood guard at the lychgate, saying: 'I am the only person who can bury people in this churchyard;' and he made them give way and conducted the service. There was some fuss about it. Also, when the Claydon church was being decorated for Xmas, some villagers forced their way in and tried to seize the Cross and candles from off the altar. He snatched the red-hot poker from out of the stove and drove them out, and had a lawsuit, for assault.

The Bishop ordered him to drop the High-Church services, and he absolutely refused and defied him to make him do so. No more seemed to be said. In later years, the village school-master, who had always reviled him strongly, retired. He could not find a house to live in, and all his furniture was turned out into the road. Up came grandfather and said: 'There is one of my glebe houses empty; you may have it.' The school-master was flabbergasted and said: 'After all my spiteful treatment of him, Mr Drury is the only real gentleman in the village.'

The room the Lady in Grey always started from was the oak-beamed room in the old part of the Rectory, which was on the right side going to the front door and I think faced north. The room under it was used by my grandfather for his hobbies. He made some splendid coloured lantern slides for his magic-lantern there. It seems a shame in a way, as they appeared to me to be the best rooms in the house. I think his study was opposite to it, and that was his holy of holies and people were rarely allowed to go in there. One of the exceptions being my Father, whom he always welcomed in.

When he was dying, he instructed his son, my uncle Drue Drury, to offer my father the living, but he did not accept it, as he considered the upkeep of the Rectory and grounds was beyond his dreams.

One other incident I remember happened in my great (or my great-great-) grandfather's time. (Both were Rectors here.) His wife, who had been ill for some time, was pronounced dead by the doctor. She was laid out, and, it is said, actually in her coffin. He was walking round the drive in despair, when it suddenly came to him that she could not be dead. He went in and got a wine-glass and put it over her mouth. A slight film came on it, and eventually she recovered from the trance and lived for several years. The doctor went through it, and wished he had never been born.

I cannot think of any more incidents and will close down and hope what I have written will be of interest to you.

Yours sincerely,

J. F. WARRINGTON-ROGERS

*Note*₁ This theory is a very natural one, but I doubt (1) whether the available masonry would have sufficed, and (2) whether any rector would loot his own church fabric to incorporate, e.g. a cherub's head, in his kitchen-garden wall. A more probable theory, held by Mr Lingard, a keen local archaeologist of Whitton Parish Council, is that these 'mock-ruins' were built by Drury from masonry, etc., once belonging to Thurlestone Church, ruined since the sixteenth century and used as a barn. The stones were known to have been brought up to the church at Whitton in 1862, to build the south aisle and tower. As Drury was at that time Patron of Whitton as well as of Claydon, he may well have used some of this material for his essay in the mock-antique. The two gazebos, or follies, are exactly like the Whitton church tower then erected.